Brian Hebblethwaite is Dean of Queen's College, Cambridge and Lecturer in Philosophy of Religion.

Edward Henderson is Professor of Philosophy at Louisiana State University, Baton Rouge.

# DIVINE
# ACTION

# DIVINE ACTION

Studies Inspired by
the Philosophical Theology
of Austin Farrer

*Edited by*
Brian Hebblethwaite and Edward Henderson

T & T CLARK
EDINBURGH

T & T CLARK
59 GEORGE STREET
EDINBURGH EH2 2LQ
SCOTLAND

First Published 1990


British Library Cataloguing in Publication Data
Divine action : studies inspired by
the philosophical theology of Austin Farrer.
1. Theology. Philosophical perspectives
I. Hebblethwaite, Brian    II. Henderson, Edward
III. Farrer, Austin *1904–68*
200'.1
ISBN 0 567 095282

BT
96.2
. D580
1990

Typeset by Buccleuch Printers Ltd, Hawick
Printed and bound by Billing & Sons Ltd, Worcester

# CONTENTS

# ACKNOWLEDGEMENTS

The conference for which these essays were first prepared was sponsored by the Louisiana State University Department of Philosophy and College of Arts and Sciences. The Society of Christian Philosophers was a co-sponsor. Financial support was provided through a grant from The Louisiana Endowment for the Humanities. We are grateful also for the generous help of Edith Kirkpatrick and Kris Kirkpatrick. The views expressed in these essays are those of the authors and are not necessarily endorsed by sponsors or supporters.

The usefulness of this book is greatly enhanced by the inclusion of indexes to Austin Farrer's major writings, prepared by Diogenes Allen. Readers of Farrer have often expressed irritation at the lack of indexes. Their provision here places us all greatly in Professor Allen's debt.

# INTRODUCTION

*Brian Hebblethwaite and Edward Henderson*

The topic of divine action in the world has rightly come to occupy centre stage in both doctrinal and philosophical theology. Whatever theological question is raised, some conception of God's action in the world will turn out to be involved in any answer proposed. The issue of objective theism – whether God-talk refers to transcendent reality or is only a symbolic expression of our highest aspirations or basic life attitudes – may seem at first to be an exception to this. It soon becomes apparent, however, that the question of divine action bears critically even on this apparently prior dispute. To approach the issue from the side of revelation is to suppose God's reality and nature to be revealed through particular events. But this assumes that the revelatory events, be they experiences peculiar to the individual or happenings preserved in tradition, are effects of God's action. To approach the issue from the side of philosophy is to suppose certain features of the world, knowable to all without dependence upon special revelation, to be effects of God's action. Even *a priori* arguments depend upon the contrast between necessary and contingent being, and it is arguable that contingency of being means being the effect of God's action. In other words the very idea of God stands or falls with the idea that God acts in relation to the world, at the very least by creating it. Thus, wherever the reality of God is taken seriously, in metaphysics or religion, the question of how to understand God's action in nature, history, and personal life becomes of crucial importance.

There are two particular difficulties, one old and one new, that make the issue of divine action especially problematic. The old difficulty is the problem of evil. So many terrible things happen in God's world that it has always been hard to maintain belief in a fatherly providence. The new difficulty is our modern scientific understanding of both the natural and the human worlds. It is not only the natural sciences but the social sciences too, and especially an informed historical-critical sense, that have held out the prospect of a complete understanding of what happens in the world in purely this-worldly terms.

It is the doctrine of providence rather than the doctrine of creation that is most problematic here. It is not too difficult for theists to achieve a reconciliation between religion and science where creation is concerned. One can quite easily hold that the entire universe depends on God for its being in being and for its being kept being, without running into conflict over how to account for what has happened within the given structures of creation. Nor is a doctrine of general providence too difficult to reconcile with contemporary scientific, sociological, and historical conceptions of reality. It is possible to hold that God has built into the nature of things a certain grain or tendency, a latent teleology, that is bound to realise God's purposes, one way or another, in the course of time. Such theological interpretations of the data of experience do not necessarily conflict with purely naturalistic descriptions. It is the notion of special providence – of particular divine acts within the created world – that raise the difficulties. Can we, in the light of modern science and critical history, practice faith as an ongoing relationship with God? Can we continue to believe that things have happened in the world that would have not happened had not God himself taken action (over and above his basic creative action), or that other things have not happened in the world that would have happened had not God prevented them? And if we can hold such beliefs, then why does God allow so much evil and suffering to happen in the world?

Examples of twentieth century Christian theology's attempts to grapple with the problem of particular divine action were collected together by Owen C. Thomas in a book entitled *God's Activity in the World: the Contemporary Problem*.[1] Two of the

[1] Chico: Scholars Press, 1983.

extracts in that collection were from a book by Austin Farrer. A strong case can be made for thinking that Farrer's contribution to our understanding of divine providence is still the most acute and penetrating to have appeared in post-war philosophical theology. For this reason, when it was decided to choose a topic dear to Farrer's heart and most worth taking further for the theme of the Fourth International Conference on the Thought of Austin Farrer, held in Louisiana State University, Baton Rouge, in April, 1986, the obvious choice was that of 'God's Action in the World'. A selection of papers from that conference is presented here. Many more papers were given at Baton Rouge, and it has not been easy to select just eleven for inclusion in this book. But the papers chosen illustrate the range and fertility of Farrer's influence on British and American philosophical theologians today. At the same time they constitute a rich and creative further contribution to the analysis of the notion of divine action.

By coincidence, at about the same time as the Farrer conference, two studies of the concept of divine action were published in England, representing opposite extremes in the spectrum of possible views on the topic. Vernon White's *The Fall of a Sparrow*[2] provides a powerful statement of the case for universal divine sovereignty, allowing nothing, not even evil and suffering, to stand apart from God's constant will and activity. Maurice Wiles's *God's Action in the World*,[3] by contrast, offers a careful and clear statement of the case against particular divine action or special providence, stressing the genuine independencies of causal power and free action bestowed upon the Creation by the Creator. For White, everything that happens is God's action. For Wiles, nothing, apart from the whole creative process itself, is God's action. Austin Farrer would strongly have opposed both these views, and none of the authors represented here would wish to follow either White or Wiles. The lasting inspiration of Farrer's work on providence, as illustrated by the present collection, lies in the possibility he opened up of articulating an

[2] Exeter: The Paternoster Press, 1985.
[3] London: SCM Press, 1986.

understanding of God's providence midway between the two
extremes. Forswearing the temptation to ascribe either everything or nothing to divine special action, our authors, like Farrer,
try to do justice at once to the religious need to ascribe some
particular effects to God's intentional activity and to the
scientific (and moral) need to recognise the God-given powers
enjoyed (and abused) by creatures.

The collection begins with a portrait of Farrer's work by
Richard Harries, now Bishop of Oxford. It was, by invitation,
the presentation that opened the Baton Rouge conference, and is,
therefore, more an appreciation of Farrer's distinctive style and
approach than a development of new thoughts about divine
action in the world. Farrer's genius, Harries claims, lay in the
combination of intellect, imagination, and spirituality which
informed his philosophical theology, as it did his sermons.
Farrer's preoccupation with questions about divine action arose
directly out of his practice of Christianity as priest, preacher, and
pastor to students. These concerns required Farrer to think of
God in terms of agency and of faith in terms of lived interaction
between God and the believer, a co-operation with God's
gracious action. Philosophy, too, contributes to knowledge of
God only insofar as if finds justification for taking things in the
world to be effects of God's action. Harries shows, however,
that, for Farrer, philosophy does not only endorse faith's
affirmation of the reality of God; it clarifies the way in which
God's real action in the world is inextricably bound up with the
*practice* of faith as a 'coinciding with God's action in one's own
life'. Harries's tone is reverent. He shows how the teasing,
quasi-poetic style of Farrer's language – something which many
readers at first find a barrier – in fact conveys an insight at once
intellectually stimulating and religiously profound. Harries is not
trying to argue us into Farrer's view of divine action. He is trying
to exhibit Farrer's work as an instance of the union of human
with divine will. 'The man', says Harries, 'is indeed in the style;
and in that style *is* the divine creativity.'[4]

---

[4] Emphasis added.

Harries's essay raises some interesting questions, not only for the theologian. Certainly we could not make the adoption of Farrer's *style* a prerequisite for those who would learn from him and carry on his work. Must we, however, require of those who write on these topics something of Farrer's own faith and spirituality? On any reckoning, the other contributors to this collection do not write in so directly engaged a religious manner as Austin Farrer usually did. And we may venture to express the hope that topics in philosophical theology *can* be explored, not only on the basis of faith and spirituality but, more tentatively, through intellectual analysis alone. Such exploration is entirely compatible, as we shall see from Diogenes Allen's contribution, with Farrer's view that faith is an epistemological condition necessary for the actual recognition of God's action in the world.

Owen C. Thomas, whose collection of key studies on *God's Activity in the World* has already been mentioned, now brings us up to date through a survey of much of the best recent work on the topic. He sets the stage for subsequent essays by focussing on the idea of double agency, the idea that both God and the human agent act in a single event or that God acts in and through the actions of finite agents without destroying their individual integrity and relative independence. This was the key notion in Farrer's treatment of providence, and all the writers surveyed by Thomas take it up in one way or another. Thomas suggests that the plausibility of the idea of double agency depends on analogies drawn from the relation of finite agents to each other. In fact, however, the analogies proposed appear to Thomas to be less plausible than actual examples of liturgical pardon, preaching, and graced actions, where human acts can be construed as at the same time divine acts in and through the human words and deeds. Thomas singles out the christological paradigm as especially significant for making sense of double agency. But the actual relation between the divine and creaturely agents remains obscure. Is this bound in the nature of the case to be so, as Farrer thought, or is there another solution to the problem of double agency? It was Thomas's challenge to the conference to tackle this question.

William Alston, of Syracuse University, New York, is well known for his seminal influence upon the remarkable flowering of philosophy of religion in America in recent decades. His contribution here clarifies the various logical and conceptual possibilities for talk of God's action in the world. Although Alston makes only one passing reference to Farrer, his precise and painstaking refutation of easy liberal assumptions about the completeness of scientific explanation and about the impossibility of speaking 'literally' of divine action, exemplifies precisely the kind of independent furthering of the enquiry itself that was the purpose of the conference. But we may be permitted to wonder how far Farrer would have supported Alston. With the latter part of Alston's essay – the comments on the univocal and the literal in talk of God – Farrer would have been in broad agreement. No doubt he would have pointed out that for St Thomas Aquinas analogy, unlike metaphor, was a species of literal discourse. And certainly Farrer had no more patience than Alston with the liberal assumption that modern science renders belief in divine intervention impossible. But in three ways he would perhaps have been less happy with the detail of Alston's defence of particular divine action. In the first place, Farrer was very much aware of theological reasons for restraint in postulating direct divine intervention – most notably, the problem of evil, but also the religious worry (expressed most forcibly by Wiles in the above-mentioned book) over the implications of hidden *manipulation* by God in the natural story of people's lives.

In the second place, Farrer was very conscious of the uniqueness of God and of God's relation to the world. That relation, Farrer insisted, must be understood as *sui generis*. It cannot – this was a major point that Farrer adapted from the Thomistic tradition – be an instance of any kind of relation holding among created things. Consequently Farrer would have thought Alston far too sanguine in his statement that 'the concept of divine action is . . . quite intelligible, coherent, and acceptable, and that impressions to the contrary stem from confusions, uncritical acceptance of shibboleths, or bad arguments'. For Farrer, the intrinsic uniqueness of God's mode of acting in the world necessarily hides divine action from us. God – and God's action – cannot be known as finite constituents of the world can be. Nor is the difficulty simply that of making sense of an agent without a body. It is that in principle we can never bring God or God's agency before us as an isolable object. Talk about God's action will always require, therefore, the use of analogies drawn from relations among finite agents, and there will always be the danger of applying the analogies without the right qualifications or of identifying the relation of God and creature with some relation of creatures to each other. We may be able rightly to identify particular effects of God's action, for these effects will after all be finite events in the world. But, Farrer thought, we can never objectify the action of God that issues in the effect. Alston, of course, acknowledges that the meaning of 'God acts' must be understood analogically, but he does not share Farrer's strong sense of the epistemological consequences of the divine uniqueness. Some of these consequences will be brought out in other essays in this volume.

The third difference between Alston and Farrer reflects the first. Farrer tried to articulate a mode of action in which God acts in and through the actions of creatures, bringing about particular purposes in naturally intelligible ways, without coercing or manipulating them. Such a conception of 'double agency' leads Farrer to propose what Alston in his discussion of conceptual possibilities seems by implication to deny: that God can act in and through the free agency of human beings and that it is precisely in the free pursuit of the divine will that we are able most clearly to see God's action in the world. This unique relation of God to creatures is the subject of considerable discussion by other contributors to the collection.

Eugene TeSelle, of Vanderbilt University Divinity School, greatly enriches the discussion by setting it in the whole context of the doctrinal tradition concerning divine action from the patristic period to the present day. Where Alston examined the logical territory, TeSelle carefully distinguishes and places the philosophical influences, Platonic, Aristotelian and Whiteheadian, that have shaped the continuing tradition, and draws out the dominant models of divine agency – self-determination within the agent, basic actions of the embodied self, more distant instrumental actions – that have characterised different periods and different schools in theological history. TeSelle, however, rebukes Farrer for his preference for the model of inner acts of self-determination by an agent – Farrer called it the model of 'agency and interior effect'. It is to be hoped that this collection will, if not resolve the issue, at least contribute to its fruitful discussion.

In fact, Farrer would have applauded TeSelle's delineation of different models, for he himself both described (in *Finite and Infinite*[5] and *The Glass of Vision*[6]) and practised (in all his philosophical works) a method of dialectically comparing and contrasting images. He held that, since God's relation to the world is *sui generis*, no one model or image could possibly do it complete justice. Different models must be proposed and the ways in which they fail to illuminate the relation must be noted. Such a dialectic of images will clarify and enable us to grasp the unique character of the God-world relation and prevent us from indentifying it with a kind of relation that can only hold among creatures. TeSelle is certainly right that it is the model of inner acts of self-determination that dominates Farrer's understanding of God's action in the world. (Rodger Forsman's essay will offer some good reasons for preferring that model.) On the other hand, Farrer did make interesting use of other models, including the model of the embodied self; and Thomas Tracy's essay, while arguing for the intelligibility of the idea of a disembodied agent, will show that the application to theology of Farrer's philosophy of action does leave room for a qualified use of the embodied self model. We can even see in Tracy's discussion that there is in Farrer's understanding an affinity with Whitehead in spite of very important differences in their understandings of God and of God's relation to the world. Farrer was not willing to say that

[5] London: Dacre Press, 1943, [2]1959.
[6] London: Dacre Press, 1948.

God *is* the soul of the world, but he did say that God *acts as* the soul of the world.

Another related and particularly important suggestion made here by TeSelle is that Athanasius's 'condescension' model of the operations of the divine Logos in the whole creation may well prove worthy of revival and fresh use. It is notable that Farrer in several places uses that very language, saying that God 'condescends' to wait upon creatures. Several of the essays will make use of this side of Farrer's thought, including those by Michael McLain, Thomas Tracy, Diogenes Allen, and Jeffrey Eaton. It is also worth noting that while none of the essays discusses the problem of evil at length, it is partly in terms of the idea of divine condescension that Farrer himself did so. Similarly the idea of divine self-limitation has frequently been used in recent theodicy, including that of Langdon Gilkey, John Hick, and Maurice Wiles. Farrer does much to develop this idea in the context of a wider philosophical theology.

TeSelle's concluding reflections on the Trinitarian conception of divine activity, especially where the immanent actuation of religious experience by the Holy Spirit is concerned, is also of great significance for the articulation of a viable theology of divine action. And there are yet other historical observations that help to provide a perspective and to suggest paths for further exploration. Certainly TeSelle's whole essay shows that it is most important for philosophical discussion of these issues to be historically and theologically informed.

The essay by David Burrell, of Notre Dame University, attempts to show the intelligibility of the idea of double agency when it is conceived as the action of eternal pure act through temporal creatures but especially in free human agents who act with an end in view. Burrell's discussion forces us to think carefully about the concept of God whose action in the world we are attempting to understand, since that concept determines what can be thought. Farrer, though much of the inspiration for his thought came from the same Thomistic tradition, had grave reservations about its ability to clarify the idea of divine action in the world. Can we be satisfied with a conception of the relation between an eternal God and his temporally structured creation that leaves all particularity on the creature's side alone? Can we seriously think of divine agency – especially of particular divine agency where there is on our part the sense of divine response to us and our circumstances – without postulating potentiality and the realisation of some potentialities rather than others in God? Moreover, the notion of God's timelessness not only tends to undermine the intelligibility of divine action, it has the effect of freezing the whole creation into a single space-time whole that only appears to be temporal to those of us within its structure. Freed from the metaphysical shackles of the idea of pure act, however, and positing in God a primordial temporality that permits the Creator to act temporally in relation to a temporal creation in a manner appropriate to the nature of what God has made, we can surely accept, as within a much more intelligible framework, all that Burrell says about God's practical knowledge of what God is doing in creating, sustaining, and acting within a temporal creation. God's knowledge of all possibilities indeed prevents God's being taken by surprise, and God's omnipotence indeed enables God to draw the threads of life and history together like a master composer or author, though without predetermining the exact course of each free agent's deeds. Such a modification of traditional Thomism may well sound like the process theology inspired by Whitehead and developed in detail by Hartshorne and others. Farrer, however, thought that by replacing the Thomistic 'pure act' with 'perfect agency' or 'the God who is all that he wills to be and wills to be all that he is', we could conceive God as *both* enjoying complete and perfect life independently of the world *and* condescending to wait temporally upon the actions of creatures, acting in their own creaturely action rather than forcing them as a transcendent cause would do, as it were 'from the outside'.

The issue raised by Burrell's essay lies at the heart of comtemporary discussion of the concept of God. Is belief in God's special action compatible with traditional notions of timelessness and simplicity? Can one admit self-limitation in God and reciprocity between God and creatures without bringing God down to the level of creaturely agents?

David Brown, of Oriel College, Oxford, is best known for his recent book on *The Divine Trinity*[7] in which he dealt with several issues related to the idea of God's action in the world. Here, in exploring the notion of divine revelation, Brown illuminates the idea of double agency by developing a theory of how revelation is effected by God in the form of divine-human dialogue carried on in the 'language' of natural symbols. The result is an original philosophical attempt to say what theologians have struggled to say ever since historical-critical scholarship made evident the presence of human perspectives, diverse traditions, and conflicting theological visions in scripture, namely, how God can truly reveal himself in a medium that is humanly, historically, and culturally conditioned. Brown argues that revelation, in order truly to be revelation, must be a matter of divine intervention – yet not intervention in a sense that requires actions contrary to nature. As our own free action takes place in the world without the violation of any natural law, so there is no need to posit any such violation in the comparable case of God's action within the structures of creation. Brown suggests, therefore, that God 'intervenes' in the world precisely through the evocation of certain natural symbols and dominant images, which then, as they are reflected on, revised, and transformed in the light of historical experience, enable God to carry on a dialogue that takes shape in history. If divine revelation does occur in something like the way Brown describes, then it is quite appropriate to say that God 'speaks' to us or that scripture is the 'word' of God. Yet it also allows us at the same time to acknowledge the human and therefore fallible component in the revelation – on the one hand to say that God 'speaks' to us and on the other hand to maintain a realistic and faithful agnosticism and openness about *what* God is alleged to say in the dialogue.

The most original feature of Brown's proposal is that the divine-human interchange occurs throught 'natural symbols'.

[7] London: Duckworth, 1985; LaSalle, Illinois, Open Court, 1985.

This idea takes further the view advanced by Farrer in his Bampton Lectures, *The Glass of Vision*, in which he argued that the medium of scriptural revelation is not word but images, progressively transformed in the history of Israel and lived out in the life of Christ. Brown's treatment is importantly different from Farrer's, however, in that, while Farrer dismissed any appeal to the unconscious psyche and focussed on those images which are part of Israel's explicit written record, Brown insists that we press behind conscious images to natural symbols. This he compares to the Freudian idea of the psyche's dialogue with the father by means of sub-conscious symbols. The idea that divine-human interchange begins at the level of sub-conscious symbols has the benefit of explaining how revelation could ever begin in the first place. It also has interesting possibilities for the interpretation of other religious traditions, for it makes it possible for Jew, Christian, or Muslim to look at other religious traditions as involving genuine revelation of God. They need not regard the others simply as human constructions.

In opting for the language of 'intervention', Brown is not, in fact, proposing a substantial alternative to Farrer's concept of double agency. His defence of his preferred analogies from dialogue, teaching, and growth in personal knowledge, is only a development of the idea of mediated, indirect communication which Farrer explored in *The Glass of Vision* and later came to call 'double agency'. For symbols and images through which the divine-human dialogue occurs carry both the action of God and the action of God's interlocutors. Surely Brown has himself given us a paradigm case of 'double agency'.

The most important part of the essay may well be the concluding section where Brown shows how the revelatory character of a transformed symbol or myth consists in the experienced encounter with God which it mediates. This is, no doubt, a statement of faith and not a proof. But, certainly, once reference to God's action is removed, the symbols lose their existential power.

Rodger Forsman, of Acadia University, enables us to see afresh the problem of meaningful *reference* to God by setting it in the context of discussion of divine action. He shows that the problem of reference here is a problem about our ability to identify certain events as effects of God's action. There is no problem about referring indirectly to real but unseen *finite* causes or agents as responsible for specific effects in the world. Reference to God takes place, in a similar way, when certain things occur which are not so easily explicable – at least in full – by reference to such causes or agents alone. Forsman cites such personal transformations as conversion as suggestive of some transfinite explanation, enabling us to identify God as the agent ultimately responsible for the change. He stresses that analogies from personal agency – in particular from teaching (cf. Brown's essay) or persuasion – are more appropriate here than analogies from some external cause/effect relation. Moreover the fact that in such cases the learner or the convert is actively engaged with the personal source of the transformation gives substance once again to Farrer's concept of *double* agency.

The next two essays are linked together by a common concern with narrative theology. Narrative theology reflects the conviction that God's identity and character are discovered in and through the *story* of God's dealings with his people in the world.

Michael McLain, of Rhodes College and Thomas Tracy, of Bates College, are in agreement (as were Alston and Brown) that the world is no more closed to divine action than it is to human action. They also agree that whatever the logical possibilities may be regarding God's action, there are good theological reasons for thinking that it does not involve the suspension or violation of the natural order of things and that it does not force or coerce creatures. The idea that best includes these provisions, they think, is that of double agency as presented in Austin Farrer's work. Beyond these broad agreements, however, their contributions lead down different paths and in pursuit of different quarries.

McLain distinguishes between the idea of direct divine action from outside nature and the idea of mediated divine action, occurring wholly within the operations of creatures. The latter is, of course, the idea of *double* agency. In double agency, God does not act directly *on* nature but rather *within* it.

McLain holds that the idea of direct divine action from outside nature is inevitably one of coercive action and that it entails the direct responsibility of God for evil. Consequently he prefers the idea that God so acts within the actions of creatures as both to be effective in them and yet to preserve their freedom and responsibility. He does not meet Owen Thomas's request for some account of how double agency works, but defends it through criticising a number of alternative proposals. But is McLain correct in thinking that direct divine action from outside nature is inevitably coercive and thus incompatible with respect for creaturely agency? Do we not rather, in order to make sense of divine action in particular times and places, have to posit direct divine action from outside as well? Tracy, at any rate, as we shall see, uses the idea of God's 'basic action', in such a way as to include that of direct divine action within the idea of double agency.

Finally McLain develops some epistemological consequences of the idea of double agency. The first is that events are not ascribed to God's particular action because of their lack of a naturalistic explanation nor because of some startling phenomenological features or psychological effects; rather, they will be recognised as effects of divine action by our seeing in them more of the divine purpose than can be discerned elsewhere. McLain makes it quite clear that such an understanding does *not* reduce to the view that special divine action is simply a matter of what seems special to human subjects. Faith may be a necessary condition of such perception, but *what* is there discerned is something of *God's* action. Indeed, it is reasonable to believe that if God acts in the world by acting in the free actions of persons, then God's effective agency will be knowable to those open to the presence of supernatural purpose and able consequently to see it is the actions, of others, say, those of a Mother Teresa.

The second epistemological consequence is that we are not bound to the idea that God must reveal himself verbally. In a discussion of Basil Mitchell's and Ronald Thiemann's arguments for this, McLain suggests that since direct verbal revelation would destroy the epistemic distance necessary for a free response, it is more plausible to think that the God of love reveals himself through the non-verbal actions of creatures. Such a view might well appeal to proponents of narrative theology. Revelation is given in actions – of Moses, the prophets, Jesus, etc. – that express and forward the divine purpose. Because these actions present us with divine purposes, the narratives depicting them tell us of God's actions, character, and will by telling us of the actions of creatures. The revelation is not *in* words; it is rather preserved and promulgated by the words of the narrative. We may observe, however, that non-coercive action by double agency does not necessarily preclude verbal revelation. Brown's view of divine/human dialogue, for example, preserves the sense of verbal revelation while making it indirect as mediated by symbols. And what would McLain say of Farrer's own claim that God can be thought to reveal himself by acting in the thoughts we freely form as we seek him in contemplative prayer?

> . . . the way in which his (God's) idea develops in us becomes his own concern . . . It is possible, then, for him to live and act *in our idea of him* . . .[8]

Surely it is appropriate to call such action of God in us both a form of verbal inspiration and a case of double agency. But it does not amount to divine coercion, and it certainly is not verbal inspiration in the fundamentalist's sense of inerrant divine dictation.

Thomas Tracy's contribution provides the most sustained and detailed effort in this collection to *explain* the particular action of God in the world as non-miraculous double agency. Tracy does this by bringing to bear on the theme of divine action the distinction between basic acts and their instrumental substructures as developed in recent philosophy of action. His account of human persons – agents with real but limited freedom who become themselves over time through their responses to limiting conditions – depends extensively on Farrer's explorations of action, self-unity and freewill in *Finite and Infinite* and

---

[8] *Lord, I believe: Suggestions for Turning the Creed into Prayer*, (London: SPCK, 1962), emphasis added.

*The Freedon of the Will.*[9] Tracy uses the concept of a basic act to refer to what Alston called God's direct actions from outside nature. They are the acts by which God's will first enters into the world: hence what Tracy calls God's 'initial acts'. Tracy agrees with Farrer and Alston in saying that we cannot in principle explain how God performs these. On the other hand, we can say how their effects can occur within creatures without violating the creatures' natures or destroying their freedom. That allows us also to explain how God's basic acts make creaturely operations into instrumental substructures in which the divine will is carried as an ongoing presence in the world.

The main substance of Tracy's contribution is found in parts III and IV of his essay. Here he describes in detail the human agent in its natural and social setting, explaining how its freedom works precisely through its responses to a variety of orienting conditions and background influences. God acts within the actions of persons, he suggests, by both directly and indirectly influencing those conditions. If this account is correct, there is a 'virtually inexhaustible multitude of different specific ways' in which God can act within our actions. God can act, for example, in unconscious and subconscious life (cp. Brown's essay), in non-religious, non-theistic, aesthetic sensibilities, in the lives of others, and in lives consciously led in faithful dependence upon and obedience to God. Tracy's account also makes sense of the frequent claim of religious souls describing the experience of conversion, that grace (God's action to help us) goes before us to enable the response of faith. It can enable the attitude of initial faith as well as the commitment of full faith, all without forcing the characters involved. Tracy's development of Farrer's ideas seems promising. Yet there are questions. Does his interpretation of divine agency return us to the 'God of the gaps'? Does the idea of divine influence through initial acts preserve the sense of the divine uniqueness, or does it treat God as one force among many others? Does the notion of God's initial acts depend upon the model of external causation, which Forsman found to be

[9] London: A & C Black, 1958.

problematical, and does that reduce God to an agent among agents?

One cannot help but notice that the account Tracy gives, both of human agency and of the divine influence within it, resembles the approach developed by the process theologians. God is not the eternal pure act of being of Burrell's account, but rather the perfect agent who acts to influence the ongoing processes of the world. Nevertheless, Tracy does not share the process under-standing of God as intrinsically and essentially limited and dependent upon the world. Tracy agrees with Farrer in affirming that God is complete in himself and the creator of the world *ex nihilo*, who, in choosing to create free finite agents, chooses to be limited in his actions. Farrer defends such an understanding in his theodicy, *Love Almighty and Ills Unlimited*, and in a short essay on 'The Prior Actuality of God'.[10] What neither Farrer nor Tracy resolve, however, is the problem of the relation of God as perfect agent to time. Is God eternal in his transcendent completeness but temporal in his actions by self-chosen limita-tion among creatures? If so, how are we to understand the inter-relation of these 'aspects' of God? If not, then is God timeless both in his independence of and his relatedness to the world? Or temporal in both? What is the nature of God's knowledge of the world? Proponents of the self-limiting idea of God need to address these and similar questions.[11]

Diogenes Allen, of Princeton Theological Seminary, con-tributes a searching discussion of the role of faith in recognising divine activity. Philosophers may well be wary of appeals to faith, lest they be efforts to by-pass the rightful demands of reason. Allen, however, follows Farrer in arguing that faith is a proper feature of the process of knowing. His appeal is to 'initial faith' as an attitude necessary for recognising God's action, not to faith as full-blown religious commitment. All forms of knowing require, according to Allen, attitudes appropriate to the

[10] *Love Almighty and Ills Unlimited*, (London: Collins, 1962); 'The Prior Actuality of God', in *Reflective Faith: Essays in Philosophical Theology*, ed. Charles C. Conti (London: SPCK, 1972).

[11] William Alston's 'Divine-Human Dialogue and the Nature of God' (*Faith and Philosophy*, Vol. 2, no. 1, Jan. 1985) would be a good place to begin.

kinds of knowledge and to the kinds of objects involved. Without the appropriate attitude, a particular kind of knowledge will not occur. Because God's actions are hidden in the actions of finite agents (double agency), the world must be approached – to use the religiously charged term for initial faith – with an 'open heart'. Allen does not claim here to give us a complete theological epistemology, of course. But inasmuch as his and Farrer's Augustinian view appears importantly different from classical foundationalism, from the Wittgensteinian view of faith as a form of life, and from Plantinga's view that belief in God is properly basic, the effort to develop the idea in the context of a larger epistemology would seem well worth making. But we are bound to raise again the question posed above in connection with Bishop Harries's opening portrait of Farrer: how far does Allen's epistemological point preclude co-operation (or even under-standing) in philosophical theology on the part of the unbeliever? Is initial faith required even for seeing the evidence as evidence and evaluating the logical coherence of the arguments? Or does it come in when the evidence has been appreciated and the theistic interpretation seen as a logically possible response to it?

Allen's essay also raises the issue of religious experience. Philosophers of religion have focussed mainly on numinous and mystical experiences, asking whether their characteristics justify our taking them as genuine encounters with God, though there has recently been more attention to less dramatic forms of religious experience. Farrer's – and Allen's – understanding of divine action does not rule out dramatic experience; but it wisely concentrates much more on religious experience in the context of a faithful form of life. The idea of double agency encourages us to put this emphasis upon everyday religious life. Religious experience, we may say, begins with the opening of the heart; it continues in the life of committed faith and its experience of dependence on and co-operation with grace. In such a context, it is reasonable to believe that we are experiencing God acting in the world in the graced action of others, in the claims which others' needs make upon us, and in the everyday prosaic blessings which we receive. Nevertheless, the hiddenness of

God's action in these actions and interactions of creatures makes it incumbent on faithful persons to maintain a certain agnosticism about the specific nature and direction of God's presence and action. Two further questions may be raised – this time from the side of the believers rather than the critic. Does the double agency view of divine action preclude all *direct* action of God? (A number of our contributors are troubled by this question.) And does the requirement of initial faith mean that God does not or even cannot act suddenly and dramatically to grasp the life of one whose heart has previously been utterly closed?

Jeffrey Eaton, formerly of Hamilton College, New York, applies Farrer's thought on divine agency and the primacy of practical faith to liberation theology. Liberation theology stresses the community over the individual, human responsibility for doing the divine will over a passive dependence that waits for God to do all, and liberation from the oppression of others over salvation from one's own sins. It is a striking fact that Farrer's understanding of double agency can be applied to all these strains of thought.

Eaton's essay is both critical and supportive of liberation theology. Surely the liberation of persons from structures which oppress them is God's will. But, for Eaton, a theology that focusses on the theme of liberation is threatened by a lack of true *theology*, especially of an understanding of God and of God's action in relation to what must be done by us. According to Eaton, liberation theologians rightly reject the formalist God of the scholastics (this would include the early Farrer). Sometimes they seem to incline towards a process God as more intelligibly related to the future and to future transformation. In other cases, liberation theologians seem to come close to a humanistic reduction of theism, explicating all theological concepts wholly in terms of their 'liberation meaning'. Given its head, that approach would turn liberation theology into an ideology. In response, Eaton reasons that if theology without praxis is empty, as the liberation theologians declare, then praxis without theology is blind. Eaton's constructive proposal is that Farrer's later understanding of God and of God's action in the world is exactly the conception liberation theology needs to keep itself both true to itself and within the circle of orthodox theism. Liberation theologians insist that thought must not leave the world of practical life behind in a cloud of abstractions. Farrer's theology does the same, conceiving God as Perfect Agent or Unconditioned Will rather than as Pure Act, and insisting that theological ideas are meaningful only insofar as they have practical verification in terms of human agency under grace. On Farrer's account of faith, this is far from being just a passive clinging to God and letting him do everything. Rather it is a matter of our active co-operation with grace. God acts in the world only insofar as creatures also act. Hence, liberation is something that human beings must actively seek; but, as Christians, they can truly seek it only in dependence on God's act. Thus, by his grace, God makes his creatures make themselves. Farrer himself, so Eaton holds, developed these ideas in terms of traditional piety. But they are eminently applicable to the liberationist's struggle, in God's name, for a better world.

The collection ends, therefore, as is only proper, in the sphere of practical application. For the burden of what our authors have learned from the theology of Austin Farrer is that God's agency and God's will are verified and known only in the doing of his will in furthering his Kingdom here on earth.

Chapter 1

# 'WE KNOW ON OUR KNEES . . .'[1]

Intellectual, imaginative and spiritual unity in the
theology of Austin Farrer

*Richard Harries*

Ronald Knox once said 'I must have a religion and it must be
different from my father's'. The comparison with Farrer is
instructive. Knox's father was an Evangelical Bishop, Farrer's a
thoughtful Baptist. Ronald Knox became a Roman Catholic,
Austin Farrer an Anglican of Catholic persuasion. Both shifted
their ecclesiastical allegiance but in the case of Farrer the inward
continuity with his father's religion was as significant as the
outward change in denomination. For Farrer affirmed the
Christian devotion of his father or, more accurately, of both his
parents, in a way that was basic to his whole intellectual outlook.

For such a private person Farrer discloses a surprising amount
about his family in his sermons: and what they reveal is a quite
remarkable degree of affection and admiration for his parents. In
one sermon he describes how, forbidden by his doctor to read
for three months, he and his father spent the summer working
together to make a hand cut oak fence round the garden. Farrer
enjoyed the work itself but above all he said there was the
pleasure of working with his father, who took an equal pleasure
in working with his son.[2] For nearly thirty years, without a
break, Farrer wrote regularly to his father.[3] The example of his

---

[1] The title of this essay is taken from a sermon of Farrer's, in *A Celebration of Faith*, ed. Leslie Houlden, (London: Hodder & Stoughton, 1970), p. 45.
[2] *The End of Man*, ed. Charles C. Conti, (London: SPCK, 1973; Grand Rapids, Mich: William B. Eerdmans Publishing Co., 1973) p. 67ff.
[3] See Philip Curtis, *A Hawk Among Sparrows. A Biography of Austin Farrer* (London: SPCK, 1985).

mother is even more telling. In one sermon he uses her as an example of Divine love.[4] In another, entitled, 'How can we know God?' he tells his Oxford audience that they will have known few women as good as his mother and continues, 'A more unphilosophical thinker it would be difficult to find.' But, 'The centre of your Christian conviction, whatever you may think, will be where my mother's was – in your exploration of grace, in your walking with God.'[5] To this we can also add his admiration for his tiny aunt who spent her life as a medical missionary in India, to whom, again, he refers in his sermons.

In short, however far he moved away from his parents socially, ecclesiastically and intellectually, first to St. Paul's School and then to Oxford and Anglicanism, he remained rooted in and inspired by the simple saint-like Christianity of his family. Faith was for him personally what later he taught philosophically and theologically that it should be, something essentially natural, something to be imbibed with mother's milk. It is a view of faith that he made explicit and argued for in the first chapter of *Saving Belief*. He also noted there the logical converse of his own happy experience, for 'The corruptions of faith herself are so many and so appalling as to allow atheism to pass for illumination.'[6] It is not therefore surprising that even in his most abtruse work, *Finite and Infinite*[7] Farrer put aside the idea of proving God from some allegedly neutral position. This view became even more pronounced later in life, as can be seen in *Faith and Speculation*,[8] which may be why some people, including Basil Mitchell found the book disappointing at first reading.[9] In a sermon delivered

[4] *The End of Man* p. 54f.

[5] *A Celebration of Faith* p. 59f.

[6] *Saving Belief* (New York: Morehouse-Barlow Co., 1965; London: Hodder & Stoughton, 1964), p. 25f.

[7] *Finite and Infinite; A Philosophical Essay*. 2nd. edn. 1958, reprinted (New York: Seabury Press, 1979).

[8] *Faith and Speculation*, (New York, New York University Press, 1967; London: Adam and Charles Black, 1967; reprinted, Edinburgh, T & T Clark, 1988).

[9] Basil Mitchell, 'Two Approaches to the Philosophy of Religion' in *For God and Clarity. New Essays in Honour of Austin Farrer*, ed. Jeffrey C. Eaton and Ann Loades (Penn: Pickwick Publications, 1983), p. 177.

about the same period as the appearance of *Faith and Speculation* Farrer showed even more effrontery:

> Since God has shown to me a ray of his goodness, I cannot doubt him on the ground that someone has made up some new logical puzzles about him. It is too late in the day to tell me that God does not exist, the God with whom I have so long conversed, and whom I have seen active in several men of real sanctity, not to mention the canonised saints.[10]

This is in no way to underestimate the sheer intellectualism of Farrer or to detract from his Herculean labours to help other rational minds see the rational truth that he saw. Nevertheless, the recognition of sanctity in others and the striving after sanctity himself, was the starting point and mainspring of all his intellectual endeavours.

Such intellectual effort Farrer regarded as essential not only for himself but for all those capable of thought. After commending the faith of his unphilosophical mother he went on to assert:

> But faith perishes if it is walled in, or confined. If it is anywhere it must be everywhere, like God himself: if God is in your life, he is in all things, for he is God. You must be able to spread the area of your recognition for him, and the basis of your conviction about him, as widely as your thought will range.[11]

Does our thought range at all? Then our thought about God, our intellectual efforts to recognise his activity in the universe, must range at least that far. Yet this theological ranging is still a secondary activity. As *Love Almighty and Ills Unlimited* concludes:

> Peasants and housekeepers find what philosophers seek in vain; the substance of truth is grasped not by argument but by faith. The leading of God through evil out of evil and into a promised good is acknowledged by those who trust in his mercy.[12]

Furthermore, Christian faith is possible, even for the philos-

[10] *A Celebration of Faith*, p.27.
[11] *A Celebration of Faith*, p.60.
[12] *Love Almighty and Ills Unlimited*, (New York: Doubleday & Co., 1961. London: William Collins & Co., 1962), p.187.

opher, with some speculative questions left unanswered. On a
number of issues, for example the fate of infants who die young
or the mentally retarded, we have nothing to go on. 'There are
few disservices more damaging to the cause of religion than the
over-weighting of its intellectual pretensions.'[13] Then, again,
theological reflection exists to serve faith. After drawing out
various analogies implicit in a statement about the atonement
Farrer suggests that this is an example of theology at work; but
this work is comparable to the way we learn grammar in order to
appreciate literature.

> We do not read the story of the cross to make theological
> deductions. We draw out our theology that we may rightly read
> the story of the cross.[14]

Few of us could stomach such statements if delivered by an
unlettered evangelist. But as they come from one of the most
sophisticated theological minds of our time, we are forced to
reckon with them. Certainly there is no understanding the nature
of Farrer's achievement without doing them justice. They grow
from the wholesome soil in which he was rooted: his familial
faith and the continuing affection in which he held it. So strong
was the hold of this ideal upon him that he wanted no intellectual
or aesthetic endeavour, no theology or poetics, that did not
enhance and reinforce the validity of such faith. The unity of
Farrer, the unity of theology and spirituality in him, which
Charles Hefling explored in *Jacob's Ladder*,[15] is a unity round
the pillar of his parent's faith. But how did Farrer achieve this
unity and in what ways does it reveal itself?

First, it would be tempting to say of Farrer that for him
*cogitare est orare*. This would however be misleading, for he
abhorred the blurring of important distinctions and prayer is
prayer, not a fancy name for thought or work. Above all he
wanted to give God his due. God is to be thought, yes, but, also
to be adored. Nevertheless, it is certainly true that Farrer sought

---

[13] *The Brink of Mystery*, ed. Charles C. Conti (London: SPCK, 1976), p.6.
[14] *Saving Belief*, p.107.
[15] Charles C. Hefling, Jr., *Jacob's Ladder. Theology and Spirituality in the
thought of Austin Farrer*, (Mass: Cowley Publications, 1979).

to make his thinking a form of praying and this as a matter of conscious intellectual and spiritual policy. In his now famous passage in *The Glass of Vision* Farrer recalled how God had used Spinoza to liberate him from an oppressive personalism:

> I would no longer attempt, with the psalmist, 'to set God before my face'. I would see him as the underlying cause of my thinking, especially of those thoughts in which I tried to think of him. I would dare to hope that sometimes my thought would become diaphonous, so that there should be some perception of the divine cause shining through the created effect, as a deep pool, settling into a clear tranquility, permits us to see the spring in the bottom of it from which its waters rise.[16]

It is hardly surprising that in the 1960s Farrer was not over-impressed by clamant calls to see God as the ground of our being. Not only had he been through it all himself many years before, he had erected a very different theological superstructure from, for example, that of Paul Tillich. For few in our time have been so uncompromising as Farrer in asserting both the transcendence of God and Divine personhood as the controlling image of Christian thinking:

> Are you brave enough to believe in God at all? . . . He can and does give an entire, an adequate and an undivided attention to every single creature and every single circumstance . . . It is not silly, childish or superstitious to suppose that God attends to your prayer or your conduct like a parent watching an infant when the parent has nothing else to do. It is merely to credit God with being God.[17]

Yet the very conviction with which he affirmed this was a measure of the personal difficulties he had once felt about such a view; and this conviction was held together with the balancing truth that God was the underlying cause of his thinking, to whom he sought to be diaphonous. The result of this is that as Basil Mitchell noted, 'There was no discernible difference of tone between preaching and lecturing or between lecturing and everyday speech.'[18] Farrer's prayers were always thought prayers,

[16] *The Glass of Vision* (London: Dacre Press, 1948), p. 8.
[17] *Saving Belief*, p. 44.
[18] *A Celebration of Faith*, p. 15.

the result of thought and the extension of thought. No less, for him, thinking was a form of praying, an attempt to be transparent to Divine truth.

The second way in which Farrer achieves a unified intellectual and spiritual vision is through his use of the dialogue form. Inner dialogue was deliberately chosen as a way into spiritual understanding. This is not always entirely satisfactory for the reader. It results in a certain allusiveness that some find difficult. But it enabled Farrer to put arguments contrary to his own and to give them all the weight they deserved. This was part of his intellectual integrity. But the dialogue form was particularly well designed to bring about spiritual, as well as intellectual, understanding. As he wrote in *Faith and Speculation*:

> I wish I had written the book better; I do not wish I had written it more formally. Reflection and discussion may permit realities to disclose themselves to us; and I would rather, if I dared to hope it, provide materials for an exercise in understanding, than formalise a chain of argument.[19]

John Henry Newman once wrote that he tried to 'say and unsay to positive effect.' It is an apt description of Farrer's method. He offers an image, shows its limitations, puts forward an alternative picture, shows how this does not work fully either but suggests how it can be used to modify the first image. Farrer's method, we might say, is to make and unmake images to positive effect. It was a method he employed to particularly good effect in *A Science of God?*[20] (*God is not Dead* in the USA) as he explored the concept of omniscience and the way it is legitimate to talk about God being, or better, acting as the *Anima Mundi*.

The Welsh poet and priest R. S. Thomas has written an essay in Welsh and a poem in English both on the theme of Abercuawg, a word meaning the place where the cuckoos sing. In the essay Thomas writes:

---

[19] *Faith and Speculation*, p. vi.
[20] *A Science of God?* (London: Geoffrey Bles, 1966); USA title: *God is not Dead* (New York: Morehouse-Barlow Co., 1966).

The fact that we go to the Machynlleth area to look for the site of Abercuawg, saying 'No this isn't it' means nothing. Here is no cause for disappointment and despair, but rather a way to come to know better, through its absence, the nature of the place which we seek . . . This is man's estate. He is always on the verge of comprehending God, but insomuch as he is a mortal creature, he never will. Nor will he ever see Abercuawg. But through striving to see it, through longing for it, through refusing to accept some second-hand substitute, he will succeed in preserving it as an eternal possibility.[21]

Farrer's dialogue form has a similar purpose and effect. It preserves that which we seek as an eternal possibility. It is an exercise in understanding that holds out the possibility of understanding. It is true that we tend to think of Farrer as a theologian of the *Via Positiva* rather than of the *Via Negativa*, in that he puts forward a stream of images for our consideration; but always these images are formed and broken: and reformed and broken again – to positive effect. One notes also the way Farrer's own method is at one with his understanding of Christian revelation. Revelation involves the communication of images. In Christ these images of Messiah and Kingdom and Sonship and sacrifice were reborn. The first Christians participated in this rebirth of images but the decisive transformation took place in Jesus himself.[22] Particularly was this true of the way in which Jesus took and lived out the images of the Book of Daniel. 'Daniel was a pattern for Jesus, a pattern he broke and remade in the living of it.'[23]

'In the living of it.' This thought is an undercurrent in all Farrer's writing. In his sermons, for all their flights into poetry and their analysis of current intellectual concerns, the undercurrent becomes the flow of the stream itself. Listeners are left with a strong practical imperative. Students were to make up quarrels with their parents and work at their books. They were to use their money wisely and their bodies chastely. They were to buy

[21] R. S. Thomas, *Selected Prose*, ed. Sandra Anstey, (Bridgend: Poetry Wales Press, 1983), p. 164.

[22] *A Rebirth of Images. The Making of St. John's Apocalypse* (London: Dacre Press, 1949; Gloucester, Mass: Peter Smith, 1970), p. 14-15.

[23] *The Brink of Mystery*, p. 166.

an alarm clock so that week by week they could take their place in the resurrected body of Christ. They were, in all the manifold experiences of their lives, to look for and adhere to the will of God in the most down to earth and severely practical ways. Such is the stock in trade of the preacher, though few are so specific. What distinguishes Farrer is the way this emphasis is fundamental not simply for living the Christian life but for knowing God's action in the world at all. This then is the third way in which Farrer's unity manifests itself. Coinciding with God's action in ones own life and knowing that there is an action of God to coincide with are inextricably bound up together. As is well known Farrer moved away from the concept of substance to that of will. In *Faith and Speculation* he wrote:

> And thus, proceeding from the 'Why is it so?' question, we may reach the God who is all he wills to be, and wills to be all he is: for his act is himself and his act is free . . . So . . . there is no discord between our pragmatic theology and the argument *a contingentia mundi*, if it is allowed its proper logic. Both come to rest in the Unconditioned Will.[24]

Farrer arrived at this conclusion by a number of different routes. One was through an analysis of what it means to exist. We only know what it means to exist in the changeable finite way with which alone we are acquainted, from our own lives. We credit existence to the galaxies and rightly so but we only know what we mean because first of all we experience existence in ourselves. But it may be that the existence we experience in ourselves is discerned as springing from some changeless and infinite cause. If so that cause will also be the cause of the universe as a whole:

> To make you or me, God must make half a universe. A man's body and a man's mind form a focus in which a world is concentrated, and drawn into a point. It may be in that point that I know existence; but it is an existence which involves the world.[25]

[24] *Faith and Speculation*, p.118.
[25] *Saving Belief*, p.30.

Another route was through an analysis of the concept of creation, which also depends on existential knowledge. If we look for God's creative hand in the origin of the universe we have no hope of seeing it. The event is too remote to us. Evolution appears to offer a better prospect for here at least we can see creation in process. But God makes things make themselves. His hand is perfectly hidden, at least until we are given a clue to interpret what is happening. The clue is in ourselves:

> If we are concerned about a creative cause, it is because, in creating all things, he is creating us; and it concerns us to enter into the making of our souls, and of one another's. To enter into the action of God thus is what we mean by religion; and as it is something we do, it is a matter of experience.[26]

In co-operating with a Divine creative action in our own lives, we have the clue to discern a hidden hand weaving up the tissue of living things in evolution; from this it is reasonable to suppose that the hand that does the weaving of the physical web created the material out of which the web is made.

Another way in which Farrer makes the same point is through his discussion of creative pressure. In nature we see innumerable entities at once being themselves and being built up into ever more complex forms. But we experience the same phenomenon in our lives. We know a persuasive leading which in no way violates or forces but works by respecting the operation of our being. Knowing this pressure through experience we read it back into the evolutionary process:

> Brute things are subject to the creative pressure, but being brute, cannot know that they are. Enlightened men can not only coincide with its dictates they can put themselves at its disposal. There is a union of wills in which God's will is inevitably directive and superior.[27]

In short, whether we analyse the concepts of existence or creation, whether we reflect on cosmology or evolution, we come back to a divine will which, if it is going to be known at all, must first be recognised under the root of our own being:

[26] *A Science of God?*, p.66.
[27] *A Science of God?*, p.106.

God acts by simple will; and we cannot see the will of God except
in what that will has created. There is only one point at which we
can possibly touch the nerve of God's creative action, or
experience creation taking place: and that is in our own life. The
believer draws his active Christian existence out of the wellspring
of divine creation, he prays prayers which become the very act of
God's will in his will. Because we have God under the root of our
being we cannot help but acknowledge him at the root of all the
world's being.[28]

So the pressing imperatives of Christian living combine with
metaphysical exploration to offer a knowledge of God's action in
the world which involves and invokes a union of human wills
with the Divine will.

It was sometimes said that Austin Farrer was a genius; the one
genius produced by the Church of England this century. What
was the nature of his genius? Normally we use the word to
indicate some overwhelming talent that a person possesses in the
light of which all their personal qualities, good and ill, pale into
insignificance. We talk of the genius of Mozart or Shakespeare or
Giotto. In such cases it does not affect our estimate of the genius
if we discover that they were childishly scatalogical, their
political opinions obnoxious or their private life a mess. Farrer's
genius was not of that kind. It consisted not of one talent but of
three; three fused together in such a way that each reached its
perfection in relation to the other two. First, there was the sheer
brilliance of his intellect, secondly there was the quality of his
imagination and thirdly there was the depth of his spirituality. It
was in this combination of intellect and imagination suffused
with a transparent holiness that his genius lies. I have looked at
the way mind and soul worked together in harmony. I want to
end by looking briefly at the role of his poetic imagination, that
is, his captivating prose style, in bringing about this unity. One
example is an early sermon on the Incarnation. It begins with the
problem posed by the existence of any power, not least the
power of God:

[28] *A Celebration of Faith*, p. 61.

The universal misuse of human power has the sad effect that power, however lovingly used, is hated . . . We have so mishandled the sceptre of God which we have usurped . . . that we are made incapable of loving the government of God himself or feeling the caress of an almighty kindness.[29]

This, one notes, is ten years before the Death of God Theologians posed the issue. How does Farrer handle the question? Christian poets, particularly those of the 17th century, like Crashaw and Donne have loved to indulge themselves in the paradoxes of the incarnation. Farrer's prose is no less evocative than their poetry. But he makes it serve a serious theological theme:

> Mary holds her finger out, and a divine hand closes on it. The maker of the world is born a begging child; he begs for milk and does not know that it is milk for which he begs. We will not lift our hands to pull the love of God down to us, but he lifts his hands to pull human compassion down upon his cradle . . . and this is how he brings his love to bear on human pride; by weakness not by strength, by need and not by bounty.[30]

A sermon which begins with a severe dilemma that is not only intellectual but of the utmost psychological, moral and pastoral importance, takes us to the hand of an infant reaching in need for milk. Along the way the dilemma is resolved and our whole perspective is altered. A spell has been cast. Magic has been at work. It is a magic in the actual words: the contrasts, the paradoxes, the specificity of the detail, the rhythms, the balanced cadences.

Another, final example. During the 1960s many of us were troubled by the principle of falsification, in particular by Antony Flew's charge that bold Christian claims like 'God loves the world' die the death of a thousand qualifications. The way Farrer dealt with this question was like no one else. He began by refusing to be apologetic about the fact that religion has to use ordinary human words:

---

[29] *Said or Sung* (London: Faith Press, 1960), USA title: *A Faith of Our Own*, (New York: The World Publishing Co., 1960), p. 34f.
[30] ibid.

God wants to give us the best thing in the world, a perfect and supernatural good. How is he going to make it known to us? He has to talk to us in the language we already know, the language of earthly things. If he talked to us the language of heaven, how would we ever understand? Inevitably the earthly words do not fit the heavenly things. The result is a good deal of initial confusion and disappointment.[31]

Does this means that the words become qualified away, that the sense is drained out of them? No, for Christ come not to dissolve but to fulfill, to make the words full, to pack them with all the meaning they can bear. He did this by taking the words and the promise they convey seriously:

We are content to think that God promises us something or other which is good, but there is no need to press very closely the sense of the words in which he gave his promises to us. Not so Christ: he pressed the sense of the words, those words 'Messiah' and 'Kingdom' for example, he pressed them so, that he ran them clean through his heart; and that was how he discovered what they mean, both for himself and for all mankind. He did not empty out the meaning of the words, he lived it out, and found it wonderful; he died for it and found it transfiguring. His fulfilling of the words was not a matter of scholastic exposition, but of death and resurrection.[32]

Look a little more closely at that passage to see how the magic works, how it is that Farrer achieves his effect. The key image is that of pressing. It begins with the word 'press' being used in the sense of asking the meaning of words. We are content with some vague belief in God's goodness. We do not press very closely the sense of the words. 'Not so Christ: he pressed the sense of the words, those words "Messiah" and "Kingdom" for example.' Here the intellectual meaning of the image is still uppermost but already there is a change of tone brought about by the repetition. Christ took the words seriously, asked what they involved for him personally. The word 'press' is then repeated a third time in conjunction with a new image that totally transforms the whole way the meaning of words is discovered. 'He pressed them so,

---

[31] *A Celebration of Faith*, p.33f.
[32] ibid.

that he ran them clean through his heart; and that was how he discovered what they mean, both for himself and for all mankind.' The sentence begins by conveying a physical image, pressing some object against ones chest, pressing it because it is precious. But what is pressed turns out to be a sword. He has run himself onto his own sword. A suicide, yet not a suicide: a death voluntarily embraced. The pressing echoes the winepress of divine wrath and the giving which is pressed down and running over. The pain recalls the words of Simeon to Mary 'And a sword shall pierce through thine own soul also'. But the sword does not just go into the heart. 'He pressed them so, that he ran them clean through his heart.' We can almost see the sword coming out of the other side: and that exactly corresponds to the total change in perspective brought about by the passage as a whole. We begin with an intellectual worrying away at the meaning of words. We end with death and resurrection. 'He did not empty out the meaning of the words, he lived it out.'

There are pious philosophers and thoughtful people of prayer. What gives the unity of Farrer, so apparent in all his work, its remarkable distinction, is the sheer quality of his prose; the product of a poetic imagination, honed by the study of ancient literature and put to the service of divine truth. The man is indeed in the style; and in that style is the Divine creativity.

Chapter 2

# RECENT THOUGHT ON DIVINE AGENCY

*Owen Thomas*

Theologians continue to talk a great deal about God's activity in the world, and there continue to be only a very few who pause to consider some of the many problems involved in such talk. So the issues raised in my book *God's Activity in the World*[1] continue to be pressing ones.

In this essay I shall offer an assessment of the current state of the discussion on this question, referring first to the books and essays which have appeared since 1982.[2] Then I will add some comments on the questions which still surround the nature of divine activity in the world.

## TRACY, JANTZEN, AND THIEMANN

A promising development of what I have called the personal action view of God's activity in the world has appeared in two recent books. I refer to Thomas F. Tracy's *God, Action and Embodiment*[3] and Ronald F. Thiemann's *Revelation and*

[1] Chico, California: Scholars Press, 1983.

[2] One book on which I will not comment further is Maurice Wiles' *God's Action in the World: The Bampton Lectures for 1986* (London: S.C.M. Press, 1986).
In these lecturers Wiles elaborates the view which was outlined in his essay in *God's Activity in the World* and which I characterised as the Uniform Action approach. God's action in the world is uniform and in no sense particular or specific, the appearance of particularity being given by varying human response to the unchanging divine action. But in this book Wiles does not develop his view significantly beyond the original essay. See my review in *The Anglican Theological Review* 69:4 (Oct., 1987).

[3] Grand Rapids, Michigan: Eerdmans, 1984.

*Theology: The Gospel as Narrated Promise.*[4] Both authors develop the theme of God as personal agent and explore the question of double agency. Neither, however, focusses on the issue of the relation of divine activity to creaturely activity.

Tracy's purpose in his book is to explore the theological possibilities and problems involved in conceiving God as one who acts, as an agent, the bearer of a personal identity made manifest in action. He agrees with the way in which Gilkey has posed the issue of divine activity, but he is critical of the ways in which Ogden and Kaufman have responded to it. Both, he believes, have drawn back from asserting that God does in fact act in history, and both have traded on a mind-body dualism (xiii–xvi)

In the first part of his book Tracy argues that in order to ascribe traits of character to God, such as love or justice, we must be able to identify enduring patterns in God's intentional action. In the second part he explores Descartes' mind-body dualism and the consequences for theology of rejecting such dualism. In the final part Tracy develops a non-Cartesian understanding of the human agent and explores and criticises the view that God is embodied in the world (Hartshorne). His own proposal is that God is not so embodied but represents the perfection of agency in being self-created, fully unified as an agent, and all-powerful (126). He believes that this constitutes a new path between classical and neo-classical theism.

What contribution does Tracy make to the question of understanding God's activity in the world in relation to finite activity? In a chapter on 'Embodiment and Identification' he argues that 'God might be identified by indicating a unique relation that he has to our shared world of objects and events located in space and time. If we think of God as an agent, might we identify God from those events in our experience that are taken to be his acts?' (77). Then he raises all the difficult questions about this which have been explored in my book, and especially those raised by Gilkey about the Exodus events. But it

---

[4] Notre Dame, Indiana: University of Notre Dame Press, 1985.

does not appear to me that he gives any indication about how he would go about resolving any of these questions.

One problem Tracy does explore further is whether the act-agent relation always points to a single agent. He states that it does not, that a single act description may be exemplified by two agents simultaneously in a single identifiable event, for example, two people pulling a rope to ring a bell. But certain features of the context of an action or characteristics of the agent can rule out ascribing a single instance of an action to more than one agent. For example, the theistic story is stubbornly monotheistic. Also the action in question can be such that admits of only one agent, for example, creation. Finally, any instance of a basic action, that is, an action without any instrumental substructure, can in principle be ascribed to only one agent. However, in actions in which there is such an instrumental substructure, two agents can be involved in bringing about a single event. This raises the question of whether God's actions in the world are basic actions or involve instrumental substructures. This depends, states Tracy, on the way the theologian formulates the theistic story (80–83). Thus the issue of the relation of divine and finite agency is not engaged.

In the chapter exploring whether God can be considered to be a fully embodied agent, a cosmic organism, Tracy returns to the double agency question as a difficulty in this view.

> Can a single event be an action in precisely the same sense for both the sub-individuals and the super-individual? If so, can they be distinct agents? Are the actions of sub-individuals to be understood as enactments of the super-individual's intentions? If so, are the sub-individuals agents in their own right at all? Is the action of the super-individual simply the accumulated effect of the actions of many subindividuals? If so, is the super-individual an agent in any significant sense? Does the super-individual act by somehow influencing the actions of the many sub-individuals? If so, is the super-individual surreptitiously being treated as a distinct entity that acts upon the society of many sub-individuals? (115)

On the basis of these and other problems Tracy dismisses this view. Yet the same problems arise in connection with his own approach, but he does not treat them there.

Mention should also be made at this point of Grace Jantzen's book *God's World, God's Body*[5] in which she argues that God is embodied in the world. God's relation to the world is analogous to a person's relation to his or her body when this relation is interpreted holistically. She argues further that the idea of God's action in the world makes more sense on the model that the world is God's body than on the traditional model. In the former view any action of God on the world is a direct or basic action not mediated by anything else. Furthermore, unlike persons' relations to their bodies, God is in control of all parts of the world. Indeed, all events in the world are God's basic actions (85–93). However, Jantzen does not explore the nature of the resulting relation between divine and finite activity.

This leads us to Thiemann's book which is a defence of the doctrine of revelation against recent criticisms and as the necessary basis for the affirmation of God's prevenience. He argues that the fatal flaw of modern doctrines of revelation has been their basis in epistemological foundationalism, and that contemporary theologians, such as Schubert Ogden, and David Tracy, attempt to avoid a doctrine of revelation by similarly flawed transcendental and foundational moves. In their place he offers a non-foundational view of theology and revelation using the category of narrated promise.

This approach focusses attention on the centrality of God's agency and self-characterisation through divine acts in the biblical narrative. (Here Thiemann is dependent upon Tracy's argument discussed above.) Thiemann notes that although God is the main character in scripture, direct divine actions are only rarely described, and the divine agency is most often depicted through the description of the acts of other agents. 'Those acts which occur through human agents are, insofar as they move toward a *telos* retrospectively discerned, the very acts of God' (90).

In exploring the intelligibility of belief in God's prevenience Thiemann inquires whether it is possible to identify God as the

<hr />

[5] Philadelphia: Westminster Press, 1984.

agent of scriptural and liturgical promises. He asserts that a liturgical pardon or absolution is a form of double agency.

> Though the speaker in the liturgical act is the presiding minister, the speaker who is committed to action is *God*. . . . These words are to be taken as the speech of God every time they are spoken. Is this notion of double agency intelligible?
> That the utterance of one speaker should be taken as the enacted intention of another presents no particular logical problem. Such complex speech-acts are a common occurrence in ordinary experience. Consider the following examples: A sister calls to her brother, 'Mom says, "its time for dinner!"'; a town crier reads a royal decree in the public square; a minister reads a Presidential proclamation from the pulpit on Thanksgiving morning. In every case one speaker speaks on behalf of another agent and enacts the agent's intention to 'call,' 'decree,' or 'proclaim.' All that is required for intelligibility is that the context and/or content of the address make clear the situation of double agency. The liturgical pardon does that in its content-reference to the primary agency of Father, Son, and Spirit or in its representative mode of speech ('by [Christ's] authority I declare to you . . .') (106).

Thiemann concludes that this notion of double agency is intelligible 'provided there are available procedures for identifying and distinguishing the acts and intentions of the two agents' (106f). The liturgical and scriptural contexts constitute a narrative identification of God as the one who gives and fulfills promises.

Then Thiemann devotes a chapter to the literary and theological interpretation of the gospel of Matthew to demonstrate that it involves a narrative identification of God. 'That description locates God as an agent of intentional action both within the scriptural text and within our common world of experience' (108). 'God is thereby identified as the one whose promises are fulfilled in the mission of the Son of God and who enacts his intention to save in the raising of Jesus from the dead' (113). It should be noted that in this interpretation the gospel story is taken as it stands without any historical critical interpretation. That is, it is at least implied that God does everything that the author of Matthew says God does.

The main area in which Tracy and Thiemann may have made a

contribution is that of double agency, and I will return to this later.

(Since the original presentation of this paper, I have learned of another important explication of the personal action view which has appeared in a book by Vernon White entitled *The Fall of a Sparrow: A Concept of Special Divine Action*.[6] After describing the demands of revelation and criticising the views of Wiles, Ogden, Baelz, and process theologians, White presents an approach in which 'God acts personally, universally, with priority and sovereign efficacy; he acts in relation to particular events' (55). He holds that divine action is thoroughly analagous to human action, which is defined by intention, and that God acts in nature as well as in history and human lives. It should also be noted that White agrees with Farrer that the 'causal joint' between divine and creaturely actions, the 'how' of double agency, is beyond our understanding.)

## McLAIN AND ALSTON

Two recent essays make similar suggestions as to how we may understand a special act of God. In an important essay which is included in this volume F. Michael McLain offers an incisive analysis of the way in which Gilkey poses the problem and a critique of the ways in which Ogden and Kaufman have responded. He argues that incorporeality is no barrier to thinking of God literally as an agent. He judges that Ogden and Kaufman have not succeeded in working out a concept of a particular special action of God. He concludes that Austin Farrer has offered the most fruitful suggestion for understanding such an action, namely, someone's perception of more than usual of the divine purpose in a particular event. Although he regularly refers to 'God acting in and through the actions of finite agents,' he does not suggest how this double agency might be understood.

In an essay entitled 'God's Action in the World'[7] William P.

---

[6] Exeter: Paternoster Press, 1985.

[7] *Evolution and Creation*, ed. Ernan McMullin (Notre Dame, University of Notre Dame Press, 1985), pp. 197–220.

Alston takes up the problem of divine agency in a rather different way from Tracy, Thiemann, and McLain. Although he holds God to be literally a personal agent, his approach to divine agency is closer to the primary cause view of Thomas than to the personal action theory.

In the first part of his essay Alston argues that almost all events in the world, including those due to natural causes, can be understood as intentional actions of God. Assuming a causal determinism in the natural order God as creator and sustainer is the agent of all events in this order. This, however, does not remove the reality of created agency, since an event in the natural order involves different roles for the divine and finite agents.

A question arises at this point. Can the results of the action of creation and preservation be properly considered the intentional acts of God? Action theory seems to imply a closer relation between agent and event than there is here. However, I suppose that Voyager II photographing the moons of Uranus in January 1986 can be considered the intentional act of the engineer who planned, designed, programmed, and executed the launch of Voyager eight years before.

Then Alston inquires whether God can be said to perform the actions of autonomous agents, if they are assumed not to be causally determined in accordance with the libertarian view, and he concludes negatively. In this connection I wonder what Alston would make of Thiemann's case of liturgical pardon and similar examples in the Bible, which are asserted to be cases of double agency. I will return to this later.

Alston also notes that the libertarian position greatly complicates the case for divine agency even of causally determined happenings, since especially today human actions have affected most events on or near the surface of the earth. What is the role of divine agency in those causally determined events which are affected by human volition? He explores the possibility of God's determination on the basis of foreknowledge but rejects it. Alston concludes that although God partly determines events influenced by human volition, God is not their agent completely.

In the second part of his essay Alston takes up the question of whether some events are actions of God in a special sense. He argues that miracles or God's direct action can be considered such special actions and cannot be ruled out by any of the arguments which have been proposed against them. However, he wants to explore the possibility of special acts of God other than miracles, such as God's guiding and strengthening people and God's providential care. Direct divine intervention is not required for this, since 'God is still intentionally doing everything done by the natural order He creates' (214). Following a suggestion by Tillich and Macquarrie, Alston proposes that an event in which someone can see the divine purpose or more of the divine purpose is a special act of God for that person. Thus the specialness is derived from the perception of the action and not from the action itself.

You will recall that David Griffin takes up a closely related question in his essay in *God's Activity in the World*. He argues that apart from miracles the claim that certain events are special acts of God is totally a function of their being perceived as special, and that there is nothing about the event in itself which makes the perception of it as special appropriate. This, he believes, leads to a relativism in regard to the revelation of the purpose of God (121). I am curious to know what Alston would make of this objection.


## DULLES, POLANYI, AND RAHNER

Another contribution to the understanding of God's activity in the world has been suggested to me by conversations and correspondence with Fr. Avery Dulles of Catholic University. During the preparation of *God's Activity in the World* he sent me an outline of his interpretation of divine agency. I was not able to persuade him to expand this into an essay for inclusion in the book, so I will try to elaborate his ideas myself.

Dulles' approach consists of an expansion and reinterpretation of the primary cause view with some help from Michael Polanyi and Karl Rahner. His outline of God's activity in the world consists of three parts: God acting simply as first cause, God bringing about a particular effect in its specificity, and God's action by grace as quasi-formal cause. I will concentrate, as he does, on the latter two.

1. God acting as first cause contributes the *esse*, the real existence, of the effect, not its specific nature. God's relation to the world in this connection is one of intimate presence to each thing which is perhaps better brought out by the participation categories of Platonic metaphysics.

2. God's bringing about a particular effect in its specificity can be compared to the effect of the mind on the body, except that God exists independently of the world, whereas the mind apparently does not exist independently of the body. The mind can be understood to act on the body not efficiently but by directing the powers that come from material nature. Likewise God can be interpreted to affect the world not by supplying a new force but by directing forces already in the world. In this fashion God may be thought to direct the world providentially.

Thus, as Rahner suggests, special divine activity in the world does not necessarily involve suspension of the laws of nature, because 'every determined level and order of being is from the very start open towards a higher level and order and can be incorporated into it, without its own laws thereby having to be suspended.' He notes that the laws of two-dimensional space are not suspended in three-dimensional space, and the laws of inorganic matter are not suspended in biology. 'Similarly, the world in its material context must be conceived as open from the outset to the reality of the spirit . . . and must be conceived as open to the reality of God.'[8]

Rahner discusses this point in more detail in an exploration of the relation of the creation of the human soul and the theory of evolution. He argues that the divine special act of the creation of the individual soul is one in which God actively enables the biological processes of human bodies to transcend themselves without changing their essences and without divine causality

[8] *Theological Investigations*, vol. 5 (Baltimore: Helicon Press, 1966), p. 467. See also *Foundations of Christian Faith* (New York: Seabury Press, 1978), pp. 259f.

replacing finite causality or inserting itself into the causal series. The ontological basis of this position is found in the basic theses of Rahner's transcendental Thomism.

The fundamental paradigm of a being is found in the being who knows and acts. The real nature of causal operation and becoming is primarily manifested in the sphere of mind and spirit. In any occasion of finite knowledge a human being is intrinsically oriented toward absolute being or God as the ground and goal of this movement of the mind. All other efficient causes are deficient modes of this causality. Therefore, any agent is able to transcend itself on the basis of the presence of God as the ground of this self-movement. This self-transcendence does not cease to be self-movement but attains its own proper nature thereby. Thus Rahner affirms the evolutionary development of matter towards spirit and concludes that the parents beget a human being and not just a human body. This, he states, exemplifies the relation between the primary cause and secondary causes.[9]

Dulles suggests the same point in a somewhat different way with the help of Polanyi's concept of 'boundary control'. Polanyi asserts that a number of different principles can control a comprehensive entity at different levels, for example, the laws of mechanics, the principles of physiology, or the principles of artifacts, such as a vocabulary or the rules of chess. The range of application of such principles is limited by boundary conditions which are controlled by higher principles.

> Thus the boundary conditions of the laws of mechanics may be controlled by the operational principles which define a machine; the boundary conditions of a muscular action may be controlled by a pattern of purposive behaviour, like that of going for a walk; the boundary conditions of a vocabulary are usually controlled by the rules of grammar; and the conditions left open by the rules of chess are controlled by the stratagems of the players. And so we find that machines, purposive action, grammatical sentences, and games of chess, are all entities subject to dual control. Such is the

[9] See *Hominisation: The Evolutionary Origin of Man as a Theological Problem* (New York: Herder & Herder, 1965), pp. 62–93. I considered using this passage in *God's Activity in the World*.

stratified structure of comprehensive entities. They embody a combination of two principles, a higher and a lower.[10]

Thus the operation of a machine relies upon the laws of mechanics and the operation of an organism relies upon the laws of physics and chemistry. These operations transcend and direct these laws but do not violate them. Likewise the special action of God in the world can be understood as one which transcends and directs the laws of finite causality without violating them.[11]

3. God's action in grace can be understood by Rahner's concept of quasi-formal cause. Rahner's departure from the traditional scholastic doctrine is his emphasis that grace is the actual self-communication of God to human beings. This is not to be understood as the giving of a created and finite reality (for example, infused habitual grace) to human beings by efficient causality, but the giving of the divine reality itself by means of what he calls quasi-formal causality.[12]

In his *Foundations of Christian Faith* Rahner drops the 'quasi' but makes his essential point about the divine self-giving as formal causality more clearly. 'Man is the event of a free, unmerited and forgiving, and absolute self-communication of God. . . . God in his most proper reality makes himself the innermost constitutive element of man. We are dealing, then, with an *ontological* self-communication of God' (116). This, he says, has 'divinising' effects in human beings without their ceasing to be finite and without God ceasing to be infinite. Therefore, 'this can and must be understood as analogous to a causality in which the 'cause' becomes an intrinsic, constitutive principle of the effect itself.' This is 'a relationship of *formal* causality as distinguished from efficient causality' (120f).

Dulles comments: 'The best created analogy is the form-matter relationship which occurs, for instance, when the soul

---

[10] Michael Polanyi, *Knowing and Being* (Chicago: University of Chicago Press, 1969), p. 217.

[11] See Avery Dulles, 'Faith, Church and God: Insights from Michael Polanyi,' *Theological Studies* 45:3 (September 1984), 548–50; *idem*, *Models of Revelation* (Garden City, New York: Doubleday & Co., 1983), pp. 146f.

[12] See *Theological Investigations* 4 (Baltimore: Helicon Press, 1966), pp. 96, 175; 5 (1966), p. 205.

animates the body, making it into a human body. This causality is not in the efficient but in the formal order. In the case of God's supernatural gift of grace, God may be called quasi-formal cause since when he communicates his personal life he remains self-subsistent and does not enter into composition with the creature. Although grace is in the order of being, not action, it affects the way the graced creature acts, so that the results may be attributed to God as something more than first cause.'

## CONCLUSION

In conclusion I want to summarise some of the main points in the literature we have surveyed. I believe that the best way to do this is to focus on the question of double agency since I am persuaded that this is the key issue in the general problem of God's activity in the world.

I noted in *God's Activity in the World* that double agency was asserted in the primary view represented by Thomas Aquinas, Protestant orthodox, and Barth, and implied in the approach of liberal theology represented by Schleiermacher, Bultmann, and Kaufman, and also by Farrer and Gilson as followers of Thomas.

What is affirmed in double agency, as I understand it, is that in one event both the divine and creaturely agents are fully active. God has not overwhelmed the finite agent so that it is merely a passive instrument, and God is not simply the creator and sustainer who allows the creaturely agent to act independently of divine agency. Furthermore, the divine and finite agents are not merely complementary, that is, they do not contribute distinct parts to the one event. As many authors have put it, God acts in and through the finite agent which also acts in the event.

Now what progress has been made in the literature we have considered on this issue of double agency? Is it an intelligible and coherent concept or not? Our authors have assumed that it is intelligible and they have suggested various analogies and examples of divine-creaturely double agency. Let us assess them in the light of the foregoing definition, and let us look first at the analogies.

Tracy's analogy of two people pulling on a rope to ring a bell is clearly not a case of double agency, since each agent contributes part of the action. The same applies, I believe, to Thiemann's analogies of the sister passing on the mother's message about dinner, the town crier reading the royal decree, and the minister reading the presidential proclamation. In each case the agents are performing distinct actions or distinct parts of one action. They would be valid analogies of double agency only if the passing on or reading were in fact the very occasion on which the message, decree, or proclamation became a reality or became effective, such that there was an identity of the actions of the two agents. For example, in the case of the royal decree, if the context were such that it actually became effective in an official proclamation, say, by a magistrate before the parliament, then this might be a fairly good analogy of divine-human double agency. Both agents, the crown and the magistrate, would be active in the one event of the proclamation of the decree.

Furthermore, Rahner's analogies (two and three dimensional space, the laws of inorganic matter and biology) and some of Polanyi's analogies (the laws of mechanics and machines, vocabulary and grammar) are also not analogies of double agency since no intentional action is involved. However, Polanyi's other analogies (physiology and purposive action, the rules of chess and the player's strategies) are possible analogies of divine-creaturely double agency. But they are analogies of double agency between God and sub-human agents rather than between God and autonomous agents. They are analogies of the way in which divine agency causes lower levels of being to transcend themselves without being disrupted.[13]

This leaves us with the two examples of divine-creaturely double agency, as distinct from analogies, namely, Thiemann's example of liturgical pardon and Dulles' and Rahner's example of grace as quasi-formal cause. Both seem to fulfill the conditions of

[13] It should be noted that in the book mentioned above Vernon White offers as analogies of double agency the following: human interpersonal influence, the relation of human agency to physical systems, and the relation of three to two dimensional space. See *The Fall of a Sparrow*, pp. 110, 115, 118f.

double agency, and they also offer examples of two distinct types of divine-creaturely double agency which I shall call promissory and gracious, respectively.

In liturgical pardon the minister relying on the promise of God (see Matt. 16:19, 18:18; John 20:23) absolves the penitent in the name of God. Thiemann quotes the Lutheran Book of Worship: 'As a called and ordained minister of the church of God, and by his authority, I therefore declare to you the entire forgiveness of all your sins, in the name of the Father, and of the Son, and of the Holy Spirit' (106). Here the divine and human agents are fully active in the one event of pardon. I am surprised that the Lutheran Thiemann did not also use the example of Christian preaching in which the hearer relying on the promise of God trusts that the human word becomes the vehicle of the word of God.[14]

Dulles and Rahner could have given many specific examples of the action of grace as quasi-formal cause. I will mention two possibilities. God inspires the prophet who says, 'Thus says the Lord . . .'. God speaks to Israel in and through the words of the prophet. This is close to the example of preaching, but it is more an example of the gracious divine presence than of trusting in a divine promise. Another example is the Christian acting in love of the neighbour by the inspiration of God (see Rom. 5:5, etc.). God loves the neighbour in and through the action of the Christian who is inspired by the divine love.

This gracious type of double agency has been central in Christian experience and reflection from the beginning, because it is based on the fundamental Christian paradigm of incarnation. The interpretation of Jesus' relation to God and more specifically the relation of Jesus' actions to God's actions has always been the basic pattern or model of the God-world relation and of divine-creaturely double agency. I referred to this in the final chapter of *God's Activity in the World*, and I want to return to it now.

In many passages of the New Testament Jesus is described as doing the works of God. Jesus is the very word of God become

---

[14] See Luke 10:16, 1 Thess. 2:13, and the Reformation principle, *Praedicatio verbi Dei est verbum Dei* (Second Helvetic Confession, 1566).

flesh (John 1:14). It is by the Spirit of God that Jesus casts out demons (Matt 12:28). The words and works of Jesus are the words and works of God (John 5:19, 19:10, etc.). Jesus is the power and wisdom of God in action (1 Cor. 1:24). I have expanded on this theme following suggestions from John Hick and W. R. Matthews to develop a christology whose main assertion is that the love manifest in Jesus' actions is numerically identical with the love of God.[15]

Since Jesus has usually been regarded as the prototype of the Christian life, we can expect to find similar testimonies from Christian experience. And this is exactly what we do find beginning with the New Testament and especially Paul. 'By the grace of God I am what I am. . . . I worked harder than any of them, though it was not I, but the grace of God which is with me' (1 Cor. 15:10). 'It is no longer I who live, but Christ who lives in me; and the life I now live in the flesh I live by faith in the Son of God' (Gal. 2:20). Then Augustine: 'Even if we do good things which pertain to God's service, it is God that brings it about that we do what God commanded.'[16] And Anselm: 'Whatever our heart rightly wills, it is of God's gift.' Finally, there are many assertions in the Reformation confessions that our good works are all by grace and the Holy Spirit.[17] We should note that these are all examples of divine-human double agency and that no valid analogies of it have been proposed with the possible exception of my interpretation of Thiemann's analogy of the reading of the royal decree.

Now is this concept of double agency intelligible or not? In *God's Activity in the World* David Griffin argues that it is not. He states that the primary-secondary cause version of double agency assumes the sufficiency of each cause and that the idea of two sufficient causes for one event is self-contradictory (117–23).

---

[15] See *Introduction to Theology*, rev. edn. (Wilton, Connecticut: Morehouse-Barlow Co., 1983), pp. 152–5.

[16] *On the Predestination of the Saints*, chapter 19.

[17] See D. M. Baillie, *God Was in Christ* (New York: Charles Scribner's Sons, 1978), chapter 5, for these references and the development of this theme.

He expands on this in an extended criticism of the philosophical theology of James F. Ross.[18]

Another critique of the primary cause view of double agency is made by Frank Dilley in *God's Activity in the World*. He holds that in double agency either the freedom of one of the agents is denied or the action must be divided between them. If there is genuine unity of action, there is no duality of causes, and if there is duality of causes, there is no unity of action, no single event. (55–57).

One solution to this problem is to loosen the definition of double agency and follow the lead of process theology. Then neither the divine nor the creaturely agent is a sufficient cause of the event. There is duality of causes but no unity of action. The two causes are complementary, and each contributes a distinct part to the event.

The other solution is to affirm double agency but also to assert that it is mysterious in character or with Farrer that the 'causal joint' is by hypothesis outside of our knowledge, even as the mind-body relation is unintelligible to us.[19]

Is there another solution to the problem of double agency? I have not heard it yet. And so I suggest that this question should be a major focus of future discussions.

---

[18] *God, Power and Evil: A Process Theodicy* (Philadelphia: Westminster, 1976), chapter 14. See also Lewis Ford, *The Lure of God* (Philadelphia: Fortress Press, 1978), p. 19.

[19] See *God's Activity in the World*, pp. 197–9, 201, 211.

Chapter 3

# HOW TO THINK ABOUT DIVINE ACTION

Twenty-five Years of Travail for Biblical Language

*William Alston*

I

There seems to be a widespread impression in theological circles, and among some philosophers who concern themselves with such matters, that the idea of God acting 'in the world' is at best problematic, dubious, and puzzling, and, at worst, incoherent, unintelligible, or radically unacceptable. I shall seek to show that this impression is quite unjustified, that the concept of divine action is, by any reasonable standards, quite intelligible, coherent, and acceptable, and that impressions to the contrary stem from confusions, uncritical acceptance of current shibboleths, or bad arguments. For this purpose I shall concentrate on the difficulties posed in Langdon Gilkey's celebrated essay, 'Cosmology, Ontology, and the Travail of Biblical Language'.[1] The attention given this essay by theologians indicated its success in articulating problems that are widely felt in theological circles. I shall take it that if I can deal with Gilkey's concerns I will have succeeded in vindicating the concept of divine activity to many of my contemporaries.[2]

[1] *Journal of Religion*, 41 (1961), pp. 194–205. Reprinted in Owen C. Thomas, ed., *God's Activity in the World: The Contemporary Problem* (Chico, California: Scholars Press, 1983). All pages references are to the latter volume.
[2] Gilkey's essay is specifically designed to display an incoherence in the then current 'biblical theology'. He argues that the proponents of that position accept certain 'liberal' tenets that are incompatible with their insistence on the reality of divine activity in the world. I am not at all disposed to quarrel with this judgement. However, Gilkey makes it quite clear that he himself shares these 'liberal' tenets and that he takes them to constitute grave difficulties for the concept of divine action. It is this latter supposition that I will be contesting.

Gilkey mobilises two difficulties for traditional conceptions of divine activity, difficulties that he takes to be closely connected. First the pervasive contemporary 'assumption of a causal order among phenomenal events' (31) is incompatible with the supposition that God has interfered with the causal order to perform the putative miracles with which the Bible is filled. 'Whatever the Hebrews believed, *we* believe that the biblical people lived in the same causal continuum of space and time in which we live, and so one in which no divine wonders transpired and no divine voices were heard . . . The modern assumption of the world order has stripped bare our view of biblical history of all the divine deeds observable on the surface of history . . .' (31) Second, and as a result, we can no longer use terms like 'act' univocally of God and human beings. We are forced to give an analogical meaning to 'God does . . .', and no one has provided a satisfactory spelling out of the analogy.

> Put in the language of contemporary semantic discussion, both the biblical and orthodox understanding of theological language was univocal. That is, when God was said to have 'acted', it was believed that he had performed an observable act in space and time so that he functioned as does any secondary cause; and when he was said to have 'spoken', it was believed that an audible voice was heard by the person addressed. In other words, the words 'act' and 'speak' were used in the same sense of God as of men. We deny this univocal understanding of theological words. To us, theological verbs such as 'to act', 'to work', 'to do', 'to speak', 'to reveal', etc., have no longer the literal meaning of observable actions in space and time or of voices in the air . . . Unless one knows in some sense what the analogy means, how the analogy is being used, and what it points to, an analogy is empty and unintelligible. . . . (32; see also 36.)
>
> What has happened is clear: because of our modern cosmology, we have stripped what we regard as 'the biblical point of view' of all its wonders and voices. This in turn has emptied the Bible's theological categories of divine deeds and divine revelations of all their univocal meaning, and we have made no effort to understand what these categories might mean as analogies. (40)

I shall now proceed to meet these challenges posed by Gilkey. First, I shall consider whether anything we are justified in accepting in the way of 'modern cosmology' rules out the possibility of direct divine production of effects in the physical universe. Second, I shall consider whether such a possibility is required to preserve a full blooded concept of, and belief in, divine action in the world. Third, I shall consider whether the factors mentioned by Gilkey force us to deny that action terms are used univocally of God and human beings. And fourth, assuming that complete univocity cannot be claimed, I shall respond to Gilkey's demand for 'concrete and specifiable content' for act terms in application to God.

## II

Just what have we learned in the last four hundred years that rules out direct divine production of worldly effects? First I want to note that Gilkey's presentation is typical of recent theological discussions of this point in failing to give a specific enough answer to this question. He uses phrases like 'the causal continuum of space-time experience' (31), 'the causal nexus in space and time' (31), and 'a causal order among phenomenal events' (31). But to affirm any of these is simply to commit oneself to the hardly startling proposition that there are causal interactions within the physical universe, that some things do happen because of the operation of natural causes. But all that is quite compatible with some natural events being, in whole or in part, the result of divine activity instead of the the result of natural causes. To find something with more of a cutting edge we must look to something as strong as universal natural causal *determinism*, the thesis that everything that happens in the universe was determined to happen just as it does by natural causes; the thesis that, given the natural causal factors that were operative, it was impossible for that event not to have occurred or to have occurred in any other way. That thesis does imply that God could have no voice in determining what happens in the natural order (except by way of a determination of that order itself, a point we shall be exploiting at a later stage of the discussion). For, according to the thesis, each natural event is uniquely determined to be what it is by *natural* causes; hence there is no room for any other influence on its constitution.

But why should we accept so strong a thesis? Gilkey, again, is typical of theologians of his stripe in simply appealing to the widespread acceptance of the position.[3] But unless we have reason to think that our age is distinguished from all others in being free of intellectual fads and fancies, of attachment to assumptions, paradigms, and models that far outstrip the available evidence, of believing things because one finds one's associates believing them, this is hardly of any probative value. A rational person will want to know, not just that the assumption is widely accepted, but what reasons, if any, there are for this widespread acceptance.

So far as I can see, the only respectable reason for determinism comes from reflection on the remarkable success of modern physical science in extending our knowledge of the natural conditions on which one or another outcome depends. On the one hand, it can be said that science assumes determinism; if scientists weren't assuming that everything has natural causes why would they devote so much time and energy to looking for the natural causal conditions of various sorts of phenomena? And on the other hand, it can be argued that the success science has enjoyed in this enterprise gives support to the thesis that there are always such conditions to be discovered. But a closer look at the situation reveals that these considerations fall far short of establishing the thesis. As for the assumption, the only thing a scientist is committed to assuming, by virtue of engaging in the scientific enterprise, is that there is a good chance that the phenomena he is investigating depend on natural causal conditions to a significant degree. These three qualifications mark three ways in which he need not be assuming the truth of the full

[3] Here is another example. 'The way of understanding miracle that appeals to breaks in the natural order and to supernatural interventions belongs to the mythological outlook and cannot commend itself in a post-mythological climate of thought. The traditional conception of miracle is irreconcilable with our modern understanding of both science and history.' John Macquarrie, *Principles of Christian Theology*, 2nd ed. (New York: Charles Scribner's Sons, 1977), p. 248.

thesis. He need only assume a significant probability, he need only make his assumption for the particular area of his investigation, and he need not assume even there (even a chance of) *complete* determination. As for the results of science, they are indeed impressive, but they fall far short of showing that every event in the universe is strictly determined to be just what it is by natural factors. All our evidence is equally compatible with the idea that natural causal determination is sometimes, or always, only approximate. After all, we have observed only a tiny proportion of natural events. Our observations are always subject to a margin of error; indeed we exploit this fact to correct observations into as good a fit with deterministic laws as is typically reported. In many cases we work with deterministic laws only at the price at taking them to be idealisations (dealing with frictionless surfaces, point masses and the like) to which actual occurrences only approximate. Thus the results of science might reasonably be taken to suggest rather a close approximation to natural determinism.

This issue is a complex and difficult one. The above paragraph only scratches the surface, but in this paper I lack the time to go into the matter properly. Before signing off, however, I do want to make one additional point that seems to me crucial. It is often supposed that the laws of nature discovered by modern physical science (or at least the laws that science has given us ample reason to accept) make it impossible that God should even partly determine the course of events, at least without violating those laws (if that is at all possible). In making this supposition one supposes that such laws specify *unqualifiedly* causally sufficient conditions. Thus a law of hydrostatics might specify as a sufficient condition for a body sinking in still water (of sufficient depth) that the body be of a density greater than the water. A man standing upright in the middle of a deep lake without sinking would be a violation of that law, and so would be impossible. But in fact we are never justified in accepting laws of this sort. The most we are ever justified in accepting is a law that specifies what will be the outcome of certain conditions *in the absence of any relevant factors other than those specified in the law*. The laws we have reason to accept lay down sufficient conditions only within a 'closed system', i.e. a system closed to influences other than those specified in the law. None of the laws we are capable of working with take account of all possible influences. Even if a formulation took account of all influences with which we are acquainted, we cannot be assured that no hitherto unknown influences are lurking on the horizon. A man standing upright on the surface of a lake will sink, *unless* he is being supported by a device dangling from a helicopter, or *unless* he is being drawn by a motor boat, or *unless* a sufficiently strong magnetic attraction is keeping him afloat, or . . . Since the laws we have reason to accept make provision for interference by outside forces unanticipated by the law, it can hardly be claimed that such a law will be violated if a divine outside force intervenes; and hence it can hardly be claimed that such laws imply that God does not intervene, much less imply that this is impossible. No doubt that is not the sort of outside force scientists normally envisage, but that is neither here nor there. If we were to make the rider read 'in the absence of outside forces of the sort we are prepared to recognise as such', our confidence in all our law formulations would be greatly weakened; for we have no basis for supposing that science has at this point identified all the factors that can influence natural phenomena.

One more point about direct divine intervention. Gilkey, again not untypically, thinks that the traditional conception of divine action recognises only Cecil B. DeMille super-spectaculars as the real thing. Thus he takes it that 'audible voices' would have to be heard if we can 'univocally' speak of God acting when prophets take themselves to have received a message from God. Again he writes, with reference to the 'biblical theology' he is attacking:

> One can only conclude, therefore, that the mighty act of God is not his objective activity in history but only his inward incitement of a religious response to an ordinary event within the space-time continuum. If this is what we mean, then clearly we have left the theological framework of 'mighty act with faith response' and returned to Schleiermacher's liberalism, in which God's general

activity is consistent throughout the continuum of space-time events and in which special religious feeling apprehends the presence of God in and through ordinary finite events. Thus our theological analogy of the mighty act seems to have no specifiable referent or meaning. (38)

But even if we are holding out for a divine *interference* in natural processes (natural events caused to be what they are, at least in part, by the direct activity of God), there is absolutely no reason to confine this category to publicly observable events, much less to super-spectacular ones. If God wills, and hence brings it about, that certain thoughts form in my mind together with the conviction that these thoughts constitute His message to me at this moment, that is as full-blooded a case of direct divine action in the world as the miraculous production of audible voices. Similarly, if God works outside the order of natural causes to 'incite a religious response to an ordinary event', that is, *ex hypothesi*, as genuine a case of God doing something in the world, outside the natural order, as a burning of a bush that is not consumed by the flames. It is but a vulgar prejudice to suppose that decibel level or number of observers is a measure of the divine activity level.[4]

## III

Thus we 'post-mythological' moderns are not constrained by anything we are justified in believing about the causal order to deny that God acts in the world outside that order. There may be theological reasons for declining to think of divine activity in this way, but here I am only concerned to argue that our general knowledge leaves the possibility open. However I am by no means suggesting that God can act in the world *only* by acting outside the natural order. On the contrary, I wish to affirm that God can, and does, act in and through the action of natural causes. However, I do not choose to allot much of this paper to a defence of that claim. We already have a number of impressive defences, particularly in St. Thomas and in the work of numerous Thomists, and I do not have time here to rehash their work. I will just say, by way of a minimal rehash, that the

---

[4] On this point see the essay by Thomas Tracy in this volume.

analogy of the artisan and his tool seems to me quite appropriate. When I split a log with an axe, it is true both that the axe splits the log and that I split the log. Similarly if God creates, orders, and conserves the natural order to carry out His purposes, then it is true both than the bee pollinates the flower and that God does so. Let me now briefly comment on a few problems that come up for this mode of divine action.

Many of those who argue that God is an agent of all creaturely happenings take God to will every detail of the world process, including putatively free choices and doings of human beings. This makes possible a satisfyingly simple picture. God institutes the natural order, realising in advance[5] all the details of its working out, and instituting it in order to bring about all those details. Every natural event, except for the first one if any, is brought about by other natural events that are used by God as instruments for that purpose. But if human free choices and actions are not willed by God (God endows these creatures with the capacity to decide such matters themselves and allows them to do so), they constitute a rent in this simple picture. God didn't institute the natural order to bring these events about; they are not (wholly) brought about by natural causes. We might try to handle this difficulty just by making an exception: God is the agent of all and only those natural events that He has willed to happen just as they do. But the trouble goes deeper. Human free actions themselves have consequences. Hence any natural happenings in the causal ancestry of which there is some creaturely free choice are not such as to be planned by God just on the basis of the kind of natural causal order He set up. Thus the biological and ecological processes involved in areas under human cultivation could not have been planned by God just on the basis of his knowledge of what would result from the beings he created and the laws of nature He ordained. Of course, if He has foreknowledge of human free actions He can take account of those in further planning. But, on the present hypothesis of

---

[5] If God's mode of being is timeless, this 'in advance' can't be given a temporal interpretation. Nevertheless the realisation can still be prior to creation, in that the latter is done in the light of that realisation.

human free will, He cannot complete His planning for the uses of created instruments prior to any creative decisions. For the foreknowledge of human free choices will be prior knowledge of what those beings actually choose in situations in which they actually find themselves. And they don't find themsleves in one set of circumstances rather than another, indeed they do not even exist, until God makes some decisions to create. Thus it would seem that in order to accommodate human free will we are forced into thinking of God as making a number of separate *ad hoc* decisions (as to how to react to free choices of creatures) after the initial institution of the natural order. We have lost the beautiful simplicity of a scheme in which, just by an initial act of creation, God thereby becomes the primary agent of every natural happening. We can, however, recapture that simplicity if we can attribute to God what the sixteenth century Jesuit theologian, Louis de Molina, called 'middle knowledge'. This is knowledge not of what actually existing creatures freely choose in actual situations, but of what various possible free creatures *would* choose in various possible situations. Armed with such knowledge God could create a total order in which everything, both naturally determined happenings and creaturely free choices, would interact to bring about just the results He is aiming at.[6]

Thus, even if natural determinism reigns, we can think of God as acting in the world through the natural order; and we can even do so if natural determinism is broken by free choices of creatures. Now let's add the point that it is conceivable that some divine actions should be outside and some through the natural order. At least we shouldn't deny that possibility without good reason for doing so, just to satisfy our yen for neatness. Indeed, anyone who believes in the outside mode will have to recognise the other mode as well. For presumably the natural order is not always being bypassed; in that case there would be no natural order. But when it is not, then, as we have seen, there is a very

___

[6] The considerations of this paragraph bring out the noteworthy point that whereas universal natural causal determinism makes difficulties for divine action outside the natural order, it facilitates divine action through the natural order. (At least it facilitates our conception of it.)

strong case, on standard theistic assumptions, for supposing that God is using natural causes to achieve His purposes. It would seem that the exclusivist position (God acts only in one of these ways) is viable only for those who deny that God ever acts outside the natural order.

The 'through the natural order only' position may seem to be faced with an embarrassment of riches. With the possible exception of free creaturely acts, everything that happens is an act of God. But then how can we accord that title to only a tiny proportion of that vast multitude? Is the raising of Jesus from the dead an 'act of God' in any sense in which the motion of a leaf in the wind outside my window is not? I believe that this formidable sounding difficulty has a simple solution. We single out some acts of God for special notice because in those cases we think we can glimpse a bit of the divine purpose, perhaps because we think God has communicated it to us. Why is that leaf moving in just the way it is? (Not what natural factors are producing that movement, but what divine purpose does it serve?) God knows. And I don't. But in the case of the resurrection we think we have some idea of what He is up to.[7] Nor does this attach only the 'mighty acts of God in history'. If I take something to be a message from God to me, by understanding the content of the message I take myself to have some idea as to what God was up to in sending the message, viz. getting me to take account of this content in my future behaviour. It is true that, on this account, what leads us to highlight certain events for special treatment is subjective, viz. the degree of our (presumed) insight into the divine purposes. But that doesn't mean that these events are acts of God only in some subjective sense. On the contrary, they share with innumerable other events the objective property of being brought about by God for the achievement of His purposes. It is only our selecting them for special notice that is subjective. And

---

[7] This point is nicely brought out in Austin Farrer, *Faith and Speculation* (London: A. & C. Black, Ltd., 1967), ch. IV.

even this may involve a non-subjective element, viz. God's informing us of His purposes in these instances.[8]

## IV

Thus far I have been considering the way in which divine action might be related to the natural causal order. I have argued that nothing we have any reason to accept (apart from theology) rules out God's bringing about natural events either outside or through the natural order, or both. The decision between these alternatives can be left to theological considerations. I have, of course, been assuming that it is *intelligible* to speak of God's bringing about natural effects. But now we must come to grips with reasons for denying this, beginning with Gilkey's reasons. To be sure, those reasons stem from the rejection of divine action in the world outside the natural order of causes, and we have already rejected that rejection. But if God does not, or cannot, act in the world outside the natural causal order, would that leave us without an intelligible conception of divine action?

In the passage from p. 32 of his essay quoted at the beginning of this paper, Gilkey purports to derive the non-univocality of 'act' from the rejection of miracles. But it is not clear how the derivation is supposed to go. According to Gilkey, when we believed in miracles we supposed that God 'performed an observable act in space and time'. But now that we have rejected miracles we 'have no longer the literal meaning of observable actions in space and time or of voices in the air'. 'The denial of wonders and voices has thus shifted our theological language from the univocal to the analogical.'[9] The claim seems to be that we have observable divine acts only if the acts are miraculous, and we can use the term 'act' univocally (with applications to human acts) only for those acts that are observable. Both

---

[8] The points in this section are developed at greater length in my paper, 'God's Action in the World', in *Evolution and Creation*, ed. Ernan McMullin (University of Notre Dame Press, 1985).

[9] Gilkey unaccountably ignores a long line of not obscure Christian theologians, e.g. Aquinas, who combine an analogical interpretation of theological language with a hospitality to 'wonders and voices'.

suppositions are demonstrably false. To evaluate the first claim we must distinguish between observation of the agent's initiatory activity and observation of the result. The typical concept of human action involves (*a*) the agent's doing something to (*b*) bring about a result of a certain kind. Thus for me to close a door is for me to (*a*) do something that (*b*) results in the door's being shut. For me to pay a bill is for me to (*a*) do something that (*b*) results in my being discharged of a certain obligation. Now observability of neither aspect (for divine actions) correlates with the act's being done outside, rather than within, the course of nature. Whether God is working through natural causes or not, in either case the result in question may or may not be publicly observable. If the result is a recovery from illness or the survival of a collision or the rout of an army, then it is publicly observable whether God is working through natural causes or apart from them. While if the result is a new insight or a new sense of purpose or a renewed confidence the result will not be publicly observable (though its manifestations may well be), whether or not God is working through natural causes.[10] As for the activity of the agent, if there is any correlation at all, it works against Gilkey's claim. The basic initiatory activity in the case of all divine action (and presumably in the case of human action as well) is something on the order of an act of will (or formation of a present intention, or whatever terminology you prefer). This will be unobservable in the divine (and human) case, whether God is working through natural causes or not. It is true, however, that in the non-miraculous cases, there may be something observable on the side of what God does to bring about the result, viz. the natural causes He uses as instruments. But this would tie observability to non-miraculous divine action, contrary to Gilkey's allegation.

So much for the supposed tie between 'outside the course of nature' and 'observability'. Now let's see whether observability is required for the application of 'action' in the sense in which it

[10] We have already noted that Gilkey is unwarranted in supposing that there must be 'audible voices' in order that God be working apart from natural causes in delivering a message.

is used of human beings. We have already seen that the initiatory act of will or intention is unobservable in the human case. As for results, they may or may not be observable; the result required for closing a door is observable, but the result required for concentrating one's attention on a certain topic is not. It is true that overt human actions typically involve observable bodily movements; I can't close a door without moving my body in some way. But *mental* actions like the one just cited show that this is not a general requirement for human actions. Indeed if it is as much as conceivable that human beings should close doors (in the same sense of 'close doors' as that in which they standardly do so) by telekinesis, e.g. just by willing that the door should be closed, then the use of bodily movements is not required by the meaning of human action terms even for overt actions that essentially involve some effect outside the agent. (This issue will be further discussed in the next section.) Finally, when an embodied human being acts, the *agent* is, of course, observable in a way that God is not. However, it remains to be argued that the observability of the agent is part of the meaning of human action terms, rather than just a pervasive feature that in fact attaches to normal human actions. I conclude that there are but dim prospects for discerning an observability requirement for action in the sense of that term in which we apply it to human beings.

Little of Gilkey's argument has survived this examination. The abandonment of miracles has no discernible implication for the univocity of 'act' across the divine-human gap. We are, to be sure, still left with questions as to just how to understand divine action, questions to which I now turn.

## V

By common consent, the terms in which we talk about God are drawn from our talk about human beings and other creatures. We first come to understand what various terms mean in application to creatures and then, when things go well, proceed on that basis to understand those terms, or others derived from them, as applied to God. Clearly the simplest possible derivation would be the univocal one: the term is applied to God with the same meaning we have learned to attach to it in talk about creatures. If 'spoke' in 'God spoke to Moses' means just the same as it does in 'Saul spoke to David' there can be no difficulty as to what it means in the former context. So let's first canvas the prospects for univocity. In this discussion I shall be concentrating on specific action terms like 'speaks' or 'makes', rather than with the category term 'action', since that's where the action is.

It is clear that divine action differs from much human action in that God doesn't perform overt actions (actions involving the production of effects outside Himself) by moving his body in various ways. Now if it is part of what is *meant* by 'Saul spoke to David' that Saul used his vocal chords in certain ways, then that part of the meaning cannot be carried over to 'God spoke to Moses' (at least if the latter is to have any chance of being true), and so 'spoke' cannot be univocal across the divine-human gap. But suppose, on the other hand, that this is not part of what is *meant* by 'speaks', as applied to human beings; it is just that this is the way that human beings in fact perform that sort of act. Here is an uncontroversial example of this latter sort of situation. Consider a door, $A$, with a handle and a swinging door, $B$. To open the former, but not the latter, one must turn the handle; but we wouldn't say that 'open' in '$H$ opened the door' *means* something different depending on whether the door has a handle. To 'open a door' is simply to do something that results in the door's coming to be open. That something can be different in different cases while 'open' is used in the same sense. It is just that what it takes to open the door differs in the two cases. Now let's suppose, analogously, that '$S$ speaks to $H$' simply means something like: $S$ brings it about that $H$ realises that a certain message comes from $S$. Or better, since $x$ can speak to $y$ without $y$'s hearing or understanding him, $S$ does something such that, if $y$ is properly attentive and has the appropriate capacities, $y$ will realise that a certain message is coming from $S$. In that sense it is not semantically necessary that one use one's vocal chords in speaking; it is just that this is the way human beings do it. God could do the same thing (i.e. speak in the same sense of 'speak') in some other way.

No doubt the formulation just given is very implausible as a meaning for 'speak', since it would equally cover written communication, and communication by other means as well. However, it might do quite well as a definition of 'communicate a message'. We shall return to this point. Meanwhile let's consider another family of common terms where the prospects for univocity are much greater. I am thinking of terms like 'comfort', 'enlighten', 'encourage', 'preserve', 'save', and 'punish'. In all these cases in saying, e.g. 'S enlightened H concerning p' (i.e. S brought H to realise that p), we are saying that S produced a certain psychological effect in H, while being quite noncommittal as to how S brings this about. Even restricting ourselves to human agents, S might have brought H to realise this by directly telling him orally, by writing him a letter, by providing him with clues that would enable him to figure it out, by sending someone else to tell him, and so on. No specification of how the effect is brought about is included in the meaning of the term. Why couldn't God bring someone to realise that something or other is the case, in the same sense of the term, even if He brings it about in some still different way, e.g. just by willing that it shall be the case, or by some direct influence on the mind of H? Of course, a die-hard opponent of univocity might claim that it is part of the meaning of 'enlighten', as used of human beings, that movements of the agent's body plays some role in bringing about the effect. But we would need some reason for supposing that, and I am at a loss to know what that would be. Since the meaning of the term is obviously neutral as between, e.g. the difference between oral and written communication and as between the difference between direct and indirect communication, why should we suppose that it is not neutral as between means that involve movements of the agent's body and those that do not? Indeed, what if a human being were able to communicate information by some sort of direct mental influence on another person? Would the former have enlightened the latter in the same sense of 'enlighten'? I would suppose so. Thus it looks as if there is a large number of what we might term 'psychological effect' action terms, each of which applies to an agent just in case the agent does something, anything, that has the appropriate psychological effect on the patient. There would seem to be no bar to applying these terms in that same sense to the cases in which God, or another non-embodied agent, brings about the crucial effect.

Let's generalise the point of the last paragraph. There are many human action terms that cannot be applied in the same sense to an agent without a body. These include the actions that simply consist in moving parts of one's body – 'kick', 'yawn', 'clench one's teeth', and the like. This category may also include action terms that involve producing a certain effect outside the agent *in a certain way*, where this way is specified in terms of bodily movements. This second sub-category may include 'speak'; it obviously includes items like 'push open a door' and 'serve an ace'. However, in many other cases all it takes for the application of the term is that the agent do something, anything, that has the right effect. In limiting cases the something done that has the effect could be as sketchy and intimate as an act of will or the formation of a present intention. Such action terms could be applied univocally to God and to us, even if what is done to bring about the effect is radically different in the two cases.

The above argument depends on some controversial dicta concerning the meaning of action terms. Not only can my position be denied; it can be argued that there is no objective, determinate truth of the matter as to what does and does not belong to the meaning of the term, as contrasted with what is confidently believed about the items to which the term applies. Whatever one may think about Quine's total rejection of the analytic-synthetic distinction, and about his pervasive scepticism concerning meaning,[11] one must acknowledge that he has highlighted difficulties in drawing the line between the meaning of terms and matters of fact. To take a nice example outside our present concerns, is it part of the meaning of 'see' that one sees with one's eyes; or is it just that in fact that is the way in which

[11] For some discussion of this see my 'Quine on Meaning', in *The Philosophy of W. V. O. Quine*, ed. Lewis Hahn (LaSalle, Illinois: Open Court Pub. Co., 1986).

human beings see? If some human beings, or humanoid creatures, were regularly to receive information via experiences that have the same phenomenal character as our visual experiences, but that are not produced by the action of light on eyes, could we speak of them as 'seeing' things in the same sense of the term in which we see things? Perhaps there is no objective answer to this question. Similarly there *may* be no objective answer to the question of whether the restriction to the use of bodily movements is part of the meaning of all human 'external effect' action terms.

However, this need not greatly concern us. It makes no real difference to the question of the intelligibility of divine action how we settle the univocality issue. The intelligibility of speaking of an *x* as *P* does not depend on using '*P*' in this context in the same sense as that in which it is used of *y*'s, even if we first learned the term in application to *y*'s. We first learned 'solvent' in application to solid substances, meaning 'capable of being dissolved in a liquid'; but that doesn't prevent us from speaking intelligibly of corporations as solvent, in a different sense of the term. I shall now proceed to utilise some points made above to show that a difference of sense need not inhibit intelligibility in this case either.

Suppose that 'comfort *H*' or 'forgive *H*', or 'command *H* to do *A*', as applied to human beings, does mean something like 'bring about effect *E* by some movements of one's body'. In that case we cannot use any of these terms of God in just that sense. But not to worry. We can simply lop off the requirement of the effect's being brought about by movements of the agent's body, thereby constructing a less specific derivative sense: *produce effect E in some way or other*. The term with that sense, which is surely intelligible if the original sense was, can then be applied univocally to God and man. And even if we don't choose ever to apply it to man, so that it is restricted to theology, it will be no less intelligible for being restricted to that field. Analogously, even if 'speak' does not literally apply to God in the sense in which it is literally asserted of human beings,[12] we can extract

[12] It can, of course, still be figuratively applied to God.

from that meaning a less specific meaning: *produce something, by whatever means, that is intended to convey a message to H.* (This meaning may well already be carried by the relatively unspecific term 'communicate a message'.) We can then proceed to apply a term with this meaning intelligibly to God. The moral is clear. Even if the meanings of human action terms are infected with elements that prevent them from being applied to God, simply shear off those elements and see what is left. It may be, and often is, that what is left is something that can be intelligibly applied to God, and in the application of which we succeed in saying what we set out to say when we talk about God's action.

To be sure, as the last two sentences suggest, there is no unrestricted guarantee that anything coherent or intelligible will remain when an element of a complex meaning is excised. We can't remove 'plane figure' from 'plane figure all points on the circumference of which are equidistant from a fixed point called the centre' and leave a viable meaning behind. It has been maintained that removing bodily movement from human overt action terms is equally disastrous. I have attempted to answer such contentions in 'Can We Speak Literally of God?'[13] Here I can only express the view that no cogent arguments have been presented for the view that bodily movement is essential to action in general, or even to overt action in general. Briefly, my position is that what is minimally essential to action is that an agent with knowledge and purposes wills, or intends, to produce certain effects in the pursuit of its purposes. If that condition is satisfied we still have action, however those volitions or intentions bring about the effects in question.[14]

This is an appropriate place to add a cautionary note about the pervasive confusion of univocity and literality, exhibited by

[13] In *Is God GOD?*, ed. Axel D. Steuer & James W. McClendon, Jr. (Nashville, Tennessee: Abingdon, 1981).

[14] We should also note that other divine-human differences have been widely regarded as subversive of the application of action terms to God. I think particularly of timelessness. On this point, see Eleonore Stump and Norman Kretzmann, 'Eternity', *Jour. Philos.*, Vol. 78, no. 8 (August, 1981), and W. P. Alston, 'Divine-Human Dialogue and the Nature of God', *Faith and Philosophy*, Vol. 2, no. 1 (January, 1985).

Gilkey along with innumerable others.[15] First of all 'univocal', unlike 'literal' is a relational term. 'Univocal' means – *with the same meaning*. It makes no sense to ask whether 'makes' in 'God made the heavens and the earth' has the same meaning, period. One must ask 'same meaning as what?' Whereas for a term to be used literally is for it to be used in some established sense it has in the language, as contrasted with being used figuratively, i.e. used in some *ad hoc* derivation from a literal use.[16] Hence a given use can be termed 'literal' or 'figurative' without thereby comparing it to some other particular use or group of uses of the term. From this it follows right away that when one is applying a term, $P$, to $X$, one need not be using it univocally with its application to $Y$, whatever $X$ and $Y$ are, in order to be using it literally. 'Force' and 'charge' are not used in physics univocally with their use in (at least pre-scientific) ordinary speech, but that hardly implies that they are being used non-literally in scientific applications. New meanings of the terms became established with the development of science, thereby enabling the terms to be used literally in these scientific applications.[17] The moral for our present concerns is that we should consider seriously the possibility that although various terms are not applied to God in just the senses in which they are applied to creatures, they may bear technical theological senses in that former use, and so be used literally, though not univocally with their use in speaking of creatures.

## VI

Thus we are not in such dire straits, with respect to understanding divine actions in the world, as Gilkey and many other contemporary religious thinkers suppose. 'Wonders and voices' need not be foresworn, and even if they are, there are plenty of

[15] '. . . today we have abandoned the univocal, literal meanings of these words.' (41)

[16] This is a very compressed statement. For more detail, see my 'Can We Speak Literally of God?', referred to above, and my 'Irreducible Metaphors in Theology', in *Experience, Reason, and God*, ed. Eugene T. Long (Washington, D.C.: Catholic University Press, 1980).

[17] That is not to say that these scientific uses were not figurative before the new meanings became established. But they are now only 'dead metaphors'.

worldly happenings putatively wrought by God in the world, most notably the psychological changes worked in devotees. Various worldly happenings can be credited to God as agent, whether or not God ever works outside the course of nature. Nor, as we have shown in the last section, need we be at a loss in understanding attributions of agency to God, whether or not any action terms can be used in precisely the same sense of God and human beings. I conclude that the equivocity bogey (or more generally, the unintelligibility bogey), like the causal determinism bogey, is no more than a paper bogey. As with all bogeys, the reasonable course is to stare them down and get on with our work.

Chapter 4

# DIVINE ACTION:
# THE DOCTRINAL TRADITION

*Eugene TeSelle*

For the purpose at hand I shall assume the mantle of the historical theologian, looking at the doctrinal tradition as it asks about divine action. This means that I shall assume a large degree of agreement about the meaning of divine action among theologians, for this is the basis of their disputes over concepts and assertions. It also means that I shall sit loose to the rival conceptualisations, recognising that they could be explored, especially in the philosophical mode, in much greater detail. I shall be looking, then, at the fundamental ways in which the problem has been stated, the principal models through which theologians have sought to understand divine action, and the analysis which has then followed from those models. The historical perspective will uncover a larger role for the notion of World-Soul than most of the literature suggests. But it will also disclose a greater complexity about this notion, and perhaps more continuity with other models and modes of analysis.

## KINDS OF DIVINE ACTS

When people speak of divine action they are referring to several distinct kinds of situations. These fall, I think, into three groupings.

First there is the creation and preservation of the things we are and the things we encounter. This is a 'radical' or 'constitutive' divine action which gives them being or makes them what they are. Traditionally things are conceived as continuing substances; but even when this notion is criticised – especially in the Whiteheadian tradition, which sees reality as microscopic 'occasions of experience' – these persisting things must be taken into account as 'societies' of occasions with a more or less steady line of inheritance from one moment to another.[1] These persisting substances or societies have their own powers of activity (and receptivity), and thus we think of them as capable of a range of experiences and actions over and above what 'constitutes' them in their continuing nature or character. In traditional theology it was usual to say that God gives to all beings their power to act and (especially in the case of rational and free beings) is not directly responsible for their actions.

Second, there are interactions among finite things, and these interactions can also be called acts of God. There are several different cases.

(a) It is always acknowledged that finite things act and interact as causes, and the divine 'concursus' is God's acting with them as they act and produce their effects. Since the Enlightenment there has been more and more emphasis upon this divine activity with and through finite things. It comes in part from a dislike of talking too glibly about radical creation or miraculous intervention; in part from an interest in redescribing divine action as something that takes place largely, or even solely, through finite interactions; in part from a response to the evolutionary understanding of the world, according to which things do not suddenly appear but arise stage by stage. Traditional theology knew that it must differentiate between generation, which occurs through the propagation of the genetic code from one generation to another, and the constitutive influence of God in the becoming of a new being.[2] But evolution magnifies the importance of generation, at the expense of radical creation and miracle. There is a stronger sense that some things must occur before others can occur, that there is a possibility for new emergents only when certain preconditions are there.

---

[1] Continuity in the midst of constant transition is especially emphasised by Nancy Frandenberry, 'The Power of the Past', *Process Studies*, 13.2 (summer 1983), pp. 132–42. Cf. also the notes in response by Richard W. Field and Dennis Cowan, *Process Studies*, 14.1 (Spring 1984), pp. 44–8.

[2] Augustine, *City of God*, XII.25; XXII.24.

(b) Before finite agents can act and interact, they must be 'positioned' for it. This is a traditional role of providence, 'disposing' things so that they will interact according to God's purposes. It is perhaps the most important meaning of 'act of God' for everyday religiosity – and for everyday theodicy. 'Why did this happen?' is the most common question about God, aroused when bad things – and sometimes good things – happen. They affect me in important ways; therefore there must be some reason for them. But such cases are also the most difficult for theological reflection, not only because it may be difficult to find any good reason at all, but because there are special problems about the 'how' of this providential positioning of things, moving them about in order to get the intended interactions.

(c) More central than both of these to the Biblical tradition are those earthly events which are called acts of God bacause they are of special significance to the community of faith. These are the classic instances dealt with in the 'Biblical theology' movement – exodus, conquest, confederacy, kingdom, exile. Events, institutions, persons are viewed as acts of God *par excellence* insofar as they are revelatory of God's purposes or mediate God's grace. We are familiar with the Biblical importance of such things, their use in the Biblical theology movement, and the subsequent criticism of most ways of construing them. It is undeniable, none the less, that finite events, institutions, and persons *can* have religious 'significance' as community-forming, or revelatory, or sacramental. A person can even speak in God's behalf, in the form of direct address. This 'significance' is what is salient about them. Whether they are to be called 'acts of God' in the more direct senses discussed earlier is what remains debatable.

(d) Often forgotten as acts of God are word, declaration, address, symbolic presentation – what the scholastics call God's *voluntas signi*, God's declared will which may or may not be fulfilled in finite events. This includes divine commands, threats, or promises, which come, through human words, into the field of our freedom, our hopes and fears, our concern for ourselves and others. In continuity with this classic notion of God's declared will, intended to lead to human response and action, is the modern notion that human beings in some sense 'complete' God's creation, which has been left in some way 'unfinished'.

Third, there is the immediate relationship with God that is usually meant by the term 'religious experience'. There can be mediating factors – especially human words or sacraments – but the human acts that are evoked have God, or God's promise, or God's grace, as their object or end. Conversion, trust, love, mystical vision have this character as God-oriented acts of intentionality. In at least this sense God is constitutive of such acts. The problem, of course, is that it is one thing to 'intend' God, and another thing entirely to be sure that God is really 'there' as the terminus of the act or approves it or has anything to do with its initiation. The traditional solution to this problem is the doctrine of grace – the conviction that God does indeed ground the meaning and validity of the act and calls it forth as a response to a divine initiative. There are some views according to which there is an immediate divine presence which both ensures the validity of the acts and evokes them; this divine presence can be understood either as something intuited within the field of understanding (as in Augustinian illumination), or as an efficient causality which is 'felt' chiefly in its effects (as in medieval notions of 'experiential knowledge' of God). And even if divine action should not be immediate, it can still be 'presupposed' as the source of coherence or focus of meaning for various finite influences or experiences.

## KINDS OF DIVINE INFLUENCE

So much for the finite effects. How is one to conceive the divine cause on the other side of them?

Thomas Aquinas several times[3] analysed the history of philosophy as a progressive discovery of the important aspects of reality. At first, he says, the 'physical philosophers' asked about things as *individuals* (*hoc ens*), and explained them in terms of the

---

[3] *Summa Theologiae*, Ia.44.2; *De Potentia*, 3.5.

movements of matter. Then Plato and Aristotle asked about *kinds* of things (*tale ens*), and explained them in terms of form. Finally others who are unnamed – perhaps the neo-Platonists, and certainly Avicenna – asked about things as *beings* (*ens in quantum est ens*), and this could be answered only in terms of a universal creative principle which is Pure Act or Being Itself.

These three levels of explanation are not neatly separated, of course; most assuredly they are not separated in Aquinas's ontology. But they do point out different concerns that philosophers may have. When there is an emphasis on the definiteness of the finite effects (*this* form or mode of life, *this* configuration of events, *this* significance of what occurs), the divine influence is understood as a choosing among possibilities, a determining how things are to be; it is understood, therefore, in a voluntaristic way. It is not that God is thought to be arbitrary, or that things can happen merely because God so decides. The point is that, when one is attending chiefly to the definiteness of the world, one is taking for granted *that* there is something or other, and the question is rather *how* it exists, *what kinds* of things there are. On the other hand, when there is an emphasis on the *actuality* of things, a sense of their contingency and a wonder *that* they are at all, one will look to divine actuality as the basis of contingent actuality.

Whitehead, who in this respect is like Plato – and Leibniz – is interested in the definiteness of the world and sees God as the principle of selection among possibilities. He is not unaware of the problem of actuality – indeed, he thinks of all finite realities as self-actualising occasions of experience; but if anything is to become actual it must have definite possibilities, it must be able to be *this* or *that*, or be in this or that *way*. Decision 'constitutes the very meaning of actuality', and '"Actuality" is the decision amid "potentiality"'.[4] Aquinas, by contrast, tends to view everything else as preparatory to actuality, which is effected by God alone; matter is in potency to form, and formed matter, the 'essence' of the finite substance, is, so to speak, fully constituted

[4] Alfred North Whitehead, *Process and Reality: An Essay in Cosmology* (New York: Macmillan, 1929), p. 68.

but is unable to be until it gains actuality, being, from divine being. We have two different conceptions of finite reality at work here. The Thomistic emphasis is upon the actualisation of potencies that are powerless by themselves and must be actuated from beyond themselves; the Whiteheadian is upon the occasion, which has the intrinsic power to actualise itself but needs concrete forms of definiteness. There will also be different conceptions of divine influence. On the one view it will consist primarily of actuation; in the other, of formation.

It is easy to talk about God acting, or doing things by just willing them to be so, or grounding the existence of finite beings. But these expressions conjure up images of the ways finite agents act, and very soon we find ourselves not simply using 'models' but thinking mythically, as though God were one more agent within our familiar web of interactions. But then, having been warned away from such heresies, we are tempted to retreat into mystery, or perhaps we begin to wonder whether 'act of God' is simply another term for the world process.

But traditional theology did not leave the matter there. It asked about the 'how' of God's influence, about the interface between God and finite things, about the 'causal joint' between them.[5] Aquinas tackled the problem head-on and saw, following Aristotle, that efficient causality is not, in the last analysis, something 'in' the agent but is efficient only because of something that happens 'in' the effect. I hit a home run not by slicing the air with a bat, but when the ball feels an impact of the right vector and intensity. The power for a moving bat to hit a home run, or for a fire to ignite something, can be there without taking effect; the efficient causality is fulfilled with the effect within the patient. Thus the 'doing' consists in the 'being done'. But it is also clear that, when efficient causation occurs, it happens only through some 'power' in the cause, and there is, at least in simple cases, the transfer of certain characteristics (momentum, heat) from the cause to the effect (there are more complex cases of mutual influence, or catalytic reactions, or the 'evoking' of actions). Following this line of reflection it is not

[5] Austin Farrer, *Faith and Speculation* (London: A. & C. Black, 1967), p. 65.

difficult to understand Thomas's assertion that there is no other divine 'action' than the finite effect and its dependence upon God as already fully in act.

But this line of analysis deals only with actuality and does not say anything about how or whether God influences the 'definiteness' of the world. God can be conceived as the flame igniting fuel (potentialities for being) already there, but how the potentialities get there remains open to question. If we do not simply call upon the evolutionary process – which may seem more random than guided, and in any case substitutes a long time for specific divine intervention – we must call in something like the Platonist/Whiteheadian notion of divine molding and shaping, the conferring of 'forms of definiteness' upon the finite process. But aside from this difference in emphasis, the Thomistic and the Whiteheadian conceptions are not far apart. Both of them stress the reaction in the effect or the percipient, and think of it as the transmitting of something from the cause (in Whitehead, conceptual feelings; in Thomas, actuation).

Austin Farrer criticises this line of analysis as a 'physicalising' of the First Cause. Farrer's alternative is one that he claims is derived from the Christian tradition. It emphasises divine freedom and the 'efficacy of decision',[6] and it is summarised in the formula 'determinators before determinants', as contrasted with the Aristotelian 'being before becoming'.[7] His argument is that in God efficacious act is not separated, as in us, from thought[8]; God's action is the efficacy of intelligence and will.

While Farrer carefully explores, and rejects, both the Aristotelian model of physical influence and the venerable World-Soul explanation (in no fewer than three forms), I do not see him adequately probing his own model of intelligent will, or the problem he himself has labelled that of the 'causal joint'. One can understand his assertion that God is intelligent will. But this says more about how God *is* than about how God *acts*. We can keep saying that God's acts are not like ours, and that God's will takes

[6] ibid., p. 139.
[7] ibid., p. 142.
[8] ibid., p. 166.

effect immediately. But this is mere assertion. Farrer has rejected the two models that have seemed more or less adequate to the theological tradition – the Aristotelian one of Pure Act which gives actuality to the finite process, and the Platonist World-Soul which influences by 'combining itself' with the finite process.

Farrer's own position, with its emphasis upon decision and the definiteness that arises from it, is closest to the human acts that we call immanent rather than transient – acts of thinking about something or other, choosing this or that action, deciding whether to act at all. The inward act is all that there is; we decide to act and it is done. Or perhaps, since Farrer wants to talk about the efficacy of God's will, it is like lifting our arm with no intermediate effort and no need to practice (for an arm action can involve complications like these). But when we think along either of these lines, our model is that of acts internal to a unified being, considered either without bodily action (immanent mental acts) or as organically embodied (in the case of simple physical movements). In the former case we have a kind of Spinozistic or idealistic pantheism, in which everything is internal to God, a modality of God's self-unfolding or self-constitution. In the latter case we have a conception of the world as God's body, and a highly unified, 'organic' one at that, in which every physical action is 'internal' to God as an animate being.[9] In neither case is the 'causal joint' examined, for any causal efficacy is considered only on the model of internal acts. Farrer seems not to have gone beyond the very positions he has criticised.

On the basis of this survey we are left, I think, with three classic models of divine action, which are often presented as alternatives to each other but may well be compatible. One is that of immanent acts within a mind or will, which gives us a strong sense of the 'agent', to be sure, but a monistic conception of how the agent acts. The second is that of embodiment, which gives us a more complex model of how the agent's decisions, in all their definiteness and directedness, are translated into the different medium of bodily movement to effect results. The

[9] On pp. 150ff., Farrer himself speaks of cosmic organism and criticises notions of pluralism, preferrings 'social' conceptions instead.

third, the one that Farrer calls the most 'physicalising', is that of act and actuation: the assumption that an agent can effect results only insofar as it is already in act and the recipient has a potentiality to be actuated. This model, 'physical' though it may be, is able, for precisely that reason, to speak about influence between distinct things. Indeed, to put the three models in this sequence is to indicate that they are based on three aspects of human agency. Some acts are private to the mind; others involve embodiment, which can be understood either as organically linked to mental acts or as more distant. I use a probe *through* the movements of my arm; more precisely, my intentions are translated to the movements of the probe through a series of neural impulses and muscle movements, and then through the instrument other things can be made to happen. I may even transmit coded signals (words, gestures, radio impulses) to someone or something in the distance which is primed to decode and follow those instructions. Thus rival conceptions of divine activity may be focusing on different aspects of human agency.

But the crucial model, one which has been dealt with only glancingly, and often negatively, is that of embodied action, thus the model of World-Soul. It attempts to explore the translation of intentions into physical action, either organic or remote. As we shall see it does not require conceptions of a single organic body, and thus it is compatible with pluralistic views of the world.

## THE WORLD-SOUL MODEL

There is not a single reason for speaking of God as World-Soul or conversely (but not correlatively) of the world as God's body. There can be various interests, which pull theological reflection in quite different directions. The seventeenth-century philosophers, confronted with the perplexities of what we label 'Cartesian dualism' (the product of our all too convincing experiences of inward thought and outward extension), tended to link mind and matter through God as the basis for space, the dimensionality of things, or even gravitational influence and efficient causality.[10] With perhaps the opposite concern to find a role for God in a world that seemed increasingly self-explanatory, the organismic or holistic theories that stretch from Schelling to Whitehead view the world process as in some sense the living out of God's life. There can also be the religious concern to speak of God as open to, related to, affected by what happens in the world. The metaphor of the world as 'God's body' may be chosen even more explicitly for its connotations of intimacy, sympathy, identification, even vulnerability.[11] In this model the world is viewed, not as something *other* than God, but as 'God's own', experienced as we feel our own bodies or perform 'basic actions' (such as blinking or moving our arms), that is, as included in the life of a single organism.[12]

These are only the expressly theological interests. There is a parallel literature, reaching from Locke and Hume up to the present, which has criticised Cartesian dualism with its distinct 'substances' and looked rather at the coherence of experiences, attended to either introspectively or in our more public discussions of 'agents'. This literature reminds us not to assume anything about the existence or nature of things called 'mind' or 'soul' or 'will'. When we use such terms, we are told, we are referring to a set of phenomena and to the 'agent' which binds them together. There are some who argue that it is meaningless to speak of any agent which is not embodied, indeed, which *is* body acting in certain ways. But it can also be argued that organic unity is not a necessary condition for conceiving of an agent, because many of our own acts are not bodily movements but are 'intentional actions', linked through meanings, not through reference to data of experience or objects of external

[10] See the discussion of their image of the world as 'God's body' in Amos Funkenstein, *Theology and the Scientific Imagination from the Middle Ages to the Seventeenth Century* (Princeton: Princeton University Press, 1986), pp. 23–97.

[11] This motivation is especially evident in Sallie McFague, *Models of God: Theology for an Ecological, Nuclear Age* (Philadelphia: Fortress Press, 1987), pp. 69–78.

[12] A thorough exploration of this model, without reference to the theological tradition, is to be found in Grace Jantzen, *God's World, God's Body* (Philadelphia: Westminster Press, 1984).

action.[13] But this literature is concerned almost entirely with the ways we use language and what is 'conceptually meaningful'. Some would insist on an embodied God, others would permit a God whose activities are 'intentional actions', independent of bodies. For the most part, however, this literature does not ask the question that concerns us here, namely *how*, assuming that God can be called an agent, God *acts*.

The modern discussion, from the seventeenth century to the present, seems to lack the breadth of vision of an older discussion, one which dominated the Platonist tradition for some centuries. The only modern to be aware of this older discussion, I think, was Whitehead. In dealing with the question whether natural law is 'imposed' by sovereign will or results from the 'immanence' of the divine, he notes the role of 'the theologians of Alexandria', who resolved the two theories by making God 'a component in the natures of all fugitive things'. Whitehead made it clear that he did not think of the World-Soul as a distinct inferior being (as it is in Plato himself, the Gnostics, and Arius); if the issue is 'the relation of reality as permanent with reality as fluent', Whitehead insists, 'the mediator must be a component in common'.[14] He later returns to the same point, noting how these theologians improved upon Plato: while Plato made the world an inferior imitation of the ideas, they thought in terms of 'God and his ideas', the direct immanence of God in the world.[15] In Whitehead's conceptual scheme, it will be recalled, this is the primordial nature of God, the one 'non-derivative actuality, unbounded by its prehensions of an actual world'. God's decision among and 'conceptual valuation' of all eternal objects is a 'unity of satisfaction', and thus constitutes a 'primordial superject' which can be an 'actual efficient fact'.[16] This efficient causality is exerted as God is 'objectified' through 'hybrid

---

[13] Thomas F. Tracy, *God, Action and Embodiment* (Grand Rapids: Eerdmans, 1984), pp. 59f., 84, 121–4.

[14] Alfred North Whitehead, *Adventures of Ideas* (New York: Macmillan, 1933), II.8.vi.

[15] ibid., II, 10, iv.

[16] *Process and Reality*, p. 48.

physical feelings' – physical, as all causal efficacy must be, but hybrid because God's own conceptual feelings are the data.[17]

Whitehead, as usual, refrains from telling us his sources. But, in the patristic writings from Justin on, we find the Logos filling the function of the Platonists' World-Soul. The exact character of the World-Soul is open to dispute, since it is described in dark language in *Timaeus* 35A and *Laws* 896D–898C, and later Platonists also saw the World-Soul in the myth in *Politicus* 269C–274D.[18] But the general principle, enunciated in the *Timaeus* (30B), is that 'intelligence cannot be present in anything apart from soul'. The sequence, then, is mind-soul-body. The Platonists did not believe, on the basis of introspection, that mind or intelligence can move matter directly. It acts only through the medium of soul; indeed, the function of soul in the Platonist tradition is to animate and form and guide matter. In this respect they anticipated, and tried to solve in advance, the problem of 'Cartesian dualism' by positing a mediating factor which shares something with each.

It is not surprising, then, to find Justin describing God as creating and ruling the world through the Logos, and describing the Logos in language which Plato uses of the World-Soul (*Apology I*, 60; *Apology II*, 6). Origen thinks of the Logos as the prefiguration or pre-actualisation of all that happens within the created world, and thus as the 'truth and life' of all that exists (*De principiis*, I, 2, 3–4). The cosmos is a huge 'animate being' held together by one Soul (ibid., II, 1, 3). Eusebius quotes both the *Timaeus* and the *Politicus* passages (*Praeparatio Evangelica*, XI, 29–35; cf. *Laus Constantini*, XII, 8). Athanasius says that the Logos, through immediate presence, is the source of coherence and order in the universe, and (probably depending on Eusebius'

---

[17] ibid., p. 377.

[18] For the development of this tradition see the discussion by P. Merlan in *The Cambridge Ancient History of Later Greek and Early Medieval Philosophy*. ed. A. H. Armstrong (Cambridge: The University Press, 1970), pp. 23–38; I have tried to trace its later use in '"Regio Dissimilitudinis" in the Christian Tradition and its Context in Late Greek Philosophy', *Augustinian Studies*, VI (1975), 153–79.

citations) mentions the *Timaeus* and *Politicus* passages (*Contra Gentes*, 40–2; cf. *De incarnatione*, 41–3).

The Nicene faith began to spell the end of the conception of the Logos as World-Soul, for in stressing the full divinity of the Word it was necessary to deny that the Word was uttered only for the sake of creation, and it became increasingly difficult to say that the Word became mixed with matter at all. But Athanasius did not abandon the view that the Logos functions as World-Soul. Instead he developed the theory of creation through condescension (*Oratio II contra Arianos*, 63–4; 78–82). The Word is begotten eternally, but accommodates to the capacities of the finite and unites with it as World-Soul, so that all things cohere in the Word as the 'first-born of all creation' (Col. 1:15).

This Athanasian theory, while viable and perhaps worthy of retrieval in our day, turned out to be only transitional. The more the full divinity of the Word was stressed, the more the Word was elevated above the firmament, so to speak, and disappeared into the transcendent divine realm. The Word could no longer fill the function of World-Soul. But the principle enunciated by Plato, that 'intelligence cannot be present in anything apart from soul', remained in effect. Augustine speculated briefly about the existence of a unitary World-Soul which is created, not divine.[19] And I have tried to demonstrate elsewhere[20] that the function of World-Soul was taken over in Augustine's theology by the angels, so that the ideas in God's mind become effective in the material world through the medium of the angels, who understand the divine mind and then act through their own subtle bodies.

In the meantime the Platonist tradition took account of some complications. The Stoics, who asserted that the soul must be material, had asked how an immaterial soul could act upon a material body. In answering them the Platonists could not

---

[19] Vernon J. Bourke, 'St Augustine and the Cosmic Soul', *Giornale de metafisica*, 9 (1954), 431–40, reprinted in *Wisdom from St Augustine* (Houston: Center for Thomistic Studies, 1984), under the title 'The Problem of a World Soul', pp. 78–90.

[20] *Augustine the Theologian*, pp. 219–22.

merely repeat Plato's statement that the body is the garment of the soul; that would, if anything, concede a lack of relationship. So they denied, on the one hand, a mere juxtaposition (*parathesis*), and, on the other, the kind of mixture that would involve a confusion (*synkrasis*). Between these two, they argued, there is a third mode of union, still a mixture or interpenetration, but forming a single composite being, without confusion or alteration of the two components.[21]

This elaboration of the sequence 'mind-soul-body' was useful to Christological reflection, especially during the controversy with Apollinarianism. Against their view that the Logos is directly united with the flesh, or that the Logos takes the place of a human mind in Christ's animated body, Gregory Nazianzen and Augustine asserted that in Christ a human mind is in immediate communion with the divine Word, and thus that the union of Word and Flesh is mediated by Christ's human mind and soul.[22]

The notion of the Logos as World-Soul was thus the victim of the Arian and then the Apollinarian controversies, which inexorably led theologians to emphasise the immutability and unrelatedness of the Logos – although there was no necessity in this, for alternative conceptions, such as the notion of 'condescension', were available to them. From time to time the Plotinian triad One-Mind-Soul was taken to be equivalent with the Christian Trinity, but mostly in passing, without serious theological reflection. And in the Western renaissances of the ninth and then the twelfth centuries there were theologians who equated the Holy Spirit with the World-Soul.[23] But such notions

[21] This line of thought, probably based on Ammonius, is found in Plotinus (*Enn.* I, 1, 10) and in Porphyry's lost 'Mixed Questions'. See Ernest L. Fortin, 'Saint Augustin et la doctrine neoplatonicienne de l'âme', *Augustinus Magister* (Paris, 1954), III, pp. 371–80, and *Christianisme et culture philosophique au cinquième siècle. La querelle de l'âme en Occident* (Paris, 1959); Jean Pepin, 'Une nouvelle source de saint Augustin. Le *Zetema* de Porphyre *Sur l'union de l'âme et du corps*', *Revue des études anciennes*, 86 (1964), pp. 53–107; and Heinrich Dörrie, *Porphyrios' 'Symmikta Zetemata'*, Zetemata, XX (Munich, 1959).

[22] See esp. Gregory, *Orat.* 2.23, and Augustine, *Ep.* 140.12.

[23] Tullio Gregory, *Anima Mundi. La filosofia de Gugliemo di Conches e la scuola di Chartres* (Florence: G. C. Sansoni, 1955), pp. 123ff.

were quickly shot out of the air as heretical.

Before we either revive or abandon the World-Soul motif we should look at the alternative suggested in the course of the late fourth-century inquiry: that the function of World-Soul may be filled, in whole or in part, by what the Platonists would call generically 'finite soul': a created World-Soul, angels, the soul of Christ, other human souls. Some years ago I proclaimed 'the abdication of the angelic powers at the apex of the hierarchy of finite causes', suggesting that this leaves a vacuum in cosmology (in that we no longer have powerful animate beings within the cosmos to move things around and cause them to interact), suggested that the evolutionary conception of the world must see it as more pluralistic and more erratic in its progress, and then alluded darkly to Whitehead. I did not go into the point, because Whitehead was not the topic under discussion.[24]

Let me take this occasion, then, to pick up the relevance of Whitehead. If, as I have argued, the function of soul is to translate the plans and intentions of mind into movements of body and physical causality, then that same function is found, according to Whitehead's conceptual scheme, in the 'mental pole' of every actual occasion, which receives possibilities for its own self-actualisation both from the antecedent universe (the source of connection and continuity) and from God (the source of novelty). Each occasion of experience has new possibilities (sometimes minimal, sometimes impressive in their range), and in the course of its concrescence it 'decides' which of these it is to actualise. When this process of concrescence reaches completion or 'satisfaction' as a unity of feeling, it 'perishes' in its subjectivity but gains 'immortality' as an object and is effective precisely through its 'physical' impact on fresh occasions.

The notion of World-Soul, then, need not be hypostatised as a single being, either divine or creaturely. It is a function which can be filled in several ways, as our survey from Plato through the Christological debates indicates. The Logos is God's ideal plan for the cosmos, 'an act of will proceeding from mind', as Origen

---

[24] *Augustine the Theologian*, pp. 222f.

says (*De principiis*, I, 2, 6 and 9), roughly equivalent with White-head's notion of God's primordial nature. But as Plato had said, 'intelligence cannot be present in anything apart from soul'. Ideas must be translated into physical motion through a soul that is 'mixed with' matter. The Platonist speculations of late antiquity, both pagan and Christian, illustrate how this function of soul can be filled by a divine hypostasis (either the Word or a Soul), or by a single created World-Soul, or by a multitude of angelic beings, or by human souls; the pagans could have added animal souls, and in the Whiteheadian reconceptualisation of Platonism, as we have seen, the function of soul is filled by the mental pole of all occasions of experience. What all of these have in common, the variable which can be given any of these different values, is that a divine Logos or Thought can take effect only through something that carries the function of 'soul'; and the importance of soul, in turn, is that it mediates between mind and matter, thought and physis, by having something in common with each, facing both ways. It is able to apprehend the ideas in God's Thought (it may even be identical with God's Thought, as in Justin and Origen); but it is also able to have a physical effect because it is combined with matter, either in a soul-body unity (as in ancient Platonism) or through the bi-polar character of all actual occasions (as in Whitehead).

## DIVINE AGENCY AND FINITE EFFECTS

At the end of the second section I suggested that models of divine agency sometimes emphasise acts of self-determination within the agent; sometimes basic actions of the embodied self; and sometimes more distant actions through intermediate physical reactions. The first of these may be utilised in a pantheistic version, but traditionally it has taken a different form, as the shaping of God's purposes in the Word or Thought. The second is closest to the World-Soul model, with its concern for the transition from mind to soul to physical movement. The third, which is the most 'physical' (or objective, or external), attempts the fullest explication of efficient causality. We have been concentrating attention upon the second model, that of World-

Soul, both in order to retrieve its classic expressions and in order to trace the full range of its possible meanings. Its special virtue is in exploring the transition from intention to physical movement. But we cannot assume that it offers a total explanation covering all cases. Let us return to the earlier consideration, in the first two sections, of the kinds of situations in which we speak of divine acts and the kinds of dependence these situations may have upon divine influence. I hope it will not appear too dogmatic to cluster them into three groupings which cut across the more casual and inductive comments in those earlier sections. Each will label a set of finite situations and at the same time highlight a specific kind of dependence upon God. Let me summarise them as *continuity*, *innovation*, and *actuation*.

We began by speaking of continuing substances (or, in Whitehead, societies). There is also the continuity of physical laws which cut across individual things. While Whitehead usually emphasises the plurality of occasions, he also recognises that forms of definiteness can be handed on from one to another. And while he tends to speak of satisfaction and closure within each actual occasion, he knows that matters are not so simple. In our experience of ourselves we are aware that what is handed on from moment to moment is not merely a set of completed experiences or decisions, influential as these may be, but also a wider range of capabilities for activity or receptivity, a 'horizon' which is, in effect, unlimited, and many of whose potentialities may never be realised. Whitehead may have undervalued persisting things and their powers, just as Aquinas may have overvalued them. What we experience in ourselves and in other things is both continuity and the potentiality for innovation and action.

Thus there is, second, the aspect of spontaneity or self-determination, certainly in human life, but perhaps in all actual occasions. This is the focus of Whitehead's philosophical theology. For him God is the source of novelty in the world, offering new eternal objects, new possibilities, new forms of definiteness which are not yet ingredient in finite occasions; these are given directly to the 'mental pole' of a new concrescence, in a manner functionally like the influence of the World-Soul in ancient Platonism. In most passages this is Whitehead's only emphasis, for creativity, as both transition and the power of self-creation in each actual occasion, is taken for granted as a factor distinct from God. Perhaps he over-emphasised this role of God as the source of novelty, in distinction from other possible roles. In human experience, at least, we are aware of powers, even powers of innovation, which are 'given' with human life itself, with its limitless horizon of thought and freedom, its capacities for imagination or perverseness. Novelty seems not to come only from God, or, if it does, it has already been given in and with the scope of consciousness far back in our lives. Divine 'lures' or 'propositions', furthermore, may not come solely through immediate prehensions of God; they may be conveyed through human words or through the significance of external events. But even with full awareness of complexities like these, we can understand the emphasis that Whitehead – like the ancient Platonists – placed on ideas and possibilities and the selection of new forms of definiteness. Innovation is important both in human life and in the cosmic emergence of new forms. And while these two cases may be more unlike than like each other, they both reinforce the openness of any current situation, the presenting of constantly new possibilities, and the pressure toward 'decision' among them, whether it is by divine, human, or natural entities, and whether it is in the mode of conscious choice, or spontaneous inclination, or 'natural selection'.

We should not slight a third aspect of finite experience, that of actuation. As we have seen, Aquinas thought of this as the most important manifestation of divine causality, even in the continuing existence of substances. I have placed it third in order to stress not substance but activity. For even after we have considered continuity and the paths of inheritance that give rise to fresh occasions, and even after we have considered the openness of the finite process to novelty, there is still a contingency about actualisation. Just as the second aspect is the crucial one from the Platonist standpoint, calling for a translation of novelty from the divine mind to temporal events through a World-Soul, the third is the crucial one from the Thomist standpoint.

We have spent some time with Aristotle's 'physical' model, the suggestion that something can come into act only because of the influence of something already in act, for it has been an important theological argument. But even on Aristotle's principle not all situations are metaphysically questionable. Action may issue from the 'active powers' of a finite being, to use Aristotle's language, or from the intrinsic ability of an occasion, to use Whitehead's language, to actualise itself and reach definite satisfaction. Furthermore, actions may be elicited or evoked by something coming from without – the proximity of several chemical compounds, or a 'hand up', or a word spoken, or a changed external situation. In some of these instances there are physical processes of actualisation; in others, only new information or a changed estimate of the situation in which one might act. Much, then, is actuated through quite ordinary intramundane relationships, either physical or mental, on the basis of active powers already belonging to finite agents, singly or in combination. A divine factor is not needed to fill any gaps of explanation; it will consist, at most, of a concursus working with and through finite causes. Frequently, therefore, we are led toward finite interactions and thus toward those situations which, in our experience of human agency, are most 'distant' from the centre of the self (muscular movements, the use of instruments, the sending of signals). Aquinas recognised this, I think. His emphasis on God as Pure Act and First Cause did not obscure for him the role of instrumental causes and the interactions of finite things. We are brought into the sphere of events which, if they are to be called acts of God at all, occur through interactions – providential coincidences, or religiously significant events, or sacramental meditation, or prophetic address. The divine influence, the 'causal joint', is to be looked for not immediately adjacent to the event but in its 'background'. Most of Whitehead's attention was directed to the way divine intentions are translated in physical process in the privacy of

concrescences in their pole; but here we are dealing with the
public interactions of physical influences or symbolic utterances
or interpretations of meaning.

Theology is most interested in the problem of actuation
when it comes to religious experience, especially those instances
which seem to lie beyond human capabilities of decision and
action, such as conversion, or endurance in spite of impossible
circumstances, or rising above oneself. Obviously all such
phenomena are susceptible of psychological analysis which
attempts to explicate them, and perhaps explain them, in strictly
immanent terms. The theological answer will usually be, not a
rejection of such lines of analysis, but an insistence that the
experiences also be understood in terms of their meanings and
motivations. This is a point at which theology has talked about
the Holy Spirit as the basis of faithfulness to God, perseverance
in the truth, or delight in the good. How one is to speak of divine
influence in the depths of human subjectivity has been a matter
of intense debate. does it act with efficient causality (which seems
too mechanical), or does it somehow evoke human spontaneity?
On either theory this third aspect of finite life, the most
volitional and affective in character, the most interior to the
human self, has been linked with the Spirit, just as the second
aspect, that of novel form, has been linked with the Word. Both
become more salient the more we find ourselves dealing with
subjectivity and spontaneity, Thus with human experience,
especially in those moments of its transcending the finite.

It will not be surprising, then, to find that my sequencing of
the aspects of finite occasions – continuity, innovation, actuation
– has some similarities with my earlier summary of models of
divine agency – subjectivity, purposiveness, efficacy – or that
both are reminiscent of traditional language about the image of
the Trinity in human life, or 'vestiges' of the Trinity in all finite

reality.[25] This is inevitable, for finite and especially human models are what we have available for speaking about divine action, and we must utilise them as best we can, revising where it seems appropriate and making due allowance for error or misconception all along the line.

As I promised at the beginning, I have tried to sit loose to specific conceptualisations and follow the drift of the problems enunciated in various times. The language used has been a (perhaps unholy, perhaps eclectic) blend of the Aristotelian and the Whiteheadian, with a good dose of the Platonist mythology of the World-Soul tossed in. But the purpose has been to take account of the full range of situations, sift them, and simplify the models used. The outcome – if this process of simplification is at all coherent – is an approach which begins with the intrinsic constitution of beings (God, ourselves, all things) and moves toward their interrelations, first in terms of conceptual novelty (always the strength of the Platonist tradition), then in terms of physical interaction (always the strength of the Aristotelian tradition). I have not ventured much in the way of testing the truth of particular assertions, but I trust that there has been some clarification of the models used in making theological assertions and the range of their applicability. The other contributions here will help to test the issues not only of meaning but of truth as well.

[25] This line of reflection has some similarities with that of Moise Amyraut, the Reformed theologian of Saumur in the seventeenth century, who in dealing with the economy of salvation spoke of the Father as the agent who wills salvation for all (but on the condition that it be received by human beings), and the Spirit as 'applying' salvation and making it efficacious within the self (for Amyraut this was also the point at which unconditional predestination took effect – a doctrine in which we need not follow him).

Chapter 5

# DIVINE PRACTICAL KNOWING

## How an Eternal God Acts in Time

### David B. Burrell

The following reflections directly address the conference theme: 'to focus thought on the crucial but difficult idea of God as one who acts in the world.' They will not engage in exegesis of the work of Austin Farrer, although their direction will certainly encourage attention to Farrer's efforts to explicate divine action, as those familiar with his thought find resonances in other contemporary Catholic thinkers like Lonergan and Sokolowski. As a way of focusing discussion, allow me to begin with an articulated thesis:

1. How does God act in time? Through temporal creatures.
1.1. God acts through all active things, but especially through us humans because God can act *in* us.
1.2. God can act in us because we are full-fledged agents who act with an end in view. (Aquinas begins his treatment of divinity [ST 1.2. Intro.] as 'the beginning and end of all things and of rational creatures especially.')
1.3. And God can insinuate the end in our deliberations (Augustine, Aquinas), confirming Moses Maimonides' judgment that only God's care for rational creatures is properly called providence.

So much for the basic position, which will involve a sustained focus on creation as the proper articulation of 'the distinction' between God and the world (Sokolowski). In response to the next query: but *how* does God act, one could respond: look at us! This approach reflects a consideration of God as 'pure act', for it makes no sense to ask *how* pure-act acts, since it is *ipso facto* in act. So God's acting involves no mechanisms, no process

93

(from potency to act), no *powers* by which divinity acts (Burrell, 1986). Moreover, pure act must be eternal (or better, must exist eternally) for reasons internal to the conception of pure act: there is no way it can be 'in time'. How, then, can an eternal pure-act act in time? Through its temporal creatures, each of which is present to it eternally, as to the source of the existing proper to each created thing.

But why insist on so elusive a denomination of divinity as *pure act*? Despite its initial opacity, the notion has three distinct conceptual advantages. (1) It incorporates Aquinas' transformation of Avicenna's fundamental distinction of possible from necessary being (*via* Aquinas' characterisation of the essence/existence distinction) into a characterisation of divinity as act without potency (ST 1.3.1, 1.3.2) and *ipsum esse subsistens* (1.3.4, 1.3.7, 1.7.1.3). (2) It can be understood as Lonergan has explicated both Augustine and Aquinas: that the primary analogue (or paradigm instance) of *act* is the act of knowing and loving, so that the human person becomes the one in which divinity can best be modelled. (3) Finally, Aquinas' characterisation of existence (*esse*, to-be) as act, taken together with the activity of knowing and loving as paradigmatic for act, allows one to capture *existence* in the judgment/decision which culminates a human act of knowing, mindful that existing is deemed to be the 'proper effect of the creator in creatures' (ST 1.45.5). (These concentric conceptual advantages are further articulated in Burrell, 1986.)

So, taken together, these classical theses, cast in explicitly *intentional* terms, allow one to invoke properly personal analogies for divine action without reducing divinity to 'a person'. For if the paradigm exemplification of *act* is, for us, intentional activity, then *pure act* is already an eminently personal notion. So God's relations with creatures are best understood in intentional rather than causal terms, without sacrificing any efficacy of creator regarding creature, and recovering a way of conceiving the interaction between both without violating divine 'unchangeableness' (Clarke). The philosophical theorems at play here dovetail with the doctrine of divine creation as the gratuitous activity of God, and with the doctrine of the incarnation as *the* way for an eternal God to act in time. Creation must be our theological starting point: to acknowledge at once 'the distinction' of God from the world as well as the connection between them. Yet historically, and perhaps conceptually, clarity about this distinction-cum-connection is attained in reflection on the 'hypostatic union' (Sokolowski).

What do we mean by creation? The doctrine shared by Jews, Christians, and Muslims comprises two interrelated assertions, to which I shall add a theological clarification from Aquinas to further our specific argument. Doctrinally, we mean (1) dependence in being, plus (2) 'the distinction', which asserts that God is no more God for creating. Dependence alone is compatible with the eternally necessary emanation of the world from divinity, so the revelation of creation as a divine gift (of grace) demands that we articulate 'the distinction' properly. It asserts that the universe does not increase God's perfection, though it adds to what there is – as in transfinite arithmetic, where infinity plus a definite amount equals infinity. Creating, then, is a free act on the part of divinity, though it is *not* best conceived as an arbitrary choice. The action can be utterly consonant with the divine nature and act of existing, yet not be necessitated thereby. For it makes no sense to say of the One whose essence is to-be that such a One is *necessitated*, since the One whose essence is to-be is without a quiddity except that of to-be (*esse*) and hence quite beyond our divisions into necessary/contingent being (Adams).[1] Hence creation can be utterly gratuitous without its needing to be conceived as a 'free choice', as though 'God could have done otherwise'. For nothing prevents one from following one's nature freely, especially when one's nature is pure-act.

What Aquinas can add to this doctrinal development, given his transformation of Avicenna's distinction of existence from essence, is the specification: the activity of creating consists in

---

[1] Our distinction lies completely within the domain of what is possible to Avicenna, who distinguishes God from all else in distinguishing necessary from possible being.

bestowing *to-be* (ST 1.45.5, 1.45.4.1). God is then the source of the existence proper to each temporal existent, and since to-be (*esse*) is to be conceived as *act* to the essence (or formal structure) of things, it can be said to be 'more intimately and profoundly interior to things than anything else [about them]' (ST 1.8.1). So God, as the One who bestows each thing's existence, is present to each thing 'in keeping with the way in which the thing possesses its existence [*secundum modum quo esse habet*]' (ST 1.8.1). At this point Aquinas even uses the soul/body metaphor, as recast by Augustine: 'immaterial things "contain" that in which they exist, as the soul "contains" the body. So God also "contains" things by existing in them' (ST 1.8.1.2). But he would never fracture the metaphor to assert literally that God was to be conceived as the soul of the world (cf. ST 1.3.8).

All this suggests that a God who is the eternal source of the activity proper to each existing thing would better be imagined *inside* the becoming which time measures than *outside* it. This image conveys the analytic fact that whatever exists, exists *now*, so evoking the presence of an eternal creator to each present thing. It also complements Aquinas' image of 'eternity *including* all phases of time' (ST 1.10.2.4) also 1.14.13) by capitalising on Augustine's paradoxical reversal of the spatial implications of 'contains' for soul and body.

Where are we then? With a God who is pure act, whose essence is simply to-be, and hence is the One from whom all that is derives – gratuitously and in the mode of existing proper to each. So the dependence of each existing thing from the One from whom all derives is manifested not in its manner of being (or nature), but in its very existing (ST 1.4.3). Yet what *manifests* each thing's createdness – its relation to the eternal source of being – is also utterly hidden, for *esse* is not a feature of things (ST 1.4.3.3 and 4).[2] So the relation whereby each thing is called a *creature* (and which relates it to the source of its being) remains hidden, though there is nothing more intimate to anything than

<hr/>

[2] cf. al-Ghazali's discussion of two of God's 'beautiful names' 'the manifest' and 'the hidden': *Ninety-Nine Names of God in Islam* tr. Robert Charles Stade (Ibadan Nigeria: Daystar Press, 1970).

that relation! If the source be eternal, this relation (which constitutes the 'truth of things' by contrast with the truth of statements [ST 1.14.8.3]) relates time to eternity (ST 1.8.1), so spanning the otherwise unbridgeable gap between time and eternity. So an eternal God acts in time primarily by creating each creature. And everything else – including God's electing a people and 'taking flesh' – is rooted here, as is (more prosaically) the working of miracles. For the root miracle, as Augustine never ceased reminding us, is the gratuitous emanation of all existents from the One whose nature is existence itself.

Yet that relation is utterly unknown, so that what constitutes each creature in existence escapes us. Thus the 'truth of things' remains a mystery though not a surd; a surfeit of intelligibility rather than a lack thereof (Pieper). The most salient sign of mystery lies in the fact that this relation purports to bridge the conceptually un-negotiable gap between eternity and time. The sign of this gap can be found in the inescapably tensed character of our discourse. Yet the gap is not between a *tensed* and *tenseless* language, as though eternity were mere timelessness, but between our tensed discourse and a *now* (or 'present tense') which never becomes the past (Burrell, 1984). And such a *now*, as creative, may be imagined both as *inside* the becoming which requires tensed discourse and as *containing* 'all phases of time' (ST 1.10.2.4).

But why locate the mystery here? Why insist that being divine entails being eternal (or existing eternally)? Could this entailment mask a mere Hellenic prejudice (Wolterstorff)? I have noted that we have no choice in the matter: there is simply no way for divinity to be in time, subject to change, unless the relation of God to the world be other than what we have meant by creation. (So, for example, Ogden proffers the analogy of soul to body, where the soul is conceived as informing a body.) So whoever affirms God to be 'the beginning and end of all things' has no alternative but to deny temporality of divinity, since there would be no reason for what is prior to 'all things' to be in time. Furthermore, if one conceptualises the difference between 'all things' and their 'beginning and end' (i.e. 'the distinction' –

Sokolowski) after the fashion of Avicenna, Maimonides, and Aquinas, identifying the One as that One whose nature is simply to–be, then whatever simply *is* must lie beyond the realm of becoming, of cause-effect interaction, and so be eternally. Moreover, whoever may be so bedevilled by difficulties attendant upon relating eternity with time as simply to bracket this question is pushed to analogous lengths in an effort to save yet other attributes of divinity – as those who claim 'middle knowledge' require a timeless use of 'is'.[3]

How might those who bow to the conceptually inevitable and assert God's eternity, however, overcome some classical dilemmas of an eternal God acting in time – especially those which emerge from such a one timelessly knowing what *will* happen in a contingent future? My strategy is two-fold: (1) keep a firm grip on our *tenses*, (2) shift our sights from speculative to practical knowing. Just such a shift is suggested by the doctrine of creation, and especially where it distinguishes itself from a necessary emanation scheme modelled on deductive reasoning. Fears which some could have about God's practical knowing leaving sufficient room for human freedom may be addressed in two mutually reinforcing ways. (*A*) Rooting the activity consequent upon practical knowing in the creation-relation assures the proper transcendence, since the proper effect of the creator's activity is the to-be of things, an activity which transcends causal patterns (linked to things' *becoming*). (*B*) An analysis of freedom as more than choice opens up the possibility of collaboration between human beings and God, so that God can act *through* us by acting *in* us without violating our freedom. When freedom is seen to embody intellect and will in a process of deliberation, and is no longer identified with a mere 'act of will', we will not be so prone to picture human and divine freedom as two wills on a collision course (Lonergan 1941, Kretzmann and Stump 1985).

The result of bringing practical knowing to the fore is to

---

[3] For they want to be able to say that God knows beforehand what the case will be, since God knows which of each pairs of disjuncts is true. But the last 'is' must be timeless.

: potter is to a pot, yet
)nveys of God's shaping
f God's activity – *esse*
al *esse* (to-be) in humans,
de of being of each thing
hat the analogy of author
; Ross 1980, 150–76).
'e is *now* present to God.
ourse. 'What will be the
ike 'what is short and
be (as in a *book* which
'e is no such thing. We
criptions framed from
 are not statements of
hat God knows each
ay be rendered (1) 'as
is each one of them is
in act in itself' (ST 1.14.13). For Aquinas, since 'eternity, which exists as a simultaneous whole, takes in (*ambit*) the whole of time. . . , all that takes place in time is eternally present to God' (ibid.). And we have continually asked since then: how is that possible? Moreover, his image of the strategically placed observer (ST 1.14.13.3) proves misleading since it implies that God's knowledge of creation is speculative. In context, however, the image is used to make a specific point: that *contemporaneity* assures a present-necessity without necessitating the event (Burrell, 1984). So the upshot of this image as well is to remind us of the *presence* of creator to creature, as of artisan to artifact, since we cannot assert literal contemporaneity when the artist is eternal and the artifact temporal (Kretzmann and Stump, 1981).

What then *can* we say? What we *must* say: (1) that not even God knows what will happen before 'it' happens, since there is as yet nothing to know, and (2) that God is not surprised by what does happen, since (a) *surprise* is a temporal category, (b) God 'has a hand in it' without determining it, as bestower of being, and (c) God's 'hands' are thoroughly intentional and hence roomy enough to include our responses (since knowing and loving are not in themsleves changes or alterations). Thus we may say (with Aquinas) that 'all of time is present to God . . . so that all that takes place in time is eternally present to God' without evacuating the reality of temporal occurrence, especially the fact that 'what will be' is *not*. For what we cannot express (or conceive) is the relation of 'being eternally present to God,' since that comprises the 'truth of things' which lies *ex professo* hidden from our view. Yet since whatever *is* is derived from God *in its present to-be*, it is – all of it – known to God by a knowledge that is primarily practical, and so not susceptible of surprise. Or rather, *all* is novelty, respecting of course the regularities of created nature. Peter Geach's image of the master improvisor captures this dimension, though his treatment presumes a relationship of God to creation more speculative that practical, as though the world were 'already out there' in the face of the creator's activity (Geach).

That is all that the logic of the matter allows us to say. But it is enough, for it allows us to affirm, with Aquinas, that 'those contingent events which are future with respect to their proximate causes, are nonetheless infallibly known to God, insofar as they come under divine perusal in their presentness (or: their presence to God)' (ST 1.14.13). This assertion presumes our differentiating the 'truth of things' from the truth of our statements about them, since 'natural things are "midway" (*mediae*) between God's knowledge and ours, for we receive our knowledge from natural things of which God is the cause through his knowledge' (ST 1.14.8.3). And that knowledge is compared to the knowledge of an artificer, so their 'presence to God' must be linked to their existence as deriving from God. So the complementary metaphors which locate eternity *inside* time as well as image it 'embracing all of time' correct each other, and are themselves guided by the master image of creating as practical knowing. So we are firmly kept from imagining an omniscient God who knows what might be as though it in fact was.

Does this mean, however, that God has no sense of how things might otherwise have been? Hardly: for artisans have a keen sense, in the course of their activity, how things might go otherwise, without having to inspect alternatives. It is the image of inspecting alternative scenarios which forfeits the master image of practical knowing, and contributes to the pseudo-worlds of 'middle knowledge' (Ross 1983, 138). What it does mean is that God is intimately involved with the world God is creating, since 'existence is more intimately and profoundly interior to things than anything else' (ST 1.8.1). And this involvement always takes place in the present: in the temporal present in which alone something exists, and in the presence of each created thing to the empowering source of its existence in the One who is creator. So the infallibility of divine knowing is not the result of a futuristic scenario which only God sees, but the consequence of the creative involvement of a God whose constitutive activity bestows existence on whatever is the case. Yet that relationship remains inconceivable to us, since our explanations are tied to causal patterns in the realm of essence – where chipmunks beget chipmunks. So we are left with analogies: artisan/artifact (Aquinas), song on the breath of a singer (Ross), or master improvisor (Geach); and the master key of practical knowing, which begs for a much clearer rendition than philosophers have provided to date.[4]

Given those limits, then, how can we say that an eternal God acts in time? (1) Freely, for time itself is created; (2) through the founding relation of creation, where being itself is bestowed (necessary or contingent); (3) as an artisan makes an artifact. As a result, (4) all that *is* is present to that from which it derives its very being, so that such a One is not surprised, and responds to intentional creatures' responsiveness in the act of creating us. In this carefully qualified sense, God can (and must) be said to know all that *is* as well as 'contain all times' in the intention to make exist what God intends to be.

---

[4] Richard Bernstein's *Beyond Objectivism and Relativism* (Philadelphia: University of Pennsylvania Press, 1983) offers a just measure of the difficulties involved in trying to characterise practical knowledge in its own right. See also Alasdair MacIntyre, *Whose Justice, Which Rationality?* (London: Duckworth, 1988).

# WORKS CITED

Adams, Robert M. 'Divine Necessity.' *J. Philosophy* 80 (1983), 741–52.

Aquinas, Thomas. *Summa Theologicae* (=ST) London: Eyre & Spottiswoode, 1963).

Burrell, David. 1984. 'Maimonides, Aquinas and Gersonides on Providence and Evil.' *Religious Studies* 20, 335–51.

1984a. 'God's Eternity'. *Faith and Philosophy* 1, 389–406.

1986. *Knowing the Unknowable God*. Notre Dame, Indiana: University of Notre Dame Press.

Clarke, W. Norris. *Philosophical Approaches to God*. Winston-Salem, North Carolina: Wake Forest University, 1979.

Farrer, Austin. *Finite and Infinite*. New York: Seabury, 1958.

Geach, Peter. *Providence and Evil*. Cambridge: Cambridge University Press, 1977.

Kretzmann, Norman and Stump, Eleanore. 1981.

1981. 'Eternity'. *J. Philsophy* 78, 429–58.

1985. 'Absolute Simplicity.' *Faith and Philosophy* 2, 353–82.

Lonergan, Bernard J. 'Saint Thomas' Thought on *Gratia Operans*'. *Theological Studies* 2 (1941), 289–324, 3 (1942) 69–88, 375–402, 533–78. (=*Grace and Freedom*. New York: Herder, 1971).

Maimonides, Moses. *Guide for the Perplexed*. New York: Dover, 1956.

Ogden, Schubert. *The Reality of God*. New York: Harper & Row, 1967.

Pieper, Josef. 'The Philosophical Act', in *Leisure the Basis of Culture*. New York: Pantheon, 1952.

Ross, James. 1980. *Philosophical Theology* (revised edition). Indianapolis, Indiana: Bobbs-Merrill.

1983. 'Creation II', in Frederick Freddoso, ed. *Existence and Nature of God*. Notre Dame, Indiana: University of Notre Dame Press.

Sokolowski, Robert. *God of Faith and Reason*. Notre Dame, Indiana: University of Notre Dame Press, 1982.

Wolterstorff, Nicholes. 'God Everlasting', in Clifton Orlebeke and Lewis Smedes, eds. *God and the Good* (Grand Rapids, Michigan: Eerdmans, 1975).

Chapter 6

# GOD AND SYMBOLIC ACTION

## David Brown

Traditional accounts of revelation, particularly of biblical revelation, have typically assumed what has often been labelled an interventionist view of divine action, that is, that God over and above his general ordering and sustaining of the world performs certain specific actions. Though I think this model requires considerable modification to account for the extent of fallibility in the scriptures, none the less it seems to me to be essentially along the right lines. We may think of revelation as a divine dialogue[1] in which God acts to speak to a community of faith and further its understanding, but always in such a way that the freedom of individual response is respected. This will explain why failures of moral insight sometimes occur, even for example in the prophets or psalms. It is because God values something more, that the individual comes to appreciate for himself what the truth is.

The first part of my paper therefore is concerned to defend just such a model against some of the more obvious philosophical objections. This will then provide a natural transition to the second half, in which I shall focus more narrowly on one particular mode for such a dialogue, that it be sometimes mediated through symbols. This was a proposal made by Austin Farrer, and I want to explore how that suggestion might be further developed.

---

[1] This dialogue model of revelation I defend in detail in chapter 2 of my *The Divine Trinity* (London: Duckworth, 1985; La Salle, Illinois: Open Court, 1985). This article is intended to supplement, rather than repeat, what I say there.

## REVELATION AS DIVINE DIALOGUE

To speak of an unembodied agent like God 'acting' does not seem to me to present any insuperable difficulties. Not only do phenomena like telepathy and telekinesis give ready intelligibility to the idea of acting without a physical medium, even in the ordinary human case where such a medium seems essential, this apparent essentiality surely stems merely from the contingent fact of constant concurrence and not because the action would be unintelligible without it. Further confirmation of this emerges from the realisation that what makes something an action is its intentionality, and we can know our intentions without first checking our bodily behaviour. In other words, because what is indispensable to the concept of action is intentionality and not a particular medium, there can be no logical incoherence in the notion of action, including divine action, that involves no such medium.

But why place such action within an interventionist framework? 'Interventionist' is perhaps not entirely a happy term. It has two principal defects. First, it suggests that God is uninvolved with the world except where he is specifically intervening. Secondly, intervention can very easily suggest manipulation or authoritarian interference. My stress in this model of divine dialogue on a free human response demonstrates clearly that the latter idea of manipulation is very far from my mind. 'Interactionist' might be a better description. But there is some truth in the first charge. For, while I wish to insist on God's creative role as sustainer and orderer of the universe, I do find it hard to locate sufficient involvement in the non-interventionist cases, such that the accusation can then be resisted that the term 'action' is here not merely being used in an attenuated sense. Thus it is only action in the same way as troops winning a battle can be described as the action of the general leading them, or the bursting of a dam as the incompetent action of the engineer who built it. Clearly in these two situations the size of possible contribution from the general and engineer can range from the merely permissive, for example a doddery, senile general giving a command to brave troops, to the absolutely decisive, the engineer building a dam unable to restrain even ordinary levels of water. So, in answer to what Owen Thomas in *God's Activity in the World* has called the 'fundamental' question, 'Does God act in all events or only in some?',[2] it is clear that we must say that there are degrees of appropriateness in speaking of divine action, but that these culminate in what I, for better or worse, have labelled the interventionist cases.

There seems to me at least two good reasons why the term 'divine action' must find its most natural application in this context. Both are linked in the sense that they are drawing out implications of the fact that 'action' belongs to the category of the 'personal'. For, as we have seen, integral to the notion are intentions and only persons can have intentions.

First, in ascribing intervention to God we are only in effect according to him the same kind of personal freedom of interaction that we would wish to ascribe to ourselves. For many, Christians and non-Christians alike, would agree that we have a contra-causal freedom that can be subsumed under no laws, whether psychological, physiological or otherwise, and that it is precisely in the exercise of that freedom that we most show ourselves to be persons and not automata. Why then should divine activity be brought under any such laws? The failure of theologians to take with sufficient seriousness this analogy with our human situation is well illustrated by F. B. Dilley's article, 'Does the "God who acts" really act?'.[3] He ends by presenting us with a stark choice between miracles and uniform natural laws, with the former discounted because of the difficulty of believing in them in the modern age. Thomas rightly points out that this is not as difficult as is often supposed,[4] but, more importantly for our purposes here, it needs to be observed that he has totally ignored a third alternative. For, just as our

[2] O. C. Thomas (ed.), *God's Activity in the World* (Chico, California: Scholars Press, 1983). p. 237.

[3] ibid., pp. 45–60; reprinted from *The Anglican Theological Review* 47 (1965), pp. 66–80.

[4] ibid., p. 6. He refers us to A. M. Greeley's *Religion in the Year 2000* (New York: Sheed & Ward, 1969).

interaction with each other can be subsumed under no natural law, so also with God's gracious interaction upon us. In short, so far from intervention necessarily involving the miraculous, it seems indispensable if we are to allow God the same power and dignity of action as we are prepared to ascribe to ourselves.

Secondly, in insisting that not all divine action is of the same kind we are doing something also to preserve our own personal freedom and dignity, as it has been given to us by God. For were we to say that it is all of the same sustaining kind subsumable under natural laws, at once both the divine distance and the divine closeness would be swallowed up in one, except perhaps subjectively, whereas both are in fact integral if human action and its relation to the divine are properly to be described as personal. Thus one needs divine distance in order to preserve room for independent human decision-making, and a non-ubiquitous divine closeness or activity if the relation is to be regarded as personal, that is, with intentions shaped in response to the free actions of the other. It is precisely bacause of uncertainty whether Farrer's theory of 'double agency'[5] meets this criterion that I find it so unsatisfactory, or at any rate the version of it which I am about to mention. For it has recently been revived and defended by Vernon White in *The Fall of the Sparrow*.[6] He develops the idea with an impressive consistency and clarity, but that in turn makes it all the more easy to see what is wrong with the idea, at least as he presents it. What White is most concerned to defend is the divine sovereignty, that nothing can be allowed to frustrate the divine intention. So significantly Barth is quoted to the effect that God 'would not be God . . . if there were a *single* point where he was . . . only *partly* active or restricted in his action'[7] (my italics), and accordingly natural events and human actions are both equally brought under the rubric that 'whatever happens is caught up to serve God's

[5] A. Farrer, *Faith and Speculation* (London: A. & C. Black, 1967; New York, New York University Press, 1967).

[6] V. White, *The Fall of a Sparrow* (Exeter: Paternoster Press, 1985), esp. chapters 4 and 5.

[7] ibid., p. 115; cf. also p. 113. The quotation is from K. Barth, *Church Dogmatics* (Edinburgh: T. & T. Clark, 1957), 3:3. 133, p. 167.

intention'.[8] But it seems to me that to insist that in any situation God is always an agent, always more than just a permitting cause, even when due qualification is made for the problem of evil, cannot but be to call into question human freedom. If we are truly in the divine image and thus truly persons, this cannot but mean an ability to frustrate the divine purpose, and frustrate it ultimately. For to suggest otherwise must inevitably mean envisaging God interfering in human freedom to ensure that his purposes are always realised.

That is of course to place a high value on freedom, but apart from the intrinsic merits of the position such a course seems to me the only plausible course open to someone willing to admit the extent of fallibility in the scriptures but at the same time concerned to defend the notion of an interactionist or interventionist God. God valued something more highly than his will and purposes for mankind always being perfectly understood, namely a free human response. As I have put it elsewhere, 'revelation is a process whereby God progressively unveils the truth about himself and his purposes to a community of believers, but always in such a way that their freedom of response is respected'.[9] Let me offer two analogies which may help to clarify the sort of process I have in mind.

First, if it does not suggest too narrow a perspective, the Oxford tutorial system may be used by way of illustration, especially where one-to-one tutorials are involved. Dialogue suggests interaction between the two parties involved, with the dialogue moving at the pace of one's dialogue partner rather than the pace of one's own knowledge, with the concern that he really understand rather than simply absorb a number of facts. Clearly there are numerous things one could say to a first year philosophy student which, though true, would not be properly understood by him. But clearly also, if the student is to know not only that certain things are true but how they are true, the teaching system is not just a matter of telling him simpler facts first but inducting him into a particular way of thinking, that has

[8] ibid., p. 133.
[9] op. cit., p. 70.

as its cost allowing him to make mistakes of assessment as he goes along, exaggerating the force of a consideration here, underestimating there, with these defects of understanding being only gradually overcome. For example, in the philosophy of religion one will only really manage to assess Plantinga's anti-foundationalism or Swinburne's probability approach if first one has understood properly the more traditional deductive approach and in turn is in a position to weigh the status of anti-foundationalism or the use of probability arguments outside the philosophy of religion.[10] But inevitably before the undergraduate gets there, he may well have made several somersaults in his position, even perhaps to the extent of denying the role of reason in religion at all.

Some may think the teaching analogy over-intellectualist, with revelation seen as essentially the communication of facts. But, if that objection is raised, my response would be that it is rather the objector who demonstrates his misunderstanding of the point of teaching. For in philosophy one is surely primarily concerned to teach a method, a way of thinking to which facts and rules are of course relevant but not the whole story. Similarly then with revelation as dialogue. The objective is teaching a method, a way of life, to which none the less certain rules of thinking and certain facts are indispensable if maximum effectiveness is to be achieved.

But the tutorial analogy is perhaps less effective at bringing out the personal character of the relationship than another possible analogy, that of getting to know someone as a friend. Seldom, if ever, do we begin to know someone in isolation. In fact, almost invariably we come to any relationship with certain pre-

---

[10] For Plantinga, A. Plantinga & N. Wolterstorff (eds.) *Faith and Rationality* (Notre Dame, Indiana: University of Notre Dame Press, 1983), esp. pp. 16–93. For Swinburne, R. Swinburne, *The Existence of God* (Oxford: Clarendon Press, 1979). For a recent, interesting discussion of the question of foundationalism without reference to religion, cf. R. J. Bernstein, *Beyond Objectivism and Relativism* (Oxford: Basil Blackwell, 1983). For the use of probability arguments outside the context of religion, the most helpful book remains B. Mitchell, *The Justification of Religious Belief* (London: MacMillan, 1973), esp. chapters 3 and 5.

suppositions, that shape the way in which that relation then proceeds and develops. Thus, the reader of this paper will already have begun to perceive me in a certain way even before he has met me, even if the facts he knows about me are absolutely minimal. Suppose that he knows just two – that I am an Oxford philosopher and that I am a priest of the Church of England. Already, that will have predisposed him to interpret anything I say in a particular light, depending on his experience of other specimens of the same two breeds. Thus perhaps the former leads him to expect this paper to be clinical and dry, the latter woolly and compromising. Nor is it true that such prejudices are easily overcome. If what he reads turns out on his view to be imaginative, then this may be explained, not in terms of this requiring some modification of his understanding of what is meant by Oxford philosophy, but instead it being said that on this occasion the author was really writing as a theologian, and so on. Again, on the latter stereotype, any chaplain of a college knows that is may well take years of very patient work to turn some atheist colleagues's stereotype of the clergy into a different shape. So often, no matter what one does, it is read in a pre-determined way. In other words, for better or worse, our perceptions are already heavily conditioned by the society about us and by our previous experience, and so whether we take the teaching analogy or the more intimate personal relationship there is just no escaping the distortions and gradualism that must inevitably accompany any dialogue that truly respects human freedom.

But, it will be objected, to describe revelation as a dialogue in this way is hopelessly misleading for at least three reasons. All of them, though accepting the fact of revelation, call into question whether what is taking place could ever be appropriately described as dialogue. The first, of which I intend to say the least, would come from those who insist on the authoritative, peremptory challenge of revelation. That it is often so experienced, as with Jeremiah, I do not for a moment deny. But even Jeremiah can at other times describe his experience in terms of just such a dialogue.[11] In fact even commands can involve complex dialogue and misunderstanding, as anyone who has had to exercise authority knows to his cost. It is the other two reasons for doubt about the model which I find more interesting, since they require its more detailed development, if it is to retain plausibility. They both concern the fact that at most what we seem to have is an inferred dialogue, since we have no independent access to what one of the interlocutors, that is God, said, only access to the resultant blend of God's and his own thoughts in the recipient's mind. Thus, except in auditions which are scarcely the norm, there is no clear parallel to speech in the divine case, and so there appears to be lacking the most obvious and essential feature in any dialogue. Coupled with that is the related fact that in human dialogue its time and place as well as an independently verifiable description of one's interlocutor seem invariably available, whereas normally all these features are problematic in a claim to be the recipient of a divine address. However, Austin Farrer in *The Glass of Vision* threw out some hints which can, I think, be used to restore the model's plausibility. It is, therefore, to consideration of the role of symbols in revelation that I next turn.

## THE ROLE OF SYMBOLS

These Bampton Lectures were certainly intended as a defence of what I have called an interventionist view of revelation, and indeed we find Farrer himself occasionally using that very word. They were delivered in 1948, but fifteen years later in 'Inspiration: Poetical and Divine' we already find him admitting that his case has been 'demolished', though significantly still then going on to say something in defence of it![12] There are a number of reasons why Farrer's understanding of revelation in terms of the communication of images failed to achieve any wide acceptance.

---

[11] Contrast Jer. 20,9, where he cannot restrain the word within him despite his wish to do so, with the more obviously dialogue form of the opening chapter.

[12] 'Inspiration: Poetical and Divine' in C. C. Conti (ed.), *Interpretation and Belief* (London: S.P.C.K., 1976), p. 39.

Two in particular stand out, both connected with the inchoate nature of his suggestion. First, he seems simply to have transferred the problem, from words to images, leaving us puzzled as to why definitive significance should be attached to one if not the other, especially as no explanation is given to account for the former's peculiar liability to error. Secondly, he offered no account of the mechanics involved, except to suggest that it was both like poetic inspiration and different from it. We are told that 'the poet is a maker, the prophet is a mouthpiece',[13] but as I have already argued, we need a more complex story than that. There is a short, intriguing passage in which Farrer summarily dismisses the idea that the matter has anything to do with images in our unconscious.[14] Inspiration, he insists, belongs to the top and not the bottom of our mind, and elsewhere too we find him exhibiting the same hostile attitude to a creative role for the subconscious.[15] However, it is precisely with that thought that I wish to engage, and through exploring the role of images and symbols in our subconscious and unconscious to argue that something like what Farrer suggested might after all be right.

First, it should be noted that this can provide us with a clear analogue for communication, for dialogue, that has no explicit verbalisation in at least one, sometimes both the partners in the dialogue. Such dialogue on the human level can be both intra-personal and inter-personal. Modern French literature provides some impressive examples of the former. On thinks of Marie Cardinal's *The Words To Say It* or some of Nathalie Sarraute's novels.[16] Thus the former describes the way in which Cardinal became mentally ill through the threatening 'It' which she discovered emerging from her unconscious, and the novel describes her fight back to sanity. Certainly she describes that fight in terms of an internal dialogue with herself, with the It

---

[13] A. Farrer, *The Glass of Vision* (London: Dacre Press, 1948), p. 129.

[14] ibid., pp. 26–7.

[15] In 'Poetic Truth', pp. 24–37 in C. C. Conti (ed.), *Reflective Faith* (London: S.P.C.K., 1972), esp. pp. 25 and 33.

[16] M. Cardinal, *The Words To Say It* (London: Picador, 1984); N. Saurraute, e.g. for her reflections on the interaction between the world of her characters and the 'real world' cf. *Between Life and Death* (London: Calder & Boyers, 1970).

expressing itself not, however, in words but in symbols, as for example in the unrestrained flow of menstrual blood.

Perhaps, however, it is with the inter-personal dialogue that we are more familiar, especially if one thinks of standard Freudian theory. The child inter-relates with its parents in non-verbal discourse, where symbols take the place of words, but where none the less we do have a dialogue, perhaps continuing into adulthood, with the child unconsciously modifying and adapting its symbols in the light of its developing relations with the parent. Thus significantly one of Freud's most recent distinguished followers, Jacques Lacan, has expressed the Freudian system in precisely these terms of symbolic discourse.[17] Significant, too, is the positive assessment he gives to the initial repression. For he argues that it is only through the child's symbolic representation of the father as the other that the child's total indentification with its mother is overcome and the child achieves a sense of its own personal identity.

Thus there seems no difficulty whatsoever in envisaging a dialogue in which one or other of the partners communicates symbolically rather than directly through words. Intriguingly in the examples quoted above, in the Cardinal case it is the sender of the signals which expresses itself symbolically, whereas in the latter case it is the recipient who relates to what he believes has been communicated by expressing it in symbolic terms. So clearly we can envisage either or both sides of the equation being expressed symbolically. It should also be noted that equally the above examples can be used to illustrate the way in which even in the human case it does not count decisively against the occurrence of symbolic dialogue that there was no recognition at the original time and place of encounter that this was in fact what was taking place.

But what then of the divine case? The idea of progressive revelation which I have been developing must I think carry with it the notion of God communicating in the context of an existing canon of assumptions, as it were – which the community of faith

[17] Pursued in lectures and talks, which have been published somewhat paradoxically under the title *Écrits* (Paris: Éditions de Seuil, 1971).

believes itself to have reached in relation to God and which in consequence conditions what the believer is led to understand by whatever God says to him. But that must inevitably raise the question of how one can best conceive this dialogue as beginning, of what mechanics might be employed in the initial stages before there really was any prior revelatory canon of assumptions.

Now I certainly do not want to deny that many a purely intellectualist or rational thought might be the result of divine promptings at the sub-conscious level, as at times when we marvel at some particular notion that has just come into our heads and can think of no obvious source for it. Nor do I wish to challenge the revelatory status of the particular images upon which Farrer concentrates, the Kingdon of God and the Son of Man, without which Farrer insists that Jesus teaching 'would not be supernatural revelation'.[18] But these, it seems to me, are already very refined symbols, and thus the story of man's symbolic dialogue with God can only be properly told if we try to penetrate further back into the more basic elements in our consciousness which God might use to communicate with us. In other words, we need to investigate the possibility of natural symbols.

Farrer in a memorable phrase informs us that 'people are everywhere wrestling with the mystery of the shadow of the infinite', but significantly the example he gives of extrapolation to the infinite is an intellectualist one, pure will.[19] However, there is no shortage of those prepared to argue that there are such things as natural symbols. A good case in point is Mary Douglas in her book of the same name. Though admitting that different social matrices will produce different symbols, at the same time she does argue for recurring patterns within the same general social form. So, for example, she contrasts societies with restricted and non-restricted codes of social rules and suggests that the latter will lead to a lack of symbols of solidarity and hierarchy, or again she notes that different conditions apply for the emergence of ritualism and effervescence but that both will

[18] *The Glass of Vision*, op. cit., p. 42.
[19] ibid., pp. 92 and 89.

have their corresponding symbols.[20] However, her concern is primarily with the transcendent as it reflects itself in social relations and this means that she loses sight of an even more basic shared naturalism in symbols.

Here Mircea Eliade has been more successful in his *The Sacred and the Profane*. He argues that primitive religion treats the world as a 'replica of the paradigmatic universe' of the gods, and that this leads to notions of sacred time and place which mean that 'nature is never only "natural"'.[21] The result is that nature is seen as constantly manifesting or symbolising the divine. As he puts it, 'for religious man, the world always presents a supernatural valence . . . every cosmic fragment is transparent'.[22] Now of course much of this will go as soon as man ceases to perceive his universe in this reflected way. But that does not mean that all natural symbols of the transcendent therefore collapse. For instance, Eliade mentions an awareness of transcendence coming through at the 'height' of the sky,[23] and it is hard not to see that as an image which will survive, whatever the social context.

Among other examples which might be given of essentially natural symbols are the two basic elements in the Christian sacraments, water and blood, F. W. Dillistone in *Christianity and Symbolism* mentions a wealth of associations for water,[24] but again it is hard to envisage the perception of water totally detached from the notion of cleansing and purification. In the case of blood he suggests that the root idea may be 'because being blood it can more easily be imagined as reaching in some way the divine mouth',[25] But this is surely quite wrong. Blood as the life-

[20] M. Douglas, *Natural Symbols* (London: Penguin, 2nd edn., 1973). For former contrast, p. 44ff., esp. p. 55; for the latter, pp. 103–4.

[21] M. Eliade, *The Sacred and the Profane* (San Diego: Harvest/HBJ, 1959), pp. 34 and 116.

[22] ibid., p. 138.

[23] ibid., p. 118.

[24] F. W. Dillistone, *Christianity and Symbolism* (London: Collins, 1955), p. 183ff.

[25] ibid., p. 226, though he does also offer as an alternative the rather vague possibility of its 'mysterious potency'.

force seems pre-eminently a natural symbol. Even today schoolboy gangs sometimes think a small surface cut and the mixing of each other's blood as the most effective sign of gang identity. Their lives are thus united, and in sacrifice what could be more natural than to offer the symbol of life back to its owner or creator?

In a discussion of *Le Mythe et le Symbole* at the *Institut Catholique* in Paris J.-R. Marello, while identifying at least four natural symbols, fire, water, sexuality and light, has warned us of the human capacity to resist any reading, however natural.[26] That is true, but we must also beware of treating as natural what can in fact bear an excluding alternative symbolic meaning. Light may be used by way of illustration. For both Cassirer and Eliade point out that darkness only becomes a symbol for evil once sun and darkness are no longer seen as part of a single cosmic unity.[27] None the less, even with all these qualifications made, we can I think endorse the view that there are such things as natural symbols, and that Jung, who has perhaps insisted more strongly than anyone else on their existence in our unconscious, was in fact on the right lines.

In *Man and his Symbols* he does not hesitate to declare that it is primarily through the unconscious and its symbols that God speaks to man: 'We are so captivated and entangled in our subjective consciousness that we have forgotten the age-old fact that God speaks chiefly through dreams and visions'.[28] I am reluctant to quantify, but that symbols exercise a crucial role in God's dialogue with man must, I think, be right. Let me therefore give three reasons for insisting on this, before going on to indicate how, starting from natural symbols, revelation might be seen as a dialogue that develops in terms of their elaboration and refinement.

[26] J.-R. Marello, 'Symbole et réalité – Réflexion sur une distinction ambigue' in Institut Catholique de Paris, Philosophie 2, *Le Mythe et le Symbole* (Paris: Editions Beauchesne, 1977), p. 155ff., esp. 162.
[27] E. Cassirer, *Language and Myth* (New York: Dover Publications, 1953), pp. 13–14; Eliade, op. cit., pp. 157–8.
[28] C. Jung, *Man and his Symbols* (London: Picador, 1978), p. 92.

A first reason for thinking that symbols might play a crucial role in God's dialogue with man is because, as we have seen, there are such things as natural as well as socially created symbols. For an implication of this is that God does not first have to create a common language of communication. This emerges naturally – the everlastingness of the hills, the purifying powers of water, blood as the essence of life, and so forth. Secondly, precisely because such language is symbolic, with one thing standing for another, it is already admirably suited to be the language of religion. For the language of religion has to be analogical, since it involves the transfer of language used in ordinary empirical contexts into a transcendent context. But, it cannot be too strongly emphasised, this is exactly what symbolic discourse is doing all the time. Hence Lacan's fondness for word play in his *Écrits*. For symbolic perception refuses to be bound by accepted categories, but instead insists on identifying comparable features outside the accepted classifications acknowledged by analytic discourse. Indeed, this perhaps gives one possible explanation of why the verbal content of religious experience is characteristically so non-logical and unargumentative. One thinks, for example, of the prophets and the strange connections of thought which they sometimes made. It is not just that they are reaching out to realities which are in any case difficult to describe, but that such crossing of categories is in any case symptomatic of the symbolic way of thinking which is at work in our unconscious. Finally, since, for whatever reason, this seems to be the primary language of our sub-conscious, God interacting with it offers a model for dialogue with the divine that no more requires the partner in the dialogue to be always recognised and acknowledged than does the creation and modification of symbols through other unconscious interaction, for example with one's father, if the Freudian theory is true. This is important because it makes it a medium through which God can act upon us, without destroying our freedom in the process. For in speaking thus he speaks without us being fully or even at all aware of who it is at work, addressing us. The crucial decision thus becomes clearly ours and not God's, in the sense that what finally matters in determining whether the dialogue continues to develop is whether we choose to bring these images to conscious awareness so that they can be creatively used and communicated to others. To all this it may be objected that it is far from obvious that the unconscious is really under our own control. Let me therefore give a personal example to illustrate the strong sense in which I believe it to be in fact just so. It was with something almost bordering on shock that I read a philosopher like Stephen Clark speaking in praise of glossolalia in his recent Gifford Lectures, *From Athens to Jerusalem*.[29] To me the loss of reason and self-control seems almost terrifyingly disconcerting. Now such fears may in their turn be irrational. But my point here is simply, to generalise, the enormous resistance one's conscious self can put up to any stirrings of one's unconscious, and so effectively the great power it has over the unconscious in continuing to maintain one's freedom.

Paul Ricoeur is another thinker who seems to accept the existence of natural symbols. Thus he writes: 'An essential characteristic of the symbol is the fact that it is never completely arbitrary . . . there always remains the trace of a natural relationship between the signifier and the signified',[30] and this he thinks pre-eminently true of what he calls 'primary' or 'archetypal' symbols. Not only that, he also attempts to bring out the creative role of the symbol, depending on whether the individual responds to the forward movement of the Spirit and produces a 'recollection of the sacred' or makes a Freudian retreat to childhood in the 'return of the repressed'. As he puts it: 'The two symbolisms are intermingled. There is always some trace of archaic myth which is grafted to and operates within the most prophetic meanings of the sacred. The progressive order of symbols is not exterior to the regressive order of fantasies; the plunge into the archaic mythologies of the unconscious brings to the surface new signs of the sacred. The eschatology

[29] S. R. L. Clark, *From Athens to Jerusalem* (Oxford: Clarendon Press, 1984), esp. p. 76.

[30] P. Ricoeur, *The Conflict of Interpretations* (Evanston: Northwestern University Press, 1974), p. 319.

of consciousness is always a creative repetition of its own archaeology'.[31]

In this connection he informs us that 'an archaic symbol survives only through the revolutions of experience and language which submerge it . . . a symbol is first of all a destroyer of a prior symbol'.[32] Whether destruction is the right term to use, when something of a family resemblance survives, is questionable, but more important for our purposes here is the fact that in *The Conflict of Interpretations* Ricoeur offers us two essays in which he analyses the way in which specific symbols can undergo just such a creative transformation.[33] One symbol he takes is that of original sin. In its case he is careful to point out that Genesis already represents a creative modification of earlier Babylonian traditions, and to draw our attention to the way in which through Israel's experience the symbol is modified from external stain to internal guilt.[34] At the same time he suggests that Augustine must take the blame for turning an originally potent symbol into a doctrine, and that for us it is necessary to 'deconstruct' Augustine to get back to the original powerful symbol. That way we escape the supposition that the story explains anything, and instead latch on to the fact that 'it has an extraordinary symbolic power because it condenses in an archetype of man everything which the believer experiences in a fugitive fashion and confesses in an allusive way'.[35] Again, in his essay on fatherhood as a symbol he notes the universality of the image in all religions as a description of God,[36] and its modification in Hebrew religion through the way in which a non-sexual word is used of creation or again the way in which Jeremiah combines it with the image of spouse, further under-

[31] ibid., pp. 333–4. Both his articles on 'The Hermenuetics of Symbols' are particularly valuable in this connection. cf. ibid., pp. 287–334.

[32] Ibid., p. 291.

[33] ' "Original Sin": A Study in Meaning', ibid., pp. 269–86; 'Fatherhood: From Phantasm to Symbol', ibid., pp. 468–97. However, in the former case it should be noted that the earlier part of the story of its development is in fact told in a subsequent essay, 'The Hermeneutics of Symbols I', p. 287ff.

[34] ibid., p. 294 and pp. 289–90.

[35] ibid., p. 283. His 'deconstruct' comment occurs on p. 281.

[36] ibid., p. 483.

mining its sexual content.[37] Then of the New Testament he remarks that not only does Jesus give it a fresh dimension with his use of *Abba*, the basic Freudian pattern is overthrown with the father's compassionate 'dying with' symbolically taking the place of being 'killed' by the child.[38]

Whether Ricoeur has chosen the best examples of such creative transformation need not concern us here. There are, of course, numerous other instances that could equally well have been taken, from a very basic symbol like blood and the way in which it is transformed from a life-force owned by God into a life-force given by God to man, to much more culture specific images like that of shepherd and its alteration from an image of authority in past tradition to one of sacrificial care in John, or the new kingdom whose recognition Luke perceives on and through the Cross.[39] But this is not the place to pursue such questions in detail. All I have been concerned to establish is the conceivability of revelation operating in this way through the creative transformation of symbols present in our unconscious, and that I think I have shown.

But, it may be objected, I have done my task too well. For in trying to make conceivable a revelatory divine dialogue through symbols it looks as though I may have removed the necessity for any talk of divine intervention or interaction. Can it not all be explained simply in terms of one initial divine act, his creation being such that it naturally produces certain symbols, and thereafter man's reflection on those symbols can be allowed to take over. Of course, it is possible to read the story like that, and give an intelligible account. But it strikes me as the poorer story, the one less attuned to the facts. Elsewhere I have suggested four

---

[37] ibid., p. 486 and p. 489.

[38] ibid., p. 492.

[39] For the transformation of the symbol of blood, contrast the absolute prohibition on drinking blood in, e.g. Lev. 17,10–14 with the injunction of John 6,53–6. Passages like Jer. 2,8 or Ezek. 34,2ff. demonstrate that the original primary significance of the image of 'shepherd' was one of authority, and so are in stark contrast to John 10,11. Likewise, the words of the penitent thief (Luke 23,42) transmute all normal understandings of kingship.

tests for what is to be classed as revelatory experience – the character of the recipient, the unexpectedness of its challenge to our existing perspectives, its congruity with other such experiences and 'the extent to which interpreting it in anything other than revelatory terms would be to denigrate it'.[40] Let me here concentrate exclusively on the last, as I think it highlights the way in which one must cease to have the same symbols, the same story, unless one tells it in an interventionist way.

Farrer informs us that 'the recipients of revelation see themselves to be addressed by God . . . And this is nothing like poetical experience, anyhow on the face of it; it is like personal encounter'.[41] But it is not just the note of personal encounter which is lost if interaction ceases to be part of the story, it is, I think, the symbols themselves. For I would wish to argue that it is integral to acceptance of a symbol (or myth for that matter since this is surely just a symbol in story form) that one accept that it conveys the reality it is supposed to represent. Roland Barthes may be mentioned as an example of a non-religious thinker who accepts this very point.[42] In an impressive discussion of myth[43] he claims that not only is there a condensation or concentration in any myth that defies any easy analytic unpacking, it is integral to the acceptance of the myth that it be seen as non-reducible. Intriguingly, Ricoeur has taken Bultmann to task on this very point, in insisting that the symbolic or mythical is irreducible, that to demythologise is already to change the meaning and in any case to pursue an impossible goal. Farrer too, in his well-known essay, 'Can Myth be Fact?' insists that on a true understanding of myth it 'was a guarantee that man's beliefs were not mere ideals or aspirations but the very laws of being', and that in consequence even the myth of Adam but still more so

---

[40] *The Divine Trinity*, op. cit., pp. 79–84, esp. p. 82.

[41] In 'Inspiration: Poetical and Divine' in *Interpretation and Belief*, op. cit., p. 44.

[42] For a discussion of Barthes on myth, cf. my *Continental Philosophy & Modern Theology* (Oxford: Basil Blackwell, 1987), chapter 2. For another treatment of symbol, chapter 5.

[43] R. Barthes, *Mythologies* (London: Granada, 1973), e.g. p. 123.

the Incarnation 'cannot be allegorised or evaporated into general statements without losing its force'.[44]

These are, I think, points too easily forgotten. As Ricoeur puts it, 'the symbol gives: I do not posit the meaning, the symbol gives it'.[45] In other words, it ceases to be the same encounter, the same conveying of reality, unless one believes that there is something interacting with us to produce those modifications of the image in us. Hence Barthes' insistence that to demythologise, to deny correspondence between the symbol and objective reality, is already to rob the symbol of its power. To take examples we considered earlier, just think of the contrast between Cardinal's 'It' and the Freudian father figure. For Cardinal, to discover that the It was only her other self was already to undermine its power; for us, to understand the possible sources of our relationship with our father makes that power now explicitly acknowledged, but need do nothing to undermine its reality, unless of course it involves coming to see envy of our father as groundless. In other words, just as we need to see interaction with our father throughout our lives modifying that unconscious image and there being a father whose inter-actions help to produce these modifications, if there is to be any continuing significance in the symbol, so I suggest the same must hold in our relation to God.

It is not that this demands any miracles. I have already argued in the first part of this paper that in suggesting such interaction all we need be seen as doing is according to God the same freedom of action which we do not hesitate to accord to ourselves. Nor is appeal to the more supernatural elements of religious experience like visions integral to my argument. No doubt on many an occasion (though not I think on all) these are simply the projection of the individual's unconscious, as for example with Jung's vision of Christ.[46] No, what is indispens-able, irrespective of whether they appear before the waking or

---

[44] In C. C. Conti (ed.), *Interpretation and Belief*, op. cit., pp. 166 and 170.
[45] op. cit., p. 288.
[46] C. G. Jung, *Memories, Dreams, Reflections* (London: Fontana, 1983), pp. 236–7.

the unconscious eye, is that their creative density can only be acknowledged satisfactorily if we see them as vehicles of encounter and interaction. For only thus are we effectively acknowledging that they could and do have a power that is irreducible and not of themselves.

Let me end with an illustration suitably drawn from the nation to which I belong. It is precisely because the symbol of the monarchy interacts with the British nation, reflecting, reinforcing and to some extent creating the nation's values that it has its power, and it is clearly this that has made it of such interest of late to semiologists.[47] Were the monarchy to cease to express these values, were it to cease to find an answering chord in the Englishman's heart, were it to cease to interact with the nation's subconscious, then it would also die as a symbol. For then reality and symbol would cease to coincide. So also then with God and the symbols through which he chooses to interrelate with us.

---

[47] e.g. D. Dayan and E. Katz on the Royal Wedding in M. Blonsky (ed.), *On Signs* (Oxford: Blackwell, 1985), pp. 16–32.

# Chapter 7

# 'DOUBLE AGENCY' AND IDENTIFYING REFERENCE TO GOD

*Rodger Forsman*

> From effects evident to us we can demonstrate what in itself is not evident to us, namely, that God exists. Now when demonstrating from effects that God exists, we are able to start from what the word 'God' means, for the names of God are derived from these effects. (*Summa Theologiae*, Ia,2,2,reply)

That God is known through his effects is the foundational principle of the cosmological tradition in philosophical theology, for it encapsulates a total conception of the objectives and correct procedure for theology. The principle presupposes that it is possible for the rational mind to gain knowledge of God without the aid of special divine revelation; and it is usually taken to imply that rational knowledge of God rests neither upon mere acknowledgement that the existence of God is self-evident nor upon an alleged non-inferential awareness of the divine nature, but rather upon inference from certain general facts about the world. Furthermore, it is implied that the inference employed is a kind of causal reasoning, or is at least analogous to causal reasoning. To note the foregoing is simply to remind ourselves of the logical context within which this tradition typically sets for its answer to the question, Is there a God?

To say that God is known through his effects, then, is in part to propose a solution to one of the main epistemological problems of theism, namely, the problem of showing on what evidence and by what kind of reasoning the judgment that God exists is to be justified if it is to be justified at all. Modern discussions of theism, however, have focused less upon the issue of the truth of, or evidence for, propositions which purport to be about God and more upon the meaning of the theist's utterances. A particularly pressing challenge to the theist from this quarter is to show how it is possible to make identifying reference to God, that is, to explain how at least some of the theist's utterances can legitimately be taken as logically well-formed statements which refer to real being. For the theist a great deal turns on meeting this challenge satisfactorily. Clearly, if the theist cannot give an account of how it is possible to identify God as a subject of discourse he will always be vulnerable to the charge that no sentence with 'God' as subject can be construed as expressing a genuine knowledge-claim (unless, of course, it is regarded as a mere tautology or a disguised and misleading way of talking about something other than the object of theistic worship).

How, then, is this problem to be handled? I proceed by outlining briefly how a problem about making identifying reference to God arises in the first place. I then examine the doctrine that God can be identifyingly referred to as the agent of certain effects. I argue that understanding this doctrine requires close examination of the notion of divine activity. In this connection I discuss two fundamentally different kinds of analogies in terms of which the notion of divine causal activity might be understood. I conclude with an estimate of the extent to which the theist can fruitfully employ the doctrine that God can be identifyingly referred to as the agent of certain effects, and state what seem to be some of the restrictions on the doctrine.

# I

## THE ORIGIN OF THE PROBLEM

Traditional theism conceives of God on the analogy of personal agency. The scriptures, the creeds, the hymns and the prayers of the Judaeo–Christian tradition are incomprehensible apart from the presupposition that there exists a divine being capable of acting so as to bring about in the world of space and time, that is the world of ordinary human activity, events which are in accordance with his intentions and purposes. The tradition holds that God reveals his nature through what he does and that God's rational creatures fittingly adore him for what he is and rightfully praise and thank him for his saving activity on their behalf; and it encourages them to commune with God in prayer and to conform themselves as much as possible to his divine nature. All of this presupposes further that much can be said about God; theism has in fact invested immense effort both at the level of practical piety, in the articulation and communication of the faith, and at the level of rational reflection, in defence of the possibility of talking about God.

Now it is reflection on our undoubted ability to talk about ordinary things that brings to light difficulties about the possibility of talking about God. If we wish to tell someone something about someone else, say Smith over there by that pile of wood building a fence, we must speak in such a way as to enable the one to whom we are speaking to identify the subject about which we are trying to speak; otherwise what we say, while not literally meaningless, is at best mystifying to the hearer; for we are not placing her or him in position to know what we are talking about. Consequently, the one to whom we are speaking is not able to determine whether what we say is true or not. In order to succeed in making a fully intelligible statement about Smith, then, we must speak in such a way as to enable the person to whom we are speaking to identify Smith as the subject of discourse. We succeed in making an identifying reference to Smith partly by distinguishing him as one type of physical object (a man) from other types of physical object which might also be present (e.g. the wood in the pile, or the hammer and nails Smith is using). Furthermore we distinguish Smith from other objects of the same type by reference to certain characteristics which he possesses uniquely, at least in the present circumstances: Smith is the man with the red hair and beard, not the blond fellow or the other one who is clean-shaven. And we also use an elementary set of spatial co-ordinates established by the relative positions of the speaker, hearer, and other objects: Smith is over *there*, *beside* the wood-pile. (And characteristically we point while saying that.) In short, we succeed in identifying

Smith as a subject of discourse because we have means, both linguistic and non-linguistic, of distinguishing Smith from other objects and which describe or indicate certain relations (e.g. spatial relations) between Smith and the speaker and hearer. Were we unable to make identifying reference to Smith we could still say a lot about Smith in the trivial sense that we could continue to utter sentences with the word 'Smith' as their grammatical subject, and which would be grammatically like sentences which we use to say something about things which we can identify as subjects of discourse in the ordinary way. But we could not say anything about Smith in the non-trivial sense of 'say about' which we intend when we make contingent statements about things, persons or events in contexts in which by making such statements we put someone in position to determine what we are talking about and whether what we say is true of the subject of discourse to which we make reference. Thus while it would still be possible to employ many sentences having the word 'Smith' as grammatical subject it is clear that such sentences would be very different logically from grammatically similar sentences about the ordinarily identifiable Smith, the red-haired, bearded fence-builder by the wood-pile.

Let us now turn to the theist's assumption that it is possible to make statements about God. If the immediately preceding analysis of the possibility of making statements about a human agent is sound (as far as it goes) and if God is to be conceived on the analogy of personal agency, fully intelligible statements about God would seem to be possible only if the theist can make identifying reference to God, that is, only if he can single out God as a subject of discourse in such a way as to enable someone to identify the being he is talking about. But it is at just this point that the theist seems to run into difficulty. For the absolute being of classical theism is plainly not an object of sense perception; he cannot be distinguished from other objects by sense-perceptible individuating characteristics. Furthermore, theists say that God is in all times and places; God is no more here than there, no more now than then. Hence God cannot be pointed to with the finger, nor located on any system of space-time co-ordinates. In fact, it seems to be the very requirements of God-hood that generate the problem of identifying reference to God; for God exists without limitation, whereas all of our ordinary ways of identifying a subject of discourse seem to require that it be subject to limitations or forms of dependence which unfit it for God-hood.

Now the general direction of the immediately foregoing discussion can be put in the form of a simple argument; it is convenient to do so in order to assist us to see clearly the kinds of moves that might be made to counter the drift of this discussion. The argument proceeds as follows:

1. Our ordinary means of making identifying reference to a subject of discourse are the only means available to us.
2. God, as conceived in traditional theism, is not identifiable by these means. Therefore,
3. God is not identifiable as a subject of discourse.

This plainly is a sceptical argument; if correct it has the effect of foreclosing on the possibility of talk about God. But any argument of this form can be reversed by denying the conclusion and one of the premises. This yields the possibility of two different responses to this kind of sceptical argument. Thus:

(a) not-3. God is identifiable as a subject of discourse.

2. God, as conceived in traditional theism, is not identifiable as a subject of discourse by our ordinary means of making identifying references. Therefore,

not-1. Our ordinary means of making identifying reference to a subject of discourse are not the only means available to us.

This argument is analogous to the intuitionist argument in epistemology. Anyone who takes this approach faces the challenge of specifying the additional and even extraordinary means of identifying a subject of discourse to which appeal is made here. I think that supporters of any form of the ontological argument are taking this approach, for they make identifying reference to God as 'that than which a greater cannot be conceived', a form of words which abstracts entirely from the ordinary identifying contexts established by the relationships of bodies with their sense-perceptible characteristics.

But there is another reversal of the sceptical argument:

(*b*) not-3. God is identifiable as a subject of discourse.

    1. Our ordinary means of making identifying reference to a subject of discourse are the only means available to us. Therefore,

    not-2. God, as conceived in traditional theism, is identifiable by these means.

Anyone who takes this approach faces the challenge of showing how God can be identified in ways not too remotely unlike the ways in which we identify more ordinary subjects of discourse. St Thomas, reflecting ancient biblical and theological tradition, takes this approach when he declares that God is named from his effects, or as I have put it for my purposes, that God is identifyingly referred to as the agent of certain effects.

The sceptical argument I have outlined shows something of the problem of identifying reference to God in that it clearly exhibits the bearing of this whole issue upon theistic belief. The two responses point to the two fundamentally different possible strategies for dealing with the problem.

Let me now summarise the discussion thus far. A problem about making identifying reference to God arises in the first place because our ordinary means of identifying a subject of discourse do not seem to enable us to identify God, or at least, it is difficult to see how such ordinary means enable us to identify God as a subject of discourse. Ordinarily we make identifying reference to something by distinguishing it from other things by its observable characteristics and by reference to its relation to the speaker, hearer, and to other objects; but this does not seem to be appropriate in the case of attempts to identify God. What might be a solution to this problem? Are we to postulate some analogue to sense perception by means of which we somehow perceive God and are thereby enabled to learn what distinguished God from other things? This is the strategy implicit in the first response to the sceptical argument just outlined; it is what St Thomas supposed Anselm to be up to. Or alternatively, are we to try to show how God, who admittedly cannot be identified as a subject of discourse in the way in which a human being can be identified, can nevertheless be identifyingly referred to by virtue of a relationship in which all things stand to God and to which direct reference can be made? This is the strategy of the second response.

There are some reasons for thinking that the second response is the more plausible of the two. First, there is something to be said for premise 1. Although this premise is neither obviously true nor obviously false it seems fair to apply the principle of parsimony here and argue that premise 1 should be denied only if there is pressing conceptual need to revise our ordinary understanding of what it is to identify something as a subject of discourse. But it is not clear that this need exists; one might of course urge that such conceptual revision is needed precisely because of the need to explain identifying reference to God; but this begins to look like special pleading. Hence I suggest that there is more reason to accept premise 1 than its negation. The second premise also is neither obviously true nor obviously false. Theists in the Thomist tradition will affirm it while many other theists and many sceptics will deny it; and it doesn't seem as easy in the case of this premise as in the case of the first to apply a burden-of-proof argument. In fact, premise 2 (or its negation) is the sort of statement which should appear as the conclusion of an argument, not as an apparently undisputed premise. Such considerations, although merely dialectical, show I suggest, that the second response to the sceptical argument is preferable to the first. In any case it is the second line of argument which I am going to examine here.

## II

### *IDENTIFYING GOD AS AGENT OF EFFECTS*

It has been proposed that God can be identifyingly referred to as agent of certain effects. How is this proposal supposed to work as a solution to the problem we are concerned with?

At the level of mere description it is not too difficult to answer this question. It is conceded first that God cannot be identified as a subject of discourse in the way in which a physical object can; but it is then asserted that certain events, e.g. the deliverance of Israel from bondage in Egypt or the rising of Jesus from the dead, have been brought about by divine activity; and so God can be identified as the agent of these effects. At a more philosophical level it is asserted that ordinary things in the world – a grain of sand, a plant, animals, human beings, mountains and stars – are brought into and maintained in existence by God's activity, and so God can be identifyingly referred to as the creator of the world.

The general strategy underlying this proposal is straight-forward. It consists first in searching for analogies in non-theological contexts for concepts or distinctions or arguments that we want to use in theological contexts, and second, in trying to show that the theological context is not so radically different from the non-theological context that the chosen analogies are not thereby rendered useless. This is the strategy adopted, for example, by Cleanthes in Hume's *Dialogues*, where Cleanthes attempts to vindicate the design argument by trying to show that analogical argument in theology is sufficiently like analogical argument in non-theological contexts that if it is a sound method in the latter contexts it should be regarded as sound in the former as well. To what non-theological matters, then, does the proposal we are considering make appeal? There are two: first, sometimes we do identify an agent by what the agent does, and second, sometimes we do argue from effect to cause. These are related to two assumptions underlying the doctrine we are examining, namely, that we can make indirect identifying reference, and that the existence of a causal relation between two things is a sufficient condition for indirect identifying reference.

I shall first say what I mean by the notion of direct identifying reference; I do not intend this to be an analysis of the notion but only a rough indication of what seems to be involved. My overriding assumption, here, is that when we are making identifying reference to something we are trying to say something about a real being, e.g. a human being. I am not concerned here with referring expressions such as 'the university', or 'the nation', not with expressions such as 'the tallest building in Baton Rouge' or 'the only seven-foot tall person in LSU'. My reasons for this restriction are, first, that theists have customarily thought that God is not like a nation or a university; and second, that identifying reference to a subject of discourse is not merely a matter of using a referring expression, even one which is uniquely referring; it is, in addition, to use such expressions in such a way as to enable a hearer to pick out the subject being referred to, then and there. Roughly, then, direct identifying reference to a subject of discourse involves the use of descriptive terms in such a way that the intended subject of discourse can be correctly identified by the hearer because the hearer can determine by observation that the descriptive words and phrases used by the speaker actually apply to something which in the determinate circumstances is there to be talked about. Indirect identifying reference, then, will be identifying reference to something which in the determinate circumstances cannot be directly identified, but can be identifyingly referred to only because of a relation in which it stands to something which can be directly identified as a subject of discourse.

Do we ever make indirect identifying reference to anything? Clearly we do. For example, we use expressions such as 'the cause of the noise', 'the author of the book', or 'the builder of the fence'. In each case there is an identifying reference to something by reference to something else (a physical object, or content of sensory awareness) along with an implied reference to a dependence relation.

It is important here to observe Strawson's distinction between identifying something as a subject of discourse, and identifying a subject of discourse as something. For example we might identify something as a subject of discourse (identifyingly refer to something) by using the words 'the red-bearded man over there by the fence'. But this is quite different from identifying the red-bearded man by the fence as Smith. The latter form of words, to use Strawson's terminology, is an identification statement, i.e. one which asserts something about a subject of discourse already identifyingly referred to. Similarly, we do refer to things in an indirect way – e.g. we refer to Smith as the man who built the fence; but as Strawson points out such sentences are used in contexts in which someone knows or believes that someone built the fence and is asking, Who built the fence? In short, a sentence like 'Smith is the man who built the fence' is not used to make identifying reference to something for the purpose of saying something about it, but to say something about a subject of discourse already identifyingly referred to. Now let us begin to elicit a few general principles about indirect identifying reference. We will proceed by considering examples.

Let us say that we are watching Smith build his fence. He is working a few feet away from where Jones, who looks like Smith's identical twin, is spading his garden. If we try to tell someone something about Smith it will not do, in these circumstances, to try to identify him as the man with the red hair and beard because that description fits Jones as well; but we can, obviously, make identifying reference to Smith as the fence-builder. But thus far this case does not help us understand *indirect* identifying reference because Smith is directly identifiable; after all, he is there in plain view. So we have to alter the circumstances a bit. Let us say, this time, that Smith is out of sight. Clearly in this case we must make indirect identifying reference to him if we wish to say anything about him. And there is no reason to think that a sentence which identifyingly refers to Smith as the fence-builder would not be a fully intelligible statement, e.g. 'The fence-builder is not working right now'.

Now why does this work? I think there are several reasons. First, we know that fences are the sort of thing that come into existence as the result of intelligent action; they don't just grow in place. Second, we understand very well the kind of activity it takes to build a fence. Third, we know that the fence-builder can be directly identified as a subject of discourse on some suitable occasion. Fourth, we know that the fence-builder can be distinguished from the effect he is alleged to have brought about, namely, the fence; to use the expression 'fence-builder' is already to imply a causal relation between Smith and the fence which precludes their being identical. Finally, we know that the fence-builder can be distinguished, on grounds other than by reference to his alleged effects, from other agents, such as Jones who is spading the garden.

Now let us change the example again and say that Smith is out of sight, in principle: he is invisible, intangible, inaudible – in short, totally unperceivable: words which remind us of Flew's allegory of the two travellers disputing about the reality of a postulated gardener – and all we have before us is the completed fence. Could we, in this case, still make identifying reference to Smith as the fence-builder?

I think we could; but it is not entirely clear what we could retain regarding the possibility of talking about Smith if too many of the above five conditions failed to hold. The first condition still holds: invisible Smith's fence is still there, it is the sort of thing we know comes about by deliberate action and in no other way. Difficulties begin to emerge regarding the second condition; for in the case of invisible Smith's fence we have no grasp of how it gets constructed. We might see boards apparently ranging themselves into proper position and alignment, and see nails sinking into the wood, and perhaps even see apparently unguided tools doing their proper work – and yet the whole thing would be a mystery to us. But I suggest that if we ever saw such a thing happening we would most certainly insist that a fence was being *built* – it wasn't just growing of itself. As for the third condition, it fails entirely. Invisible Smith just cannot be identified directly and this fact has consequences for the last two conditions; for since we cannot identify Smith independently of what he is alleged to be doing we really are unable to determine the scope of his alleged activity. Perhaps Smith's identical twin built the fence, and not the Smith we are talking about; and how could we tell the difference? If we can't distinguish between Smith and another agent, how could we tell whether Smith did *this* rather than *that*? And yet it is just this that we must be able to do if we are to talk about *the* builder of the fence. But if all we have to go on is the completed fence it is difficult to see how these necessary distinctions can be made. Finally, there is the nagging suspicion that perhaps invisible Smith really isn't there at all. We believe that good fences make good neighbours; and perhaps there is something like the Whiteheadian principle of the augmentation of value that brings about such aids to good neighbourliness, a principle that operates from time to time, we know not why or how. The word 'Smith', in short, is a mere short-hand expression for the longer and more cumbersome expression, 'the $X$ which generates fences'.

Despite all of these difficulties, however, I think we could still make identifying reference to Smith (as a personal agent and not merely as a fence-building $X$) as long as we knew or were reasonably assured that the fence is indeed a fence in the ordinary sense of the term, i.e. an artifact, a product of intelligent activity. Of course we would have to be quite agnostic about Smith's character, his manner of operation, his aims, and so on. But as long as we were in position to correctly describe something as the effect of an agent's operation, we could successfully make identifying reference to the agent of the effect, by reference to the effect.

I said earlier that the doctrine that God can be identifyingly referred to as agent of certain effects rests on two assumptions. The first, that indirect identifying reference is possible, has just been discussed and I turn now to the second, namely, the notion that the existence of a causal relation between two things is a sufficient condition for identifying reference. It was not really possible, nor desirable, to keep discussion of these two assumptions entirely separate; and in fact I have already stated a somewhat limited conclusion about the second assumption to the extent to which I have said that indirect identifying reference to something as an agent of an effect is possible if we can be reasonably assured that the alleged effect is indeed an effect of intelligent activity. But more needs to be said on this matter, as the following discussion should show, for plainly not every relation which is in some sense or other a causal relation will be a sufficient condition for indirect identifying reference.

To call some thing or event or process an effect is to say that it stands in some sort of dependence relation to something else. It is worth noting that to call something an effect is not to say that it stands in one specific kind of dependence relation which is the same for all effects. For example, our statements of causal relations between things frequently take the form of statements of observed regular sequence in events; i.e. sometimes when we say that A caused B we mean no more than Hume says we mean: that whenever an event of type A occurs an event of type B occurs. Now if we already have to hand a regularity statement such as 'Hurricanes damage houses', and we see a part of a town devastated after a strong wind has passed through, we can legitimately make inferences about the force of the wind. This is to argue from an effect to a conclusion about the nature of a cause. But this kind of case is of no help to the theist for as Hume pointed out in *Dialogues* we cannot arrive at regularity statements of this kind without being in position to observe both what we call cause and what we call effect and also their invariable conjunction; and as he dryly notes, no one has seen worlds being created. Whatever the relation of the world to God is, it is not the relation described by Hume's analysis of causality. No doubt the mutual interaction of many things is for some purposes adequately described by complex sets of regularity statements of the Humean sort; but God is certainly not the cause of effects if 'cause' and 'effect' are understood in Hume's sense.

But Hume's analysis of causation ill fits a form of dependence relation with which we are very familiar, namely, our own agent causality as we experience it in making things happen by our action, for example, putting materials together to make a fence which did not hitherto exist. William Paley tries to exploit this analogy, arguing that material things are so like products of intelligent design that we really must acdept the thesis that they are the result of the action of an intelligent agent. And so for Paley, God is to be identified as the designer of the world. But are natural things really products of design? There's the rub; and Paley had the misfortune of having had his argument refuted a quarter of a century before he published it.

With clearer insight into the logical demands facing metaphysical theology than was possessed by the deists of Hume's day, St Thomas in *De Ente et Essentia*, tried to show that natural things are composite beings whose compositeness is such that it must be attributed to the operation of a being which is not composite. But again, are there composite beings in the sense required by St Thomas' argument? The metaphysical vocabulary of essence and existence in terms of which the distinction between composite and non-composite being was made no longer has any connection with what we now ordinarily and correctly understand as the explanation of things or events in the world. Furthermore, even if the distinction could be made fully intelligible, the argument would offer little comfort to the theist, for he wants to be able to say more than that the word 'God' is the name of an *X* which brings things into existence but is otherwise unknown.

Considerations such as the foregoing help us considerably in understanding the logical relevance of the strong drive in much of theistic argument to describe certain events or phenomena in such a way as to make them appear to be inexplicable apart from divine activity, which is then postulated as cause of the effects adduced. And without registering all the necessary qualifications, I think that theism of the sort we are considering must proceed in somewhat this way; for as the foregoing discussion suggests, God can be identifyingly referred to as agent of certain effects only if we can be reasonably assured that the alleged effects are indeed effects, not merely in a Humean sense, but in the sense of being the results of something very like agent causality. But it is not totally misleading to say that the historical path taken by theism is littered with the wreckage of attempts to carry out this very programme. Why then should we think that there is hope for progress along the same lines as taken by previous efforts?

At an impasse like this I think we should remind ourselves of how theistic thinking proceeds, namely, by applying in theological contexts analogies drawn from non-theological contexts. I want to suggest, without arguing the point, that much of the difficulty with theistic argument arises from the habit of focusing on the wrong sort of analogy. A statement such as this serves only to prompt the question, What is the right sort of analogy? I proceed in the final part of this paper to examine one answer to this question.

## III

### 'EXTERNAL AFFECTION', 'INTERIOR EFFECT', AND 'DOUBLE AGENCY'

In *Finite and Infinite*, his first major treatise in philosophical theology, Austin Farrer employed a distinction between what he called 'agency and interior effect', and 'operation and external affection'. The latter signifies the relation that obtains when someone acts so as to bring about an effect in something other than itself; e.g. we walk in the meadow and the daisies get trampled. This is the sort of relation which obtains when someone builds a fence, or when a watch-maker makes a watch. The expression 'agency and interior effect', on the other hand signifies the relation which obtains when an agent by doing something gives rise to the agent's own next phase. The effect is 'interior' in the sense that what an agent becomes is in part due to what the agent does. For example, to love is to foster the well-being of another. I become a more loving person by becoming more effective in fostering the well-being of others. I become more loving, not by reflecting on the meaning of the world 'love', nor by generating in myself certain feelings for someone, but by acting caringly, in *caritas*, for the other. In this sense I can make myself what I become, within certain limits.

Now I think that many of the difficulties about identifying reference to God arise from modelling divine activity on analogies of the former type, that is, on watch-maker and fence-builder analogies. We have already seen how easily these can be pressed beyond the point of usefulness to the theist. But what if divine causality does not take effect in such an exterior manner, anyway? What if God's active relation to the creature is not like Smith's relation to the fence, but is like the relation between successive phases of Smith himself as one phase brings about the next? Are there any analogies which would make this notion intelligible?

I think there are; but first let us remind ourselves of what such analogies are supposed to accomplish for the theist; they are supposed to demonstrate by example that there is in non-theological contexts a distinction, relation, concept, or argument which is already acknowledged as sound, and which can be employed in the context of theological analysis without such radical qualification as to unfit it for its intended use. Now as I suggested earlier the doctrine that God can be identifyingly referred to as agent of certain effects depends on the possibility of a reasonable assurance that certain alleged effects are in fact effects, and effects of an agent. But as the foregoing discussion seemed to show, any analogy useful to the theist will have to allow for certain obscurities about how the agent brings about the effects he is known to bring about, and even for uncertainty about how to distinguish between what one agent does and what another does. It is in the sphere of what Farrer calls 'agency and interior effect' that we are most likely to find such analogies.

I can think of two analogies which seem to be useful to the theist in this regard. The first is suggested by Professor Basil Mitchell in his book, *The Justification of Religious Belief*. Mitchell argues that the relation of God to the creature can be modelled on the relation of a pupil to a teacher, for the purpose of understanding the relation of divine agency to creaturely effect. Thus a teacher says and does many things in giving instruction, but the pupil's learning is her/his own achievement. Nevertheless the pupil might acknowledge with wonder and gratitude that he would not be the person he is without the teacher's activity.

Now I'm not sure how fully this analogy could be developed. But on the surface, at least it seems to give body to the notion of a sort of dependence relation between two beings which can be readily recognised by the indisputable effects of the actions of one agent upon the other, but which is nevertheless an internal effect in the sense described above. This seems to be precisely the sort of analogy from the field of inter-finite causation which Farrer signified in his last book in philosophical theology, *Faith and Speculation*, by the elusive term, 'double agency', the type of operation in which two agents, one divine and infinite, the other creaturely and finite, do one and the same action although not as agents on the same level.

The other analogy is developed from a remark by Farrer in a short essay entitled 'Causes', in *Reflective Faith*. He speaks there of changing one's mind, i.e. of having one's mind changed by another. This seems to be a very interesting notion. Two questions arise concerning it. First, how do you, by your own actions, change my mind about something? We do in fact speak this way, and there is a whole vocabulary associated with the reality we signify be speaking thus: we can think here of terms such as 'persuasion', 'inducement', 'convincement'. In many such cases we actually recognise in the law that one person can act causally in the mind of another and sometimes be morally and legally responsible for so acting, even though it is recognised at the same time that the person who is persuaded or induced to do something is also responsible for what was done. This consideration gives rise to the second question: is changing my mind your action or mine? Or is it both yours and mine – certainly not on the same level, as Farrer would put it, but nevertheless an effect in me which you have brought about, as well as I? For you might have set out deliberately to change my mind; and I might have begun with a determination not to be swayed from my position.

At one level of description you change my mind by talking to me, and this of course involves modulation of wave motion in an elastic medium which results in the generation in my brain of certain electrical events. But we would not accept such a description as an explanation of my changing my mind, for the description does not tell us what reasons you gave me for changing my mind. In short, you change my mind by offering me rational or moral persuasion, and if I grasp your reasons, I can make them mine as well, and so change my mind on the matter under discussion. Now is this action yours or mine? Well, in a way it is clearly yours; you can say that you *succeeded* in changing my mind, or that you *tried* but *failed*. On the other hand, it is obviously something that I do. I have to take responsibility for it; in many (but not all) circumstances we think it childish to try to blame someone else for the opinions we hold. Again this seems to be a very natural context in which one person might say, 'I wouldn't be what I am except for what he/she did on that occasion'. And in so saying the person would not be referring to causality of an exterior kind. Clearly if someone acts so as to injure my brain in certain ways I could also say later that I would not be what I am except for that person's action on a certain occasion, but we would mean something different by it, we would be signfying a different kind of dependence relation, and a different kind of causation.

No doubt this example, too, needs much more careful analysis. Yet it seems to point to a kind of dependence relation between two beings in which what an agent does as his own act is nevertheless naturally spoken of as something brought about by the activity of another.

Now I want to acknowledge – even insist – that we cannot apply such analogies neat in the theological case; after all, the voice of God is not propagated in an elastic medium (except in Monty Python films). Yet, how damaging is this fact to the theist's case? As I argued previously we need an example of agent causality in a non-theological context, an example in which the effect is clearly identifiable as an effect, and clearly an effect attributable to an agent. The case of someone changing someone else's mind furnishes those features nicely. It might be objected, of course, that we know the causal mechanism whereby one agent is enabled to persuade another to change her or his mind, e.g. we understand voice production, the stimulation of the auditory nerve, and so on, whereas the voice of God, if such there be, is not of that sort. But I doubt that this is a convincing rebuttal; for as a matter of fact we don't explain a change of mind by reference to psychological facts. On the contrary we go directly to talk of reasons, evidence, goals, purposes, aspirations, and so on. It is in such rational and moral terms that we try to persuade one another, and in these terms that we explain whatever stance we take. Persuading someone to change her or his mind, then, is something I can try to do, deliberately; I can plan how to do it, I can modify my tactics in relation to responses I get from the other person, and so on, all without taking any account of the psychological operation of the instruments and media which enable me to do what I am trying to do. Thus the degree of obscurity about how my causal activity actually brings about the change of mind in another person is not so much a disadvantage in the analogy but a similarity to our situation when we try to understand how divine causality passes over into creaturely effect.

I shall now try to apply the analogy. Let us imagine a somewhat morally lazy person who is thrown by circumstances into a situation in which he is forced to take a moral stand. Perhaps he has mildly aspired towards being a better person, and has occasionally had twinges of regret he is such a weathervane, drifting constantly with the prevailing winds of doctrine. He knows he should be a better person – more perceptive, more sensitive to the minds of others, more sensitive to their unique personal qualities. He might even recite prayers asking God to strengthen his moral backbone; but in practice this person does nothing about the matter, and rationalises his lackadaisical stance by saying that he is waiting for the working of divine grace upon him. Then one day he trips over poor Lazarus collapsd on the street, and he suddenly acknowledges that it is his own responsibility to do the right thing, and discovers that in doing it, again and again, he is a changed person.

Now there is always the possibility that such a person will attribute his change of character to late maturation of the moral sense, or to recognition that it just feels good to be nice to people, or something of that sort. An atheist is certainly not denying any scientific fact by denying what the theist takes to be the realities of the life of faith. But what if this person does not deny them? What if he takes his change of character as the effect of something like personal agency? Could he not legitimately refer his new character to the activity of God, and refer to God as his saviour, or as the one who has created his life anew? The effect in question, after all, is very like what can happen when another person acts in such a way as to change someone's mind, despite the obvious differences: someone might physically take me by the shoulders and point me in the direction of my moral duty, whereas God does not do this. Nevertheless, some reports of conversion experiences do indeed express the vividness and compellingness of those experiences in that same physical terminology.

I suggest, in conclusion, that there are in the sphere of inter-personal relations certain analogies which can quite plausibly be regarded as shedding considerable light on the classical doctrine that God can be identifyingly referred to as the agent of certain effects.

I want in closing to point out an important limitation of the argument in this paper. The conclusion I have proposed cannot stand by itself. It needs the support of a more general analysis of the epistemology of theism, one which would set forth the epistemic conditions under which the theist might justly claim to be reasonably assured that certain interior effects are the grounds for belief in God. But that is not the topic of this paper.

Chapter 8

# NARRATIVE INTERPRETATION AND THE PROBLEM OF DOUBLE AGENCY

*F. Michael McLain*

It has been suggested that the central contribution of narrative analysis to theological method is its reminder of 'the close connection between God's *identity* and *narrative* structure'. This is due to the fact that an agent's identity is revealed in certain of his/her actions, just in case those actions are disclosive of that person's character and purposes. For what we mean by 'identity' in this connection is the substance of the agent's personality and character as revealed in a pattern of action. Narrative is the form in which we render in a coherent fashion the agent's actions across time and thus the agent's character. So if God is an agent who acts in the world so as to disclose divine character and purpose, then narrative is the appropriate form in which to render God's identity.

Writing in summary about the promise of 'narrative theology', Professor George Stroup has noted that the attempt to develop such a theology faces several difficulties. Having suggested the importance of the idea of revelation for narrative theology, Stroup writes:

> Revelation refers to an event in which God, or that which is ultimately real, is disclosed in the midst of human finitude. God is traditionally understood to be the primary agent in this event, but for some time theologians have recognised that a host of difficult theological issues surround any attempt to speak of God as an agent and a particular event as 'God's act'.[1]

[1] George Stroup, 'Revelation', in *Christian Theology: An Introduction to its Traditions and Tasks*, ed. Peter C. Hodgson and Robert H. King. (Philadelphia: Fortress Press, 1982); p. 111.

He is, of course, quite correct in this. The issues are not only theological; there are difficult philosophical issues involved in claiming that God is a personal agent who acts in the world. This paper focuses and examines some of those theological and philosophical issues.

Fundamental among them is the intelligibility of the idea of 'double agency', and the difficulties surrounding the notion of *particular* divine action in the world. The first problem is due to the fact that God's identity-revealing-agency is most often depicted in Biblical narrative in and through the agency of the people of Israel and Jesus. It has been alleged, however, that the idea of two agents for the same act is unintelligible, and indeed the dominant mode of philosophical theology at this time, process theology, renders it impossible.[2]

The intelligibility of the idea of double agency requires as a minimal condition the coherence of the supposition of a mode of action radically different from our own, a mode of action belonging to an unrestricted, disembodied agent. Unfortunately, the shape this problem has been given in recent theology obscures the correct approach to it, and thus the possibility of taking literally the concept of God as an agent who acts in the world which a 'realistic' reading of Biblical narrative pre-supposes. We must begin with Langdon Gilkey's influential essay, 'Cosmology, Ontology, and the Travail of Biblical Language', and the subsequent responses to it by Schubert Ogden and Gordon Kaufman.

In addition to its failure, as I see it, to grapple correctly with the problem of predicating action of God, much theology, with the notable exception of the work of Austin Farrer, has failed also to articulate correctly the matter of particular divine action in the world. If narrative is taken to depict such action, then

---

[2] Lewis Ford, *The Lure of God: A Biblical Background for Process Theism.* Philadelphia: Fortress Press, 1978, p. 19. Commenting on classical theism's supposition that 'when I act, it is also God acting through me', Ford says, 'This identification is not possible in process theism, which sees self-decision and divine persuasion, along with the multiplicity of past causal conditions, as distinct but indispensable and complementary aspects of every act of freedom'.

some basis must be provided for singling out as special some of God's actions. The way in which this problem has been construed has obscured the most promising approach to it.

Finally, it is widely assumed that, if God is disclosed in such actions, we *must* construe them as God's direct act of communication which is verbally self-interpreted in the Biblical text. This concept of 'revelation' has not been easy to sustain in the face of critical assessment of the Biblical materials. It will be argued that at least we are under no conceptual constraint to think of divine self-disclosure in this fashion. Indeed, if we take seriously the idea that God acts in and through the actions of finite agents it seems more appropriate to think of this as *indirect, non-verbal* communication.

## I

The well-known thesis of Gilkey's article is that while Biblical narrative presents God literally as an agent who acts in the world, the writings of contemporary Biblical scholars and theologians often do not. He sets out this claim in the following way:

> Put in the language of contemporary semantic discussion, both the Biblical and the orthodox understanding of theological language was univocal. That is, when God was said to have 'acted', it was believed that he had performed an observable act in space and time so that he functioned as does any secondary cause; and when he was said to have 'spoken', it was believed that an audible voice was heard by the person addressed. In other words, the words 'act' and 'speak' were used in the same sense of God as of men. We deny this univocal understanding of theological words. To us, theological verbs such as 'to act', 'to work', 'to do', 'to speak', 'to reveal', etc. have no longer the literal meaning of observable actions in space and time or of voices in the air. The denial of wonders and voices has thus shifted our theological language from the univocal to the analogical.[3]

[3] Langdon Gilkey, 'Cosmology, Ontology, and the Travail of Biblical Language', in *God's Activity in the World: The Contemporary Problem*, ed. Owen C. Thomas. Chico, California: Scholars' Press, 1983, p. 32. Many of the important articles on this subject have been included in this volume and I shall refer to it for ease of reference.

In arguing for this thesis Gilkey develops two lines of thought which may and should be kept distinct. One strand of this argument deals with what it is *possible* for us to conceive, given our concepts of human action and agency; the second strand, which is independent of the conceptual question, provides a reason for describing divine action in a certain way, given our belief in the causal continuum. As we shall see, the two issues are easily confused and have been so by Gilkey and other thinkers we will consider. Since William P. Alston has substantially met the challenge(s) presented by Gilkey's article, I shall frequently refer the reader to Alston's chapter in this volume for the relevant arguments.[4]

The prior issue has to do with what is conceptually possible. Gilkey contends that we do not employ the literal meaning or univocal sense of 'act', 'speak', etc. because we do not give such words the sense 'of observable actions in space and time or of voices in the air'. As Alston reminds us, it is crucial to distinguish 'literal' and 'univocal'.[5] Once we do so, Gilkey's substantive point is a thesis about the meaning of action concepts, namely, that the meaning of all action concepts contains a bodily movement component or requirement. If it does, then such concepts cannot be applied univocally to God, a disembodied agent, and if such concepts are rendered meaningless when shorn of this component, then they may not be applied meaningfully to God at all.

It is worth noting that this matter has frequently been confused with the different issues of *identifying* a divine action and *justifying* the claim that one has occurred. These errors, hardly trivial, have been made, I shall argue, by such sophisticated writers as Frank Kirkpatrick and Basil Mitchell. In addition, we cannot handle Gilkey's problem as some have thought by construing divine action in terms of 'inner' episodes in the divine life. On a certain construal of mental predicates, one I believe to be correct, this strategy fails, insofar as it purports to

[4] Chapter 3 of the present volume, 'How to Think About Divine Action' by William P. Alston.

[5] Alston, pp. 68f. above.

be a way of rendering intelligible the idea of disembodied action. Once we set aside these mistakes, we can proceed in setting forth a positive strategy for dealing with Gilkey's first challenge.

The basic issue, then, as concisely stated by Basil Mitchell, is 'whether our concept of action is such as to render unintelligible all talk of incorporeal agency'.[6] And in dealing with this issue we must not confuse the question of meaning with those of identification and justification. Thus Kirkpatrick, in a fine article on the notion of an act of God, sets forth his approach to the intelligibility of a disembodied act.[7] Like Mitchell, he begins by noting that the conceptual scheme we employ in describing actions is logically distinct from the one used to describe physical movements or 'occurrences in which intentions play no role'.[8] Furthermore, if (some of) our acts are free, Kirkpatrick believes that those acts cannot be causally necessitated, that is, cannot be brought about by antecedent events which amount to causally sufficient conditions. In this sense, free human actions transcend the causal order and provide us with a model for divine action.

It is plain, however, that none of this shows that our action concepts do not carry with them a bodily movement requirement. For it may be that the concept of free human action is the concept of bringing about some event by freely performing a bodily movement. If this is so, then the model does not give us a model for *disembodied* divine agency. Kirkpatrick's reflections amount to the specification of some of the conditions under which we would be *justified* in claiming that a putative action is not susceptible of causal explanation, but this does not advance the case for the meaningfulness of the concept of disembodied action.

Mitchell's handling of this issue misfires and ends up, in fact, as a consideration of how we might justify the claim that a disembodied action has occurred. He claims that, under three

[6] Basil Mitchell, *The Justification of Religious Belief*, London: Macmillan, 1973, p. 7.
[7] Frank G. Kirkpatrick, 'Understanding an Act of God', in Thomas, pp. 163–80.
[8] Kirkpatrick, p. 173.

conditions, we could pick out an event as an action performed by a particular agent without recourse to observation of that agent's body. The indication, he says, would be a combination of the following:

(a) The unlikelihood of the event's occurrence apart from the intervention of some agent.

(b) The event's contributing to some purpose.

(c) The agreement of that purpose with the independently known character and purposes of the putative agent.[9]

When we reflect on these conditions, however, it seems clear that, if present, they are conditions which would warrant someone in claiming that some event had been brought about by a particular agent. Furthermore, they are conditions which would warrant this ascription whether or not the agent was embodied. That we could be *warranted* in ascribing an event to a disembodied agent, *if it makes sense to speak of such*, is an important consideration. However, the prior question is precisely whether or not the concept of disembodied action is meaningful. The matters considered by these authors do not provide a way of answering this question, though they are frequently thought to do so.[10]

It is tempting to meet the issue of disembodied agency in yet another way, a temptation to which theologians whom we shall discuss later in some detail have succumbed.[11] Events in an

---

[9] Mitchell, p. 8.

[10] The *approach* one takes to the question of the meaningfulness of talk about disembodied agency and action may have substantive implications for a range of issues. Thus, Mitchell appears by his first condition, 'the unlikelihood of the event's occurrence apart from the intervention of some agent', to commit himself (unnecessarily) to a notion of particular divine action as something *extraordinary*, as an event which has no plausible natural explanation. This does not seems to be the import of Wisdom's famous invisible Gardener parable, with which Mitchell begins his reflection. The point of the parable is that the facts are compatible with either interpretation, there is a gardener or there is not. Also, Mitchell's third condition appears to commit him to the view that we must know the agent's purposes in some way other than by noting her (alleged) actions, e.g. through the agent's disclosure of those purposes. This view of 'revelation' is the one Mitchell in fact holds, as we shall see below. However, we need not commit ourselves to that view, I think, in order to make sense of the notion of disembodied action.

[11] I have in mind Schubert Ogden and Gordon Kaufman.

agent's inner life such as 'deciding', 'choosing', 'willing', 'thinking' and so on, are plausibly termed actions and they are neither observable nor embodied, at least in the same way as, say, raising my arm is embodied. Perhaps, then, we should think of God's action on the model of a human agent's inner world of activity, and use our concepts of inner activity in a straightforward, literal way in speaking of the divine agent.

This proposal fails, I think, for at least two reasons. Biblical narrative speaks of God's *overt* behaviour, not just the inner life of the divine being. If we set aside talk of God's overt actions, therefore, we should be clear at least that we are departing from a straightforward rendering of the narrative's intention.

The more telling objection to the 'inner' action strategy is due to the so-called logical connection thesis advanced by Strawson and others.[12] Strawson's claim, which I believe to be correct, is that our mental predicate terms (for example, those we are inclined to ascribe to God, 'forgiving', 'judging', 'commanding', 'intending', etc.) have both subjective and objective reference. That is, it is part of the meaning of such terms that they can be applied to a subject *only if* overt action predicates are also applicable. This is because such predicates involve dispositions to behave in certain ways, e.g. in the case of 'forgive', the disposition to utter, 'I forgive you', on appropriate occasions and so on. Thus if we accept Strawson's thesis, it will be true that God can literally 'will', 'love', 'command', etc. only if God can literally perform overt actions.

Given the logical connection thesis concerning mental concepts, a more radical challenge than Gilkey anticipates can be put to those who would ascribe *either* inner or overt actions to God. Since according to this thesis mental predication is dependent upon the capacity to perform overt action, and since overt behaviour seems to require bodily movements, then if God is understood to be an incorporeal being, God cannot have the requisite dispositions to bodily behaviour. Therefore, we can

---

[12] The 'logical connection' thesis put forward by Peter Strawson arises in connection with his critique of dualism, see *Individuals: an Essay in Descriptive Metaphysics*. Garden City: Doubleday Anchor Books, ch. 3.

ascribe *neither inner nor overt* action to God, either literally or analogically. Such language as used of a disembodied agent will be logically incoherent.[13]

This problem will not have the same force, perhaps, for theologians who claim that God is an embodied agent, that to be God is to have a world. Clearly, for those who think of God as a disembodied agent, the challenge must be met. And if a successful answer is forthcoming, it will show, in part, that it is not necessary to adopt the requirement that God should be embodied.

The crucial issue, obviously, is whether overt behaviour is dependent upon bodily movement. We must not allow this issue to be prejudged by the fact, as Gilkey apparently does, that cases familiar to us typically involve bodily movements of the (human) agent. The key consideration is this: Putnam and others have persuasively argued that even if we learn the meaning of a term from a certain class of denotata, and even if this class contains the only denotata with which we are familiar, a feature that is pervasive of the familiar class *may not* be reflected in the *meaning* of the term. Thus the feature of bodily movement may not be reflected in the general concept of action. To assume otherwise is to suppose that, in the case at hand, we must form our concept of 'action' in a way limited to the class of actions from which we learned the concept. This is plausible only on a strict verificationist account of meaning, which is surely wrong and which Gilkey himself rightly rejects.

How, then, shall we decide the question: Does overt action require bodily movement? In approaching this issue we must begin by distinguishing between basic and non-basic actions.[14] A basic action is one that is performed not by or in simultaneously performing some other action. A non-basic action is done *by* performing a basic action. Thus if raising one's arm is not done by doing something else, it is a basic action. Signalling a friend by

[13] Kai Nielsen, *Contemporary Critiques of Religion*. New York: Hernden and Hernden, 1971, pp. 119–28.

[14] This distinction is due to Arthur C. Danto, 'Basic Actions', American Philosophical Quarterly, 1965, 2, pp. 141–8.

raising one's arm or 'throwing a ball' by moving one's arm in a certain way, on the other hand, provide examples of non-basic actions. Since non-basic actions are accomplished by performing basic ones, if every human basic action consists in moving some part of one's body, then a *human being* cannot do anything overt without moving some part of his body. Either an action is basic, in which case it simply is the moving of some part of one's body, or it is non-basic, and thus performed *by* moving some part of one's body.

By this route we arrive at the not implausible view that bodily movement is part of the meaning of *human* action concepts. For the sake of the argument, let us assume that this is so. Does it follow that things must be this way *in general* with action concepts? Intuitively, no. We can readily distinguish the questions: (1) How do human beings bring about the actions they perform, and (2) Is movement of an agent's body part of the concept of action? It seems obvious that even if our experience suggests, 'by moving some bodily part', in answer to (1), it does not follow from this fact that (2) deserves a positive answer. Moreover, even if we decide that (2) is true with respect to human action concepts, we may be able still to form recognisable action concepts which do not contain a bodily movements requirement.

I find Alston persuasive in his analysis of both points. We recall that his arguments yield the conclusion:

> Briefly my position is that what is minimally essential to action is that an agent with knowledge and purposes will, or intend, to produce certain efforts in the pursuit of its purposes. If that condition is satisfied we still have action, *however those volitions or intentions bring about* the effects in question. (my emphasis)[15]

If Alston is correct, incorporeality is no barrier to thinking of God literally as an agent who acts in the world. As Alston notes, there may be other barriers to such literal ascription, but not the one singled out by Gilkey.

---

[15] Alston, p. 68 above.

## II

The second problem posed by Gilkey's piece for any attempt to take Biblical narrative's intention to speak of divine action in the world in a straightforward, 'literal' way is that of the so-called 'causal continuum'. In what is perhaps the most familiar move of contemporary theologians, Gilkey avers that as moderns all of us are firmly committed to belief in 'the causal continuum of space-time experience'. This is the central issue requiring attention from those who would encourage the primacy of narrative in theological reflection. As Gilkey observes:

> Now this assumption of a causal order among phenomenal events, and therefore of the authority of the scientific interpretation of observable events, makes a great difference to the validity one assigns to Biblical narratives and so to the way one understands their meaning. Suddenly a vast panoply of divine deeds . . . in the Biblical history of the Hebrew people become what we choose to call symbols rather than plain old historical facts. . . . Whatever the Hebrews believed, *we* believe that the biblical people lived in the same causal continuum of space and time in which we live, and so one in which no divine wonders transpired and no divine voices were heard'.[16]

Gilkey does little in this essay to characterise our alleged belief in a causal continuum or to examine reasons which might be given in support of it. He simply assumes, as so many theologians do, that contemporary reflection has, should and/or must accept this belief as central to the context in which we do theology. It is crucial to be clear about the supposed way(s) it renders problematic the notion of divine action in the world. And, on this score, we may begin with some preliminary comments.

The problem, I take it, is a general one. We may or may not believe that those events singled out in scripture were done by God; what is unclear is the general idea of divine action in the world. Gilkey's reason for rejecting the scriptural accounts to which he gives attention is that the general account of divine action they presuppose, namely, the claim that God is their *sole*

[16] Gilkey, p. 31.

cause is unacceptable to the modern mind. It is important, then, to keep in mind that the issue before us is the general concept of particular divine action in the world and the reasonableness of the belief that such events transpire. Furthermore, this is not the same issue as the one we have just considered and with which it is so often confused, namely the *meaningfulness* of the claim that God acts. If the proposal of that problem is satisfactory, we can literally ascribe actions to God. (Actually there is another purely conceptual issue which has been offered as a decisive barrier to this belief, namely, the claim that the concept of a natural event entails that its explanation be found in antecedent causes of the same kind. We shall consider below this claim, as it is formulated by Gordon Kaufman.) But if we accept the causal continuum, we cannot, perhaps do one or more of the following: explain any particular event as an act of God, or identify such events, or be reasonable in our belief that a particular event was caused by God. It is to this host of issues which we turn our attention.

The dominant way in which particular divine action in the world is construed by Gilkey is in terms of God's acting outside the causal continuum in extraordinary, spectacular ways, that is, as one who acts miraculously. There is a persistent tendency in the literature, owing perhaps to Bultmann's influence, to think of particular divine action in this way.[17] The problem is given another influential form by Gilkey. If we deny the miraculous, and assume with theological liberalism that God's action in the world is uniform and pervasive, then we have no basis for picking out some particular occurrence as a divine action which contributes *uniquely* to the fulfillment of divine purpose. Uniqueness enters in only *subjectively*, when recognition occurs of God's all pervasive, purposive activity which is everywhere objectively the same. But unless an occurrence can be said to

---

[17] Articles on this subject display a remarkable variety of ways to characterise particular divine action. God is said to act 'outside' the causal continuum, to act in some (phenomenologically) extraordinary way, to be the sole cause of some event, to be the author of an event without adequate finite causes, and so on. I trust that my discussion of such action will make it clear what I take to be the decisive issue(s) in all of this.

contribute uniquely to the realisation of divine purpose, it is claimed, then it can have no 'special' status.

These two ways of characterising the problem of particular divine action are typically taken to be exhaustive: either such action is specified as an event which is outside the course of nature or as an event which contributes uniquely to the realisation of the divine purpose(s). Insofar as theologians have sought to affirm divine action in the world, but eschewed either of these ways of doing so, their attempts have indeed proved to be perplexingly vague. This may be due, however, to the general acceptance of Gilkey's criterion for picking out such events, namely, his claim that an event in which God does something:

> 'special' . . . must in some sense be more than an ordinary run-of-the-mill event. It may be epistemologically indistinguishable from other events to those without faith, but for those of faith it must be objectively or ontologically different from other events. Otherwise, there is no mighty act, but only our belief in it, and God is the God who in fact does not act.[18]

In what follows I will be aiming at the general conclusion that Gilkey's options do not exhaust the ways of characterising a particular divine action and that his statement of a criterion is deficient. I am not satisfied with the efforts of others to meet the challenge he poses. It will be obvious that the place to begin is with a characterisation of a causal continuum. We may usefully do this by considering how belief in it is supposed to rule out taking particular events as acts of God.

One of the most extensive characterisations of the causal continuum thesis, and defenses of it, is found in the writings of Gordon Kaufman. According to him, the intellectual epoch to which we all belong it characterised by:

> The gradually developing awareness of the interconnected web of events which has made possible the high-level description and understanding characteristic of modern science and history. Therefore, it is no longer possible for us to think (when we think clearly and consistently) of individual or particular events somehow by themselves: every event is defined as a focal point in

[18] Gilkey, p. 37.

a web that reaches in all directions beyond it indefinitely; it is never grasped (in our modern experience) as an independent substance that can exist and be thought by itself alone.[19]

This way of viewing evens poses an apparently insurmountable problem for conceiving of particular divine action in the world:

> Our experience is of a unified and orderly world; in such a world acts of God (in the traditional sense) are not merely improbable or difficult to believe: they are literally inconceivable. It is not a question of whether talk about such acts is true or false; it is, in the literal sense, meaningless; one cannot make the concept hang together consistently.[20]

Kaufman's basic point concerning 'the web of events' is not entirely clear. One plausible construction of his position is this: the concept of an occurrence which has 'adequate finite causes', where 'adequate' seems to mean causally sufficient conditions.[21] If this is what is *meant* by an event, then obviously acts of God are inconceivable; there is a buried contradiction in the idea of such an act.

On this construction, Kaufman's view commits him to the principle *every event has causally sufficient conditions*, as a principle which follows from the very concept of an event. When interpreted this way, Kaufman is making what I take to be the quite implausible assumption that this principle is analytic. Kant did not judge is so, and its proponents are few, if any. The principle at best is a contingent truth, one which the determinist holds to be true. Construed as a logical truth it has probably been proved false, due to William Rowe's argument that there must be at least one positive contingent state of affairs.[22]

Kaufman's frequent reference to Kant suggests that he would settle for the weaker claim that this principle is only a presupposition of reason, a condition of the possibility of any experience whatsoever, but one which we cannot know to be

---

[19] Gordon Kaufman, 'On the Meaning of "Act of God"', in Thomas, p. 147.
[20] Kaufman, p. 148.
[21] Kaufman, p. 159, note 11.
[22] See William Rowe on the principle of sufficient reason in *The Cosmological Argument*. Princeton: Princeton University Press, 1975, pp. 99–112.

applicable to 'things-in-themselves'. If he were to follow Kant in this manner, he would be claiming that the principle is a synthetic *a priori* one, derived by a 'transcendental deduction'. It is beyond our purpose here to assess Kant's philosophy (and its enormous influence on contemporary theology) but it is quite clear that if this is Kaufman's thesis he is caught in a fatal inconsistency. For Kaufman thinks that we structure our experience at times in another way quite inconsistent with this one. That is, we conceive some events as not following others upon a causal rule but as a self-determined by the agent who performs them.[23] In such cases, we conceive our experience in terms of 'an agent who performs the act', and this means as an event, the agent's action, which does not have causally sufficient antecedent conditions. The idea of 'agent causality' does seems to be conceivable, as Kaufman assumes, though it may be false, of course, to claim that such causality exists. The point is that its admitted use in 'structuring' our experience renders inconsistent the Kantian interpretation of Kaufman's views.

The final argument for determinism suggested by Kaufman is the evidential one. He writes:

> The success of modern natural science in describing, predicting, and in some measure controlling events in the natural order is due precisely to the discovery of ways to discern and formulate fundamental structural regularities obtaining between events (laws of nature), but this growing success makes it increasingly difficult even to conceive what an event occurring somehow independently of this web might be.[24]

This passage can be interpreted to mean that the 'growing success' of natural science makes it reasonable to believe, on the basis of the evidence, that determinism is true. This argument, like the second one above, does not rule out logically the claim that the determined natural order has been freely created by a self-determining agent. But it does rob him of the model in terms of which Kaufman proposes to illuminate the 'master-act' by which God has enacted the world of nature and history. For if

[23] Kaufman, p. 146.
[24] Kaufman, p. 145.

we believe determinism is true, then we *should* analyse human free-will in a way which is *compatible* with determinism. The compatibilist notion of freedom, namely, the idea that freedom means absence of constraint from anything outside the agent, is not adequate to express God's freedom in creating, viz. the performance of an action from which God could have refrained. And this notion of freedom, the notion that the agent could have done otherwise than he chose to do, will not be available at the human level to serve as a model for God's creative choice, if we construe Kaufman's reasoning in this final way. Thus, again, he may be caught in an inconsistency.

The prior question, obviously, is whether scientific evidence renders reasonable the claim that determinism is true. Assuming the evidence is relevant to the question of determinism's truth (as opposed to the claim of some that the question can be settled in the negative on purely conceptual grounds), it seems fair to say that the evidence to date is compatible with the view that causal determination is sometimes (or always, as process theologians believe) only approximate. On this account, the antecedent causal factors only establish limits within which an agent's free or spontaneous responses must take place. One may hold this view at the present time without fear of being labelled irrational, and, indeed, in some passages Kaufman himself appears to embrace it.

I conclude, then, that Kaufman has given no good reasons to interpret 'adequate' finite causes to mean causally sufficient conditions. But, and this is the crucial point to note, it is only on that reading of 'adequate' that God's direct, particular action in the world would constitute a violation of the laws of nature. At the present stage of scientific development, our laws state what must happen under certain conditions *all other things being equal*. The qualification here is crucial. Statements of monologically sufficient conditions do not (at present) purport to take account of all possible influences relevant to the determination of an occurrence. Thus, if the natural laws we employ in understanding phenomena leave open the possibility of the influence of forces not mentioned in the law, divine 'interference' would not be a violation of a particular law.

Kaufman's point may boil down to little more than this, then: those imbued with the scientific mind look for an explanation in terms of a natural, not divine, force. That may be true, but it gives us no *reason* to rule out the latter. Of course, Kaufman may share the view of those who believe that the day of a unified science is at hand, and that on that day we may expect the specification and connection of *all* the factors that can effect a given kind of outcome. Eschatological hope springs eternal in all of us, no doubt, but until that day arrives, we may properly remain sceptical about its appearance.

I do not mean to suggest in all of this that I do not share the *bias* of our scientific culture. I do. It is just that when I reflect on the matter, I do not find that my bias is rationally warranted. I do not, however, for a variety of reasons, wish to drift back in the direction of an uncritical acceptance of Biblical narrative. Five come readily to mind.

First of all, we often think it reasonable to set aside as legendary accretion certain spectacular occurrences presented in Biblical narrative or provide alternative interpretations involving natural conditions for events given supernatural explanations by the Biblical writers. A case illustrating the later point would be demonic possession and its cure. The account given in scripture of the symptoms may incline us to say that this was in fact a case of epilepsy, for which we are prepared to offer a well-confirmed medical diagnosis. It is, perhaps, not unreasonable to hold, therefore, that there is a plausible natural explanation (not amounting to a statement of sufficient conditions) for those events taken by Biblical writers to have been outside the usual course of nature.

Secondly, although it may not be, as Hume argued, in principle impossible to be justified in believing that a 'wondrous' event has occurred, for example, that Sarah's child is due to the direct action of God, it is nevertheless difficult to justify such a claim. To do so we would need to rule out as possible a naturalistic explanation. But that would require that we have a complete account of Sarah's condition, as well as one of all the natural causes relevant to that kind of occurrence. It seems improbable that we could ever be in a position to meet these conditions.

Thirdly, it does not seem uncharitable to attribute to the Biblical writers a lack of understanding and credulity which we neither share nor should want to share. The other side of this coin is that it seems plausible to think that God would work through natural causes to an understanding of which God commends our attention. A contemporary believer may hold that God's action in and through natural causes is not so spectacular and obvious as earlier generations believed. Many of the cases in which believers are prepared to find the divine actively at work possess no striking phenomenological qualities such that we should even be inclined to count them as falling outside the usual course of nature. A woman prays that she will be strengthened so as not to pass along to her children the racial prejudice with which she grew up. She successfully avoids doing so and credits God with having strengthened her in her resolve. A plausible natural explanation for her success comes readily to mind, and there is nothing spectacular in the occurrence to make the natural explanation seem excessively strained.

Fourthly, as Austin Farrer has reminded us, typically when we take an event to be an act of God in some special sense, it is not the belief that God has acted outside the natural order that prompts us to do so, but rather the nature of *the outcome* as engaging our practical response, as providing occasion to join our purpose to the divine purpose we take to be carried out in the occurrence. Thus, the practice of selecting as special certain alleged actions of God does not hinge on a belief in miracles.

Finally, there are plausible theological considerations for taking the view that God works through natural causes so as to make it always [somewhat] reasonable to assume that only natural factors are at work in bringing about some event. In particular, I have in mind John Hick's claim that an epistemic distance between persons and God is required as a necessary condition of entering freely into a relationship of love with God.[25]

---

[25] John Hick develops this thesis in a provocative way in his *Evil and the God of Love*. San Francisco: Harper & Row, 1978.

Surely, then, the only constraint operating on one who wishes to claim that God always works through natural causes is that plausible reasons, particularly theological ones, be offered in support of this contention. For the converging set of reasons given above, I am in sympathy with the efforts of theologians like Schubert Ogden and Gordon Kaufman to work out a conception of particular divine action in the world which does not require us to conceive the specialness of such action as consisting in its being outside the natural order. In the section that follows I shall argue, however, that neither has succeeded in providing a viable alternative account of such action. In arguing this case, I will not be assuming that they must, alternatively, make out the case that particular divine activity must be ontologically distinguishable or contribute *uniquely* to the realisation of divine purpose. Thus, the dilemma which Gilkey's essay seems to pose may not be a real one.

## III

In considering the work of Ogden and Kaufman on divine action in the world, I shall focus only on their success in stating a sense in which we may single out for special attention particular divine actions.

Ogden's well-known claim is that just as I am the soul or mind of my body, by analogy, God is the soul or mind of the world. He delineates two models for understanding, respectively, God's actions as a self and God's relation to the world. First, the primary sense in which a person, and by analogy God, acts is in terms of those private acts of decision 'by which the human self acts to constitute its own inner being. . . . It is only because the self first acts to constitute itself, to respond to its world, and to decide its own inner being that it 'acts' at all in the more ordinary meaning of the word.'[26] The second analogy offered by Ogden involves the claim that we as persons stand in a direct

[26] Schubert Ogden, 'What Sense Does it Make to Say, "God Acts in History"'? in Thomas, pp. 77–100.

relationship to our bodies at the point of the individual cells which constitute the brain. 'We respond with virtual immediacy to the impulses that come from our brains, and it is over our brains (or their individual cells) that our decisions as selves or minds exercise a virtually direct power or control'.[27] This provides Ogden with the analogy he thinks necessary to grasp the relation between God and the world.

By employing these two analogies or models, then, Ogden believes we can have some understanding of that recurring divine act in which God 'ever and again actualises his own divine essence by responding in love to all the creatures in his world'.[28]

It is clear that Ogden has given us a powerful set of analogies for conceiving God's *transcendent* activity. As he says, God's action 'is not an action *in* history but an action that *transcends* it'.[29] Nevertheless, he claims also that it is possible to designate two senses in which God acts *in* history, and Ogden seems anxious not to jettison the practice of picking out as special particular divine acts in the world.

However, his first sense of divine action in the world *cannot* illuminate the practice of picking out some events as acts of God in a special sense. Just as *all* our bodily actions are to some extent our actions as selves, so by analogy, says Ogden, every creature is to some extent God's act.[30] The limits within which creaturely freedom is exercised are 'grounded in God's own free decisions', and thus the responses of creatures reflect, as it were, the actions of God. Obviously, we have here no basis for singling out certain events as having some special significance.

It is the second sense of divine action in the world on which Ogden rests his case for a full-blown designation of some events as God's special acts. Ogden notes correctly that 'some of our outer acts of word and deed . . . are . . . *our* acts in a way that others are not. Because certain of our actions give peculiarly apt expression to what we are . . ., these actions *are* our actions in a

---

[27] Ogden, p. 89.
[28] Ogden, p. 90.
[29] Ogden, p. 90.
[30] Ogden, p. 91.

special sense'. Citing as a specific example his relation to his wife, Ogden says: 'Who she is for me is who I understand her to be in terms of certain quite particular events, having a "once-for-all" historical character, that I take to be revelatory of her person and attitude as they relate to me.'[31]

Now due to the human capacity for symbolic expression, our capacity 'to grasp the *logos* of reality as such and to represent it through symbolic speech and action', it is by analogy possible, Ogden claims, for our acts of representing the ultimate truth about our life to become acts of God. Thus,

> whenever or insofar as particular religious symbols appropriately re-present God's action as Creator and Redeemer, they actually are or become his act in a sense strictly analogous of the sense in which some of our own symbolic actions are acts in a way others are not.[32]

> Therefore, what is meant when we say that God acts in history is primarily that there are certain distinctively human words and deeds in which his characteristic action as Creator and Redeemer is appropriately represented or revealed. We mean that there are some human actions, some specific attempts to express the ultimate truth of our existence through symbolic words and deeds, that are vastly more than merely human actions. Because through them nothing less than the transcendent action of God himself is re-presented, they are also acts of God, that is, they *are* acts of God analogously to the way in which our outer acts *are* our acts insofar as they re-present our own characteristic decisions as selves or persons.[33]

This is curious. If we press the analogy of Ogden's relation to his wife, then it would seem that it is either *Ogden's act* of grasping the point of his wife's characteristic action or the symbolic expression of what is grasped by Ogden, say, the sentence, 'She loves me', that is analogous to our attempts to express symbolically the ultimate truth of our existence. But, surely, neither *Ogden's* act of grasping or uttering, nor the content of what is uttered, are his *wife's* acts. They are Ogden's

[31] Ogden, p. 93.
[32] Ogden, p. 94.
[33] Ogden, p. 95.

more or less accurate understandings and expressions of what his wife intended to convey by her action. They are *revelatory* of who she is in relation to him in a way that other of her actions are not, to be sure, but not because they are *her actions*. Their revelatory nature is due to the fact that they reflect accurately those actions.

By analogy, our religious expressions will be more or less accurate representations of 'the act whereby (God) ever and again actualises his own divine essence by responding in love to all the creatures in his world',[34] that is, of God's *transcendent* act, but they will not be divine actions, nor even representations of divine acts, *in* history. But what is being expressed, then, gives us no basis for singling out as a special act of *God* any particular event constitutive of nature and history.

Like Ogden, Gordon Kaufman follows Gilkey's advice in his attempt to work out a conception of what it means to say that God acts. In proposing his model for divine action, he proceeds first to provide a conception of how God acts in 'ordinary' events. Kaufman's suggestion, roughly, is that God's primary act is the act by which God enacts the whole of nature and history, what he terms God's 'master act'.[35] Just as human agents perform various particular actions ('sub-acts') in order to accomplish some long term, overarching goal (their 'master act'), so also all of nature and history may be regarded analogously as God's master-act. In a manner formally paralleled to Ogden's account, Kaufman proposes that the 'whole complicated and intricate movement of all nature and history should be regarded as a single all-encompassing act of God'.[36]

Kaufman's analysis of the concept of action requires that a master-act be implemented by sub-acts. Thus, just as I implement my master-act of making a table by driving nails, planing boards, and so on, we are led to expect, by analogy, some specification of those sub-acts by which God implements the divine master-act. In his way Kaufman's scheme promises to

[34] Ogden, p. 90.
[35] Kaufman, p. 142–4.
[36] Kaufman, p. 150.

illuminate the problem of particular divine action in the world. However, we are disappointed. It seems that Kaufman is inclined either to equate God's sub-acts with the single act of laying out the essential structure of the world process in founding it, as when he writes:

> 'It is God's master-act that gives the world the structure it has and gives natural and historical processes their direction'.[37]

Or, he is inclined to pick out divine sub-acts within the world process without providing an account of his basis for doing so. Thus, he writes:

> 'Assuming (on the basis of Christian claims) that God has revealed something of his purposes for man and the world, one finds it possible to discuss with the help of modern knowledge of nature and history, some of the stages (sub-acts) through which the created order has moved as God has gradually been performing his master act. The creation of the solar system, the emergence of life on earth, the evolution of higher forms of life and finally man – each of these ... represents an indispensable step toward the realisation of God's ultimate objectives for creation.'[38]

Presumably, however, all of God's actions with respect to this world share the status of being a step toward the realisation of God's overarching purpose(s). That status alone gives us no way of understanding why we select some events as special, particular divine actions in the world. What we need in principle is something like those acts which are presupposed in Kaufman's allusion to the fact that, 'God has revealed something of his purpose for man'. Without awareness of those purposes we cannot, *ex hypothesi*, pick out sub-acts as contributing to God's master act. But, then, it is the events in which those purposes are disclosed that will provide the examples of particular divine actions in the world, and it is precisely acts of that sort for which Kaufman has given us no criterion.

We have come full circle. The failure of Ogden and Kaufman to give us a basis for designating particular divine actions

[37] Kaufman, p. 150.
[38] Kaufman, p. 154.

illustrates the dilemma posed by Gilkey's original discussion. If a theologian chooses not to single out certain events as special acts of God due to the fact that they occur or appear to occur outside the natural order, then specialness seems to be a function only of our subjective response to events which are all in the same way God's actions or reflections of them. We have, then, the typical solution of theological liberalism to the problem of divine action in the world. Perhaps liberalism is the desirable answer to this issue, but, if so, Biblical narrative cannot have any special status and function as singling out particular divine actions in the world and as encouraging the practice of continuing to do so within the Christian commumity.

The clue to a viable alternative lies, I believe, in Austin Farrer's suggestion cited above, namely, that what a believer typically takes to be specially significant about an act of God is *the outcome* of that event as a carrying out of God's purposes.[39] Thus, in the earlier example of the woman who was strengthened, what she takes to be significant is God's strengthening her *in order to* carry out the purpose of not passing along racial prejudice, in order, further, she might suggest, to carry out God's purpose for humankind that humans relate to one another in respect as persons. What makes this an act of God for her, then, is not that God acts in an unusual or more basic way than in other events, but that in this case her sense of divine purpose is corroborated, as it were, and advanced by the strengthening. Others, like her children, may come to see in her action the expression of divine purposive action, and thus in turn attach special significance to this occurrence as an act of God.

The difference, then, between an act singled out in this way and what one takes to be the ordinary acts of God – what Gilkey calls run-of-the-mill events – is not that God acts differently but that one believes in certain instances she has *discerned more of divine purpose* than usual. In either case, God's action is as 'objectively there' as you please, but whereas mostly one is prepared to suggest no more than that God intended the event, in

[39] Austin Farrer, *Faith and Speculation*. London, A. & C. Black, 1967.

some cases one believes she sees something of the purpose for which the event is intended, for what further purpose that event was brought about. Farrer is undoubtedly correct in suggesting that it is the believer's involvement in the supposed divine purpose, her effort to join her action to God's, that looms large in assigning the degree of specialness she attaches to certain events. In all of this, the believer may well be wrong in her alleged discernment of divine purpose, but nothing in principle stands in the way of getting the matter correct.

I propose, then, that the claim to discern more of divine purpose in some events than is ordinarily discerned can serve as the criterion by which it is singled out as a special occurrence. It does not have to be, or appear to be, an event which occurs outside of nature, nor do we have to claim (though we may) as the only alternative that special events contribute uniquely to the realisation of divine purpose.[40] The dilemma suggested by Gilkey is apparent only. Furthermore, it is not the merely subjective response of the believer that is involved in picking out such events. Rather it is her belief that she has discerned something more of divine purpose such that she can act appropriately in relation to it.

## IV

It will be obvious that the account of particular divine action developed here has implications for our alleged knowledge of God's nature and purposes, and thus for the much debated topic of 'revelation' to which we alluded at the outset. Such actions are singled out, I have suggested, because they are received as

[40] Compare Thomas F. Tracy in his paper 'Enacting History: Ogden and Kaufman on God's Mighty Acts', *Journal of Religion*, 64 (1984) 20–36, where he writes: 'If we cannot speak of God acting in *a unique way* in specific historical events, then most traditional Christological claims must be set aside. It will be impossible to speak of Jesus Christ as that individual life in which God acts to establish a new relationship with fallen humanity', p. 21. I am claiming that acting in 'a unique way' is not a necessary condition of singling out as special Jesus' life. If one claims to discern this divine purpose here (or some other one), that is sufficient to make reasonable talk about particular divine action in this case.

disclosing something more of divine purpose (and nature) than is disclosed in ordinary events. Insofar as Biblical narrative is taken to be a unified account of such disclosures and their reception, it would seem that by implication the category of revelation looms on the horizon. Our particular concern in this section will be to focus some conceptual constraints under which we operate in the use of this category, and to assess arguments that have been put forward in support of certain ways of understanding revelation.

It is a widely shared assumption that if we use the concept of revelation we *must* take it to mean that God communicates or seeks to communicate *directly* with us in some kind of *verbal* way. Furthermore, it is often thought that it is *incoherent* to suppose that God is not revealed to us. Do these suppositions represent some sort of conceptual constraint on thinking which employs the theistic scheme we have been examining?

The reasoning for the latter assumption, which I consider *prima facie* plausible, is nicely expressed by Basil Mitchell. Citing this line from H. R. Niebuhr, 'The only word which does justice to the knowledge of persons or selves is "revelation"', Mitchell proceeds to argue in this fashion:

> Theism makes a reasoned case for the creation of the world by a transcendent personal being who had certain good purposes in creating it, purposes which have to do with the development of creatures with the capacities to think and love and worship. If, in addition, there was reason to believe that God had found ways of communicating to his creatures fundamental truths about his nature and purposes *which they otherwise could not discover*, it would enormously strengthen the overall case for his existence. Indeed, there is *an obvious gap* in a form of theism in which God, having made a world of rational creatures able to love and worship him, did not *in any way* communicate with them. (my emphases)[41]

Mitchell's reasoning is entirely plausible, but we may ask if it marks out conceptual constraints, as it purports to do, within which we must operate in taking God to be a personal agent who has created us. It seems that this reasoning fails to do so, since we

---

[41] Basil Mitchell, 'Does Christianity Need a Revelation'? *Theology*, 83 (1980): p. 108.

can conceive the *possibility* that God, having created a world with such creatures, has a *reason* for not communicating or seeking to communicate with them. Surely the only conceptual constraint which binds us is that, if God acts or chooses to *refrain* from acting, God *must* have a *reason* for doing so. To perform an action or, having entertained it, to refrain from performing it, an agent has to have a reason for acting or refraining. Furthermore, as Hampshire reminds us, the agent must act for a purpose and see the action, or the refraining from it, as a good thing.[42] This seems to be the only logical limit we may legitimately place on divine action.

Let us assume, however, that God does communicate or try to do so. Is it necessary to claim that what is communicated in this way is information we could not otherwise discover or obtain? Surely this also does not represent a conceptual constraint. If, for example, we discover within ourselves a capacity to 'love and worship', we may infer that we have been created by an agent whose purpose for us is that we should exercise those capacities. Our inference may be confirmed by the divine disclosure of this purpose which we correctly receive. That kind of confirmation of our inference would add to the strength of the case for theism without requiring that any otherwise undiscoverable knowledge be included.

Finally, *must* we assume that the way God communicates with us is *verbally*, or for that matter, in some *direct* form of communication? No doubt this is a traditional assumption, but is it an assumption which exercises a conceptual constraint over our employment of the theistic scheme? I shall argue that it does not. It is worth noting at the outset how widely shared is this assumption. Thus, in his critique of Thomas Torrance, Ronald Thiemann does not challenge the claim that it is the Biblical texts which are the form in which God reveals God's identity.[43] He does not claim, as does Torrance, that God is the author of the

---

[42] Stuart Hampshire, *Freedom of the Individual*. London: Chatto & Windus, 1965, p. 41.

[43] Ronald Thiemann, *Revelation and Theology: The Gospel as Narrated Promise*. Notre Dame: University of Notre Dame Press, 1985.

text, a view of which he is sharply critical. But he does claim that the texts, in their narrative structure, give them a reliable 'identity-description' of God because God *intended* them to. This amounts to the claim, it would seem, that God chooses verbal communication as the means by which to make God known. Thiemann's subtle Barthian way of handling the point does not alter this implication of his claim.

But, apart from the argument from tradition, is it necessary to construe divine communication as taking this form? The most plausible supporting argument available also has been articulated by Mitchell. The contention arises in this way: let us suppose that God, a disembodied agent, communicates with us by acting through particular events in the world. We must then ask how we are to identify those events as actions, as well as the agent to whom they are to be ascribed. Normally, bodily movement of a person is a reliable guide to both questions, that is, the question as to whether an event is an action, and if so, whose. But *ex hypothesi* we do not achieve this means of identification in God's case. However, we could in principle make this determination, if other indications were present. Mitchell claims, we recall, that these must be three:

(1) The unlikelihood of the event's occurrence apart from the intervention of some agent;
(2) The event's contributing to some purpose;
(3) The agreement of the purpose with the *independently known* character and purposes of the putative agent. (my emphasis)

I have argued above in effect that we need not commit ourselves to (1) in understanding the claim that some occurrence is an action.[44] We can reasonably judge that an event contributes to some purpose, even though there is a plausible explanation of its occurrence in non-purposive terms. Thus all we are required to argue, against the excesses of Kaufman and others, is that no 'complete and entirely adequate' account is available for a putative divine action, viz. an account in terms of causally

[44] See note 9 above.

sufficient natural conditions such as to preclude personal explanation of the event. But what of Mitchell's third condition?

Commenting on it, Mitchell reasons in this way against those who would argue that the Biblical texts and other supposed *loci* of divine revelation are 'merely' the 'response of . . . men of religious insight to the events in question'. We are required to ask, he suggests, what makes their response an *appropriate* response?

> For it to be appropriate they must recognise that the state of affairs does indeed express the divine personality; but how are they to tell whether it does or does not? As H. R. Niebuhr argued, the basic analogy is that of one person disclosing his character and purpose to another. Although if I do not know you I can learn a certain amount about you by observing and responding to your behaviour, unless I am very familiar with the work you do and the way you live I am likely to find this somewhat ambiguous. And even if I have this kind of background knowledge and you behave always as someone of your sort might be expected to do, I can have no warrant for supposing that this bit of behaviour, rather than that, represents your distinctive character and intentions. If, however, you talk to me about yourself and tell me what you are trying to achieve, and if some of your behaviour is evidently directed to your avowed ends, then I can use the clues thus provided to interpret behaviour of yours which has not been explained to me.[45]

Let us concede that what I learn about another from observing and responding to another's behaviour remains somewhat ambiguous. Does it follow that I can have no warrant for supposing that *this* bit of behaviour rather than *that* represents your *distinctive* character and intentions? I do not think so. The warrant will lie in the evidential *pattern* which I claim to discern (though, obviously, I could be wrong). Thus close observation of Mother Teresa over a long period of time could reasonably produce the judgment that her main purpose is to alleviate dire suffering out of love for the sufferers. Clearly, one could be mistaken in the account both of her purposes and of her motive; but the judgment about the pattern the evidence suggests would, just as clearly, be a warranted judgment.

[45] Mitchell, 'Christianity', p. 108.

Mitchell's criticism of this way of viewing the matter has another aspect to it. Of Kaufman (and Maurice Wiles), he supposes that, perhaps:

> They are not denying that God 'speaks' to man; they are explaining how he speaks to man, viz. in and through the ordinary processes of human cultural development. My trouble with this reply is that, so far as I can see, the process they are describing is analogous not to the situation in which I come to know your character and intentions through what you tell me, but to the situation in which I conjecture your character and intentions from your non-verbal behaviour alone. And this is precisely not a situation in which it is appropriate to talk of your communicating with me.[46]

But, again, it does not seem that Mitchell has located a *conceptual constraint* on our thinking. Suppose Mother Teresa believes that God desires or commands us all to adopt as our purpose the comforting of the destitute, and further that she desires to share with us her belief. Suppose also that she does not have time, or think it wise, to try to communicate *directly* to us her conviction. It does not follow that she will be unable to intentionally communicate with us. She can intend to do so, and perhaps succeed, simply by doing in an observable way what she believes we should all be doing. On the assumption of conditions present such that we could reasonably be expected to see her task as one we should share, e.g. our possession of altruistic impulses, the possibility of judging that her actions reflect a quite full enactment of them and that we should do more to act upon ours, etc., Mother Teresa could be properly understood as communicating with us indirectly in a non-verbal way. We could reasonably take her as an example to follow, and as seeking to communicate that example indirectly simply by doing what she believes we all should do.

Whether this analogy can and should be developed as a way of understanding God's communication with us, I am not prepared to say. I see nothing which rules it out as an incoherent

---

[46] Mitchell, 'Christianity', p. 109.

supposition. If it fits the evidence available, and if there is a plausible reason(s) for proposing it (e.g. God's maintenance of an epistemic distance between God and persons, so as to ensure that their response to God may be one of uncoerced love), then I think it is open conceptually for a theologian to construe divine communication accordingly. It goes without saying, perhaps, that the analogy fits nicely 'the pattern of hiddenness and presence' taken to be fundamental to a narrative account which depicts divine agency as present in the world *through* the agency of the people of Israel and the man, Jesus of Nazareth.

## V

We may conclude, then, that the concept of a disembodied agent is coherent and that the absence of embodiment presents no bar to literal predication of action concepts to such an agent. The idea, upon which narrative theology hinges, of particular divine action in the world is intelligible apart from construing such action as occurring outside of nature or even as contributing uniquely to the realisation of divine purpose. Nor must we, as a matter of conceptual necessity, take such actions as we consider disclosive of God's nature and purposes to be *direct* communication requiring verbal self-interpretation. We may be led to hope by these conclusions that the philosophical issues basic to narrative theology can be solved.

Chapter 9

# NARRATIVE THEOLOGY AND THE ACTS OF GOD

*Thomas F. Tracy*

## HOW MIGHT WE CONCEIVE OF GOD'S ACTIVITY IN THE WORLD?

Stated in this general way, the question is a tempting occasion to launch some speculations into the thin air of philosophical theology, where so many strange intellectual contraptions have been set in motion. This is an opportunity I will not pass up. But before offering some suggestions about one important way in which God has been said to act, I want at least to note the hermeneutical context of such discussions, since we should not conclude too quickly that we know what particular claims or types of claims Christians (or other theists) are committed to making about God's acts.

## I

## *BIBLICAL STORIES OF GOD'S MIGHTY ACTS*

Worship in the biblically based traditions typically involves a movement back and forth between the scriptural texts, in which God's acts are depicted, and the contemporary context, in which the ongoing activity of God is affirmed. The recital of these ancient stories tells the worshippers *whom* they worship and what sort of story is even now unfolding between them and this God. But precisely this poses the problem, for the contemporary believer can hardly avoid recognising the gap between the world of the bible and his or her own world. The oppressed of our world, for example, are not liberated through spectacular displays of divine power in plagues, pillars of fire, and parted waters.

Theology has struggled for some time, therefore, with questions about how to understand biblical stories about God's mighty acts in history. It is always possible, of course, to cut through this Gordian knot by taking the biblical narratives strictly as symbolic expressions of a type of religious experience or of a possibility for self-understanding that was evoked by the historical experience of Israel. This, in fact, is a characteristically modern move; we begin with narratives of God's mighty acts and we arrive at statements about religious subjectivity, avoiding (if we are careful) any claim that God acts in particular historical events.[1]

Not surprisingly, this interpretive strategy provokes the response that it thoroughly dehistoricises God's relation to human beings. But those who have thought it important to affirm that God acts in the events of our history have been unable to develop their claims with sufficient detail and explicitness. The 'biblical theologians', of course, are the prime example here. As Langdon Gilkey pointed out, they appealed to the biblical portrayals of God as One Who Acts, yet they were unwilling or unable to say *what* it is that God does.[2]

Against this background, there has recently appeared a fruitful reconsideration of biblical narrative. Hans Frei, in particular, has urged us to look more carefully at the way a 'realistic narrative' bears it meaning.[3] A narrative that presents a 'history-like' interaction of character and circumstance is not about something

[1] On such an account, our consciousness of God's activity (e.g. as the Whence of our existence) may and perhaps must be tied to certain events or persons that serve as the occasion for its emergence in us and that remain powerfully expressive. Biblical narratives about God's acts witness to such occasions and continue to function evocatively. But it is a contingent fact about us and our religious traditions that these events have called forth our consciousness of God. No claim is made that God acts in these events in a distinctive way, that here God enacts some particular purpose.

[2] 'Cosmology, Ontology, and the Travail of Biblical Language', *The Journal of Religion*, 41 (1961): 194–205.

[3] *The Eclipse of Biblical Narrative* (New Haven: Yale University Press, 1974), and *The Identity of Jesus Christ* (Philadelphia: Fortress Press, 1975).

that lies behind the story, say, the events or experiences that triggered the process of composition or the intention of the authors in telling it. Rather, the subject matter of the story just is the story it tells about agents acting in some natural and social world. In presenting an unfolding pattern of action-in-context, the narrative provides an identity description of an agent, i.e. it displays *who* the agent is. As Frei puts it, we are concerned here with 'the kind of story in which "the signified", the identity of the protagonist, is enacted by the signifier, the narrative sequence itself'.[4]

Read this way, the function of biblical narratives is to introduce God as a character within a set of stories. We do not need to look outside the unfolding story-line in order to grasp what these narratives are about; indeed, if we do so we miss the point, which is precisely the presentation of this agent in action. The actions that identify who God is are first and foremost the actions narrated in the biblical stories, and not some set of events that we have reconstructed given our best historical conjectures about what might actually have happened.

It is worth noting parenthetically that there are important exegetical questions about how to construe the biblical narratives as a complex but coherent whole. The Christian canon does not present a *single* narrative but rather is a collection of diverse genres of literature including a variety of different stories. To the extent that theologians identify significantly different story-patterns in scripture, they may differ in their understanding of the identity of the divine agent.

Questions of exegetical detail aside, this recognition that biblical narratives can be read as depicting the identity of the divine agent provides an important key to generating theological uses of scripture that are more nuanced than those pursued by

---

[4] Unpublished paper titled, 'Theology and the Interpretation of Narrative: Some Hermeneutical Considerations', p. 29. There are clearly some important anthropological claims at work in these hermeneutical remarks. For Frei's discussion of the personal identity of an agent of intentional actions, see chapters 4 & 9 of *The Identity of Jesus Christ*.

the biblical theologians.[5] The point I want to stress, however, is that this interpretive strategy does not somehow rid us of the question about what we mean by an act of God – rather, the question simply arises in a somewhat different form. Simply put, the narrative theologian will almost surely want to affirm the reality of God. The faithful do not undertake a life of devotion to the main character of what they take to be a purely fictional story. Rather they understand the God they worship to be the God of the history they *live*, and not simply of a history they tell or are told in a piece of imaginative literature. The question about God's acts arises as soon as we affirm that the God of biblical narrative is the lord of our actual history. This affirmation presents us with the task of explaining how we might think of the activity of *this* God (as presented in biblical narrative) in *this* world (as we believe it actually to be). We must explain how the divine character presented in the biblical narratives can be understood to be an agent in our history.

Any systematic effort to offer such an explanation will need to address at least three clusters of issues. First, there are historical issues. Narrative theologians affirm the aptness of the biblical stories (construed in some particular way) as an identity description of God. But they also acknowledge that much in these stories cannot be treated as describing actual historical events. Some subtle questions arise about the relations between the *stories* we tell in order to depict an agent's personal identity and the *actions* that we are prepared actually to ascribe to that agent. Second, christological issues clearly will occupy an important place in the discussion, for the stories about Jesus lie at the heart of the Christian's account of what God does and who God is. Third, we will need to think through how the God identified in the biblical narratives can be understood to engage us now to influence the character of our lives. As Augustine richly illustrates in his *Confessions*, the biblical stories of God's acts provide the impetus for Christians to tell the stories of their

[5] See, for example, Frei, *The Identity of Jesus Christ*, Thiemann, *Revelation and Theology*, esp. chapters 5 & 7, and Michael Root, 'The Narrative Structure of Soteriology', *Modern Theology*, January 1986.

lives as histories of interaction with God.

In the discussion that follows, I want to explore this third way in which the God identified in biblical narrative can be tied to the history we understand ourselves to live. The question here concerns how we might conceive of God's action in the lives of finite agents. Speculation about how God acts to affect the development of our lives is, in the nature of the case, an uncertain enterprise. There are obviously many ways to go wrong with such a discussion, so many in fact that we may wonder whether there is any hope of giving an account that does not generate various theological embarrassments or leave itself open to a hostile *reductio*. We can minimise somewhat the magnitude of our virtually inevitable missteps by recognising some intrinsic limits upon what we can say about *any* form of divine action in our world. We need to pause, then, before proceeding with the question about God's action in the lives of finite agents, and note two general constraints upon such discussions.

## II
### *SOME LIMITS ON THEOLOGICAL SPECULATION*

We can never expect to give a complete account of God's dealings with us precisely because it is *God's* actions about which we are inquiring. There are two principal considerations here.

First, we will not be able to explain *how* God brings about effects in our world. This is due, at its root, to conceptual limitations on our ability to spell out what it is to be the divine agent and to act as God acts. Care is required in stating this point, however. I am not denying that we can conceive of God as an agent in the sense that we can preserve the formal, or logical, properties of the concept 'agent' (its various entailments) in our talk of God. I have argued at length elsewhere that we can coherently speak of God as an unembodied agent, indeed as the 'perfection of agency' (viz. as that individual in whom the capacities that define agency find their maximal expression).[6] By stripping away limitations peculiar to human agency, we can

[6] See my *God, Action, and Embodiment* (Grand Rapids: Eerdmans, 1984), esp. chapter 7.

generate an abstract description of the form of God's agency. But we cannot provide more than various fragile analogies for the nature of God's activity an an unembodied agent or for the manner in which God's activity engages our world. Instead, we must look to the effects of God's activity, to what the texts and tradition understand God to have *done*.

This, I take it, is parallel to Austin Farrer's point in telling us that, 'the causal joint (so to speak) between infinite and finite action plays and in the nature of the case can play no part in our concern with God and his will'.[7] We must be careful to deploy this point about the 'causal joint' at the right stage of the discussion, however, and not assume that it releases us from every sort of question about how God acts. In order to see how this is so, we need to take up briefly a familiar consideration in philosophical discussions of human action.

Often when we ask how an agent did some particular thing we are inquiring about what might be called the 'instrumental substructure' of the agent's action. Complex intentional actions are organised in hierarchies of instrumental relations; we do one thing in order to do another, e.g. we turn the key in order to start the car in order to drive to a political meeting in order to help elect a worthy candidate. If we ask '*How* did you get to the political meeting?' we are inquiring about *what* the agent did in order to bring about the outcome in question. Here we seek an answer that moves down the instrumental hierarchy of an intentional action series.

In our talk about God's acts, it will not do to offer descriptions only of high-level intentions (i.e. intentions fairly far up in an intentional action series). Precisely that was one of the ways in which the biblical theologians ran into trouble. It is not enough simply to say that God acts redemptively on our behalf in the history of Israel. We must be able to give an account of *what God does* in order to redeem. If we reply that, e.g. God frees the Hebrew people from bondage in Egypt, then once again we need to indicate what this act of 'freeing the Hebrew people' consists

[7] *Faith and Speculation* (New York: New York University Press, 1967), p. 65.

of. We must, in short, be prepared to give some account of the instrumental substructure of God's acts. Unless we can do so, our talk of God's acts will (as Gilkey suggested) finally be empty of the cognitive content we thought we could claim for it.

How far down the substructure of God's acts must we be able to carry our analysis? In principle, regress down an instrumental action series comes to an end when we reach a 'basic action', viz. an intentional action that the agent initiates without having to undertake any prior intentional action in order to bring it about.[8] If we ask how basic actions are performed we are no longer calling for a further step down a hierarchy of instrumental actions, but rather are seeking an explanation of the agent's capacity to act intentionally. Precisely this cannot be provided, however, when the agent in question is God; if God is the unembodied perfection of agency, we will not be able to analyse the nature of God's agency and explain what it is to act as God acts. The point about the causal joint, then, is that as we approach the lowest level in the substructure of God's acts, we will reach a point at which it follows from what we mean by 'God' that we cannot say more about how God acts. Specifically, we will not be able to say how God brings about those events that lie at bottom, at it were, of the instrumental action hierarchies that achieve God's purpose in our world. The question remains, however, about how far we can go toward identifying particular events or types of events in which God initiates action in our world. And in considering this question, we must note another limitation on theological speculation.

Second, we cannot comprehend *fully* either what God intends or the range of actions in which that intention is enacted. God acts with a scope (over all creatures) and an intimacy (to every

---

[8] On basic actions see, e.g. Aurthur Danto, *Analytical Philosophy of Action* (Cambridge: Cambridge University Press, 1973), Alvin Goldman, *A Theory of Human Action* (Englewood Cliffs: Prentice-Hall, 1970), chapter 3, and Roderick M. Chisholm, *Person and Object* (La Salle, Illinois: Open Court, 1976), chapter 2. There is dispute over which actions should be identified as basic actions, but the idea of a basic action is reasonably clear: regress of intentional explanation can come to an end only in an action that we perform *not* by undertaking any prior intentional action as the means to it, but simply by initiating it.

creature) that dwarfs our capacity to imagine it. We can form only a partial conception of God's activity from those events in which we identify God's purposes at work. These epistemological limitations – combined with our tendency to form a view of the world that reflects our idiosyncratic interests and resentments – suggest that we should be cautious about attempting any very precise identification of where and how God is acting in our world. There will be particular difficulty in specifying lower level actions, ecpecially the initial acts, within the instrumental action series that enact God's higher level purposes for us. God may enact a single high level intention (e.g. that creatures be fulfilled in fellowship with God) in an inexhaustible variety of particular ways in individual lives. Given this inventiveness of God's action in response to the actions of creatures, we cannot expect to trace the details of God's workings in the world.

Our account of God's actions, therefore, will ordinarily become progressively less detailed and more qualified as we move down the substructure of divine action toward those events in which God initially brings his will to bear in our world. We do need, however, to give an account of the general sorts of events we envision as God's initial acts. If we fail to do so, then our talk of God as one who engages us redemptively in history will be referentially hollow, attributing high level purposes to God without indicating what God might be doing to achieve those purposes. At this point Gilkey's challenge – viz. to explain what we mean by the expression 'act of God' – comes to rest with stubborn unavoidability.

## III

## DETERMINISM, HUMAN FREEDOM, AND THE POSSIBILITY OF DIVINE ACTION IN HISTORY

Bearing in mind these limits on the theological speculation, our project is to explore ways of conceiving of the initial acts by which God affects the lives of human agents. Any effort to do so, however, immediately faces certain preemptive objections. It has become a familiar feature of contemporary theological discussion to hear that our participation in 'the modern worldview' means that we can no longer hold that God acts within our world to bring about particular effects. One thinks, for example, of Bultmann's insistence that any talk of God acting within the 'objective' world inevitably portrays God's action as an alien power that 'breaks into and disrupts the continuum of natural, historical, or psychical events – in short as a "miracle"'.[9] Miracles, we are told, are no longer thinkable for us whose view of the world 'has been moulded by modern science and the modern conception of human nature as a self-subsistent unity immune from the interference of super-natural powers'.[10]

I think that it is in fact possible to refute most such claims about the inconceivability of miracle in the modern world. But given the epistemological and theological problems with miracles, it is ill-advised to tie one's account of God's action primarily to divine interventions that disrupt the regularities we have come to expect among natural events. The more important point at which to resist Bultmann is in his claim that any talk of God affecting the course of nature or human history constitutes an appeal to miracle. The crucial supposition at work here is that modern understandings of our world are deterministic, i.e. they present to us a closed causal continuum tht leaves 'no room for

[9] From Bultmann's reply to his critics in *Kerygma und Mythos*, ed. H. W. Bartsch (Hamburg: Herbert Reich-Evangelischer Verlag, 1951), vol. 2, pp. 196–7, as translated by Ogden and quoted in *Christ without Myth*, pp. 91–2. cf. English translation by R. H. Fuller, *Kerygma and Myth*, ed. H. W. Bartsch (New York: Harper & Brothers, 1961), p. 197.

[10] Bultmann, *Kerygma and Myth*, p. 7.

God's working'.[11] That supposition leads Bultmann to suggest that we think of God acting 'within' events to address us as (noumenal) selves in such a way that the outward (phenomenal) course of events (including psychological events) remains utterly untouched.[12] If we find this solution too obscure to be very helpful, then we seem to be left with the options of embracing miracle or concluding that God does not act responsively *in* history but only initiates and sustains it as a whole (as was said, for example, by the deists).[13]

It is open to us, however, to challenge the deterministic supposition. If we do so, then it may be possible to conceive of our world as structured in such a way that God can act within it to influence the direction of events without overriding its intrinsic structures. Our world may be both a natural order, comprehensible for a variety of purposes without reference to God, and also be the scene of God's ongoing creative activity.

We can pursue this possibility, as we reflect on God's active relation to our lives, by exploring the claim that human beings are free agents of intentional actions. Philosophical reflection on human action has long struggled with questions about the relation between descriptions of human beings as (1) causally

[11] Bultmann, *Jesus Christ and Mythology* (New York: Charles Scribner's Sons, 1958), p. 65.

[12] See Bultmann's reply to his critics in *Kerygma and Myth*, p. 197. Also see *Jesus Christ and Mythology*, pp. 60–6.

[13] In an important article, 'Providence and Divine Action', (*Religious Studies*, 14, 1978, pp. 223–6), Brian Hebblethwaite argues that talk of divine providence is *not* dependent upon an indeterminism that creates gaps in our explanation of events. Even if there are 'no gaps here, not even psychical ones', (p. 225) we can still think of the whole series of events as 'pliable or flexible to the providential hand of God' (p. 226). That is an appealing claim; the difficulty, of course, is to give an account of *how* we can coherently say both of these things. If every occurrence has causally sufficient conditions in the finite events that precede it, then it is difficult to see how God can affect the overall series of events except by determining its initial conditions and laws of development. If, on the other hand, God acts within history in such a way that events develop differently than they would have otherwise, then the natural causes of those events will not alone be sufficient to account for them; there will be a causal and explanatory gap. Some account must be given of how we can have flexibility without gaps. Hebblethwaite appeals to Farrer's remarks on 'double agency' here, and I will comment briefly on this idea in the last section of this paper.

structured organisms, (2) agents of intentional action, and (3) centres of free decision in the determination of at least some of their own actions. I want to explore briefly two ways of handling these issues both of which affirm human freedom in a sense stronger than that allowed by the soft-determinist.[14] I will call these two positions 'conceptual compatibilism' and 'a libertarianism of situated freedom'.

The key issue that divides these two views concerns the relation between descriptions of human beings as causally structured organisms and as free agents of intentional actions. A movement of the body (e.g. a movement of arm and hand) often can be described not only as a neurophysiological sequence but also as an intentional action. We could ask someone, 'Why did you raise your arm?', and we might be told that she was waving to a friend. We could also ask her (since, conveniently, she happens to be a neurophysiologist), 'Why did your arm go up?'. In this case we expect to hear about nerve impulses, muscle contractions, and so on. The physiological story provides a causal explanation of the arm going up. The intentional action story provides reasons for the agent's action of raising her arm. How are these stories related to each other?

The conceptual compatibilist contends that these two descriptions do not need to fit together at all. Each is coherent and complete in itself. They cannot conflict because, though they describe the same event, they do so in vocabularies that are systematically disjoined. The subject and predicate concepts they each employ are defined in such a way that statements in one vocabulary never have among their truth conditions statements in the other vocabulary. As a result, the two vocabularies can never generate subject-predicate assertions that conflict; even if they seem to contradict each other, they will in fact be asserting

---

[14] Typically, soft-determinists say that an agent is free when she is not prevented by factors beyond her control (e.g. coercion) from doing what she wants or intends to do. This is compatible with granting that all events, including the agent's desires and intentions, are causally determined by antecedent conditions. By contrast, traditional defenders of 'free will' want to claim for the agent a power to make self-determining choices which are not causally necessitated by prior circumstances.

different predicates of different subjects. We run into problems only when we make the mistake of crossing categories and trying to say, for example, how the agent's reasons explain her arm going up or how neurophysiological processes explain the agent's action of raising her arm. The arm movement can be understood in each way, without intrusion of either explanatory pattern on the other.

If a position of this sort could be sustained it would open up some interesting options for theological reflection about God's activity in the world. For on this account, we could understand events as part of a closed causal continuum and yet also describe them as enacting God's purposes. Just as a deterministic physiological story would have no bearing on talk of intentional action (including talk of free action), so a universal causal determinism would have no bearing on talk of God as the personal and purposive lord of history. Theological statements about God's action would not entail that the scientist's causal explanations of events must at some point be incomplete. We could show, for example, that the deists were wrong in thinking that Newtonian determinism required that we give up talk about *particular* divine actions in history; a strong east wind at the reed sea can perfectly well both be necessitated by prior meteorological conditions and be the mighty act of the God of Israel. God's agency does not need to be inserted between or among creaturely causes; the language of purpose and the language of causation simply do not interact and compete in this way.[15]

---

[15] John Compton seems to take a position of this kind in a helpful exploratory essay, 'Science and God's Action in Nature' in *Earth Might Be Fair*, ed. Ian Barbour (Englewood Cliffs: Prentice-Hall, 1972). He argues that 'the entire logic of bodily event and the logic of actions – each equally applicable to me and my behaviour – are different' (p. 38). Hence he can conclude that God does not 'need to find a "gap" in nature in order to act, any more than you or I need a similar interstice in our body chemistry. Each story has a complete cast of characters, without the need for interaction with the other story, but quite compatible with it' (p. 39). Compton also says, however, that 'consciously held reasons and intentions *are* causes of our actions, and they do effectively modify bodily conditions. But this is not inexplicable physiologically; it is true because these reasons and intentions have a basis in certain complex states of our brains and

The difficulty with this approach, attractive as it is, is that the vocabularies of intentional action and causality do appear to be relevant to each other. What one says about a series of events as caused has a bearing on what one can say about it as intended, and vice versa. In particular, there are some causal stories about human behaviour that rule out intentional action stories. If (i) someone grasps the agent's arm and raises it or if (ii) the arm twitches convulsively, so that its movement is beyond the agent's control, then that movement is not an intentional action. It certainly looks as though the reason we do not regard the convulsive jerk as an intentional action is that here an automatic reflex runs its course beyond the 'reach' of the agent's intentional control. The agent's action of raising her arm depends upon the causal regularities of bodily life, but it also requires that those autonomic processes be open to modification in accordance with the agent's intention. What makes the agent's action of raising her arm different from the convulsive jerk is the agent's intentional initiation and control of the action.

It appears, then, that we cannot avoid difficult questions about the interconnections between descriptions of causal series and descriptions of intentional actions. One of the central tasks of action theory is to offer some account of the agent's capacity to act intentionally, the capacity to put the autonomic processes of bodily life to work to serve the agent's purposes. This is disputed territory, and it is not possible here to undertake an exploration of it.[16] For my immediate purposes, however, it is enough to

nervous systems' (p. 41). At this point Compton seems to embrace an event-causation theory of action (and perhaps some version of soft-determinism). This would still allow him to sustain the claim than we can describe bodily behaviour both as causally determined and as intentional action. But it abandons the claim that the language of intentional action and that of physical causation do not interact and cannot conflict (for it suggests that explanation by appeal to an agent's intention can be analysed in terms of the causal efficacy of certain complex brain states). And having given up this claim, the position loses its power to free us from difficulties about God's action within a closed causal order.

[16] For a theory of 'agent causation' see, e.g. Roderick Chisholm, *Person and Object*, chapter II. For a theory of 'event-causation' see, e.g. Alvin Goldman, *A Theory of Human Action*.

note that if we deny the compatibility of freedom with causal determinism, then whatever account we give of the 'machinery' of intentional action, our affirmation of human freedom will entail that an agent's *free* acts are not causally necessitated by their various background conditions. We envision, instead, an agent whose future is not exhaustively specified by his past, who faces open alternatives for action, and whose decisions represent a creative movement beyond what is given. This, of course, is not to say that all of our actions are free or that our actions are not profoundly conditioned by the matrix of events in which they are rooted. Our freedom can only be a freedom to determine what is left determinable within a nexus of ordered processes that are largely beyond our control and that may often rather narrowly delimit the range of possibilities open to us. We live toward a future that is partly open to our creation and partly determined by what has been. Hence, we live by imagination and experimentation; we envision what is not yet but might be, and we try out these possibilities, discovering the hard contours of a world that does not always yield to our intentions for it.

It is in this context that I want to speak of God's interaction with human beings. If a human agent's life does not constitute, in Bultmann's words, a 'closed weft of cause and effect' in which each episode is rigidly determined by its predecessors, then the possibility opens up that God might interact with persons without disrupting the intelligible order of events in our lives. God might in various ways contribute to the content and development of our actions as free agents without disarranging the network of natural interactions in which our lives are embedded. Specifically, I want to suggest that we think of God as continuously shaping the direction of each individual's self-determination by contributing to the network of influences that condition our actions from moment to moment throughout our histories. In order to see how this could be, we need to explore somewhat further the relation of our free actions to the complex texture of events in which they arise.

IV

## HUMAN CREATIVITY AND GOD'S ACTION
## IN OUR LIVES

We operate as agents of free intentional actions, I have suggested, in the transition from what we are given to what we create. In free action we make something new of what is given to us, but the possibilities for what we make are structured by what is given. We can observe this subtle interaction of givenness and creativity, destiny and freedom, in our ongoing activity of recognising possibilities for action and choosing between them. This process is shaped by an extraordinarily complex network of conditioning factors not all of which are accessible to critical reflection, much less to our intentional modification.

Note, for example, three important categories of these orienting conditions ingredient in action: bodily life, memory, and social context. The capacities of bodily life determine the repertoire of basic actions available to us. However sophisticated we may become in using technological means to achieve our ends indirectly, our projects are crucially structured by the fact that we possess these particular powers of bodily action. In addition to establishing our basic capacity to act, bodily life also shapes what we do with that capacity. The life of the body generates an agenda for action, a set of needs and drives that orient our activity. Hence Austin Farrer can speak of 'the bodily bias of the will'.[17] Our powers of action come already aimed at satisfying a range of biologically established vital interests.

Memory, as well, plays a fundamental and fascinatingly subtle role in the formation of our actions. We carry our history with us into our present context of action in a variety of ways, many of which are not self-conscious. As we project a future before us that we take to be open to various constructions through our free action, we do so along lines laid down by our perceptions, of our past. This mnemonic structuring of our expectations (and imaginations) is easy to recognise when it takes the form of well-

[17] *Finite and Infinite*, 2nd edn. (London: A. & C. Black, Dacre Press, 1959), chapter XV, pp. 171–82.

evidenced items of knowledge about the natural or social world we inhabit. But our effective memory includes much more than just those episodes that are subject to immediate recall and those patterns of experience that we have learned to formulate in inductive generalisations. We also live from our past in less articulate ways, reacting to or repeating patterns of emotion and action that are buried deep in the sedimentation of our experience. Our mapping of the future in light of the past, therefore, takes place within a matrix of mnemonically informed emotions, attitudes, anticipations, interests, and so on, that display various degrees of reflectiveness and that may be (at their deeper levels) very difficult for us to identify and describe.

Third, the social context of our lives as agents deserves comment. Precisely because the pattern of activity in a human life is not exhaustively specified by the body, we are capable of and require a complex social existence. Our capacity to determine the course of our own lives is exercised in a network of personal relationships set within wider social structures. The possible courses of action that we project before us in time are located in a social landscape, and the alternative among which we choose are thoroughly shaped by the social world we inhabit. Indeed, we ourselves are formed socially from our very beginnings; the social world in which we live calls forth and cultivates certain ways of being an agent.[18] In our central relationships from earlist childhood we learn our roles, powers, responsibilities, and limits. Knowingly and unknowingly, we take others as models for what we might be and we absorb suggestions about what we should want, what projects are worthwhile, and how we should regard ourselves and others. Our much vaunted autonomy as agents consists not in a capacity to constitute ourselves independently of a social context, but rather in our powers of analysis, criticism, and imaginative flexibility – powers which are variously acknowledged or ignored, cultivated or suppressed, in different social settings.

[18] Stanley Hauerwas presses this point perceptively and argues that communities shape character through the stories they perpetuate. See, e.g. *The Peaceable Kingdom* (Notre Dame: University of Notre Dame Press, 1983).

A great deal more might be said, of course, about the web of influences that constitutes the orienting conditions out of which we act. But perhaps this is enough to remind us of the richness and complexity of those conditions. We might say that our lives as agents unfold as an ongoing experiment in integrating the multitude of influences that bear upon us from the natural and social worlds in which we act, from bodily life, from memory, and so on. In free action we creatively focus these influences into a new unity defined by our intentions. This suggests a simple way of indicating the co-presence of necessity and freedom in our lives. We always act under conditions that structure and limit the range of possibilities we can recognise and pursue. But when action is free, these orienting conditions do not exclude all options for the future except one. Rather, a free action is a creative response to the conditions under which it is initiated; it draws this network of influences into a new configuration in an action that becomes the next phase of the agent's history. Each action, in turn, gives rise to further interaction with our world, to changed bodily circumstances, to fresh memory associations, to evolving emotional intonations – in short, to new occasions for the integration of a network of influences in action.

As this process unfolds, our actions develop out of one another and display complex patterns of continuity across time. It is these patterns of continuity that we try to identify when we describe the distinctive personal identity of an agent. We look, that is, for the agent's characteristic responses to situations, his enduring interests, his persistent attitudes, his operative scheme of values, his distinctive style, and so on. These continuities reflect the formation of the agent's actions as part of a developing history, each new moment of which is conditioned by those which went before. An agent's free actions build creatively upon this history, incorporating it in a distinctive way and becoming part of it for the actions which follow. In this way, each action is firmly rooted in the agent's historical identity and contributes in its particular way to the development of that identity.

If we think of human agents in this way, then we can conceive of God as continuously influencing each finite agent without disrupting the intelligible order of events in the agent's life. God can do so by contributing to the network of orienting conditions from which the finite agent acts. In this way, God can be understood to bring to bear within every agent's life the insistent pressure of his intentions for us. In response, therefore, to our question about the nature of God's initial acts, we can give the following partial answer: at least one of the ways God initiates action in our world will be by contributing to the orienting conditions, or network of influences, from which human agents act.

Immediately, of course, we want to know what it is for God to 'contribute' to the orientation of our actions; what exactly are we claiming that God *does*? In pushing this inquiry as far as we can, we must keep in mind the limits on theological speculation discussed earlier. God's activity will exceed our capacity to describe it, I suggested, because we can comprehend neither (1) how God's activity engages our world nor (2) the full scope and content of God's acts. The first limit entails that we cannot expect to explain how God brings about the effects that are his initial acts within our lives. The second limit entails that our descriptions of what God brings about in us will inevitably be incomplete. Yet in spite of these limitations, and in partial mitigation of them, we can fill out our talk about God's acts within the lives of human agents in two ways. First, we can delineate the role God's activity plays in relation to the network of creaturely influences that affect us. Second, we can indicate what sorts of effects we envision God to bring about in us. In these ways, we can sketch the rough contours of God's active relation to us, indicating how we might envision the general 'mode of entry' of God's activity into our lives as agents.

I want to touch briefly upon the second of these two topics before turning to the first in more detail. When we attempt to identify particular episodes or developments in our lives as especially reflecting God's activity, we confront a two-fold mystery. There is, as we just noted, the mystery of a divine agency whose full purposes and scope we cannot grasp. There is also the mystery of one's own life as the bearer of a personal identity developed out of a skein of influence and action so intricate that we cannot describe it in a fully definitive way. We should be cautious, therefore, about embracing any single account of God's dealings with us (e.g. a description of some form of experience or mode of consciousness) as *the* manner of God's action in our lives. Given the variety and complexity of the background conditions at work in human actions, God's activity can engage us in a virtually inexhaustible multitude of different specific ways. In addition, God's activity will very often remain hidden within the flow of ordinary events in our lives. As I will suggest below, God's acts need not disrupt the network of creaturely influences upon us, and so need not announce themselves. There is no reason to think that God's activity will always, or even very often, register in our awareness as *God's* influence upon us.

God's dealings with us can go unrecognised, therefore, precisely because they are so integrally and extensively woven into the fabric of our lives. But for this same reason, when we set out to identify God's workings in or upon us, it will be possible to cite a tremendous variety of events as bearing God's influence. The language of Christian practice reflects this. The tradition has characteristically claimed, for example, that God is actively present in the liturgical life of the community (e.g. in hearing God's word in preaching, and in the reception of the sacraments), and in special episodes of religious experience or in deep structures of religious consciousness. In addition, Christians have recognised God's influence in a wide range of episodes from ordinary life that shape what sort of person one becomes, e.g. in insights into the needs or character or experience of others, in the courage to take risks for the sake of justice or love, in moments of joy and wonder or of exhaustion and despair, in nagging dissatisfactions with the character of our attachments, in a drive to deepened self-knowledge and richer relationship with others, in an expansive desire for fullness of life, and so on.

If there is an objection to this talk of God's acts, it is not that it fails actually to attribute any actions to God but rather that it appears to attribute too many. We may wonder, that is, whether the integrity and relative independence of the finite agent can be preserved if the divine agent is so intimately and pervasively involved in the creature's life. At this point we turn to the first of our two topics above, viz. the relation of God's activity to the web of creaturely influences within which we exercise our limited freedom. There are three considerations here that emerge out of our discussion of the human agent.

First, God's influence upon us will be thoroughly integrated with the developing network of creaturely conditions that constitutes the intelligible history and reliable context of each of our actions. When we say that God contributes to the matrix of influences that shape our actions, we are *not* saying that God unilaterally produces in us affect and cognition or decision and action. We need not think of God inserting alien or contextless thoughts and feelings into our lives from above. Indeed, if God's contribution to the finite agent's life were to appear as a 'bolt from the blue' – an event unrelated to the rest of the agent's experiences, feelings, thoughts, values, aspirations, and so on – we would have to wonder whether it could be counted as a development in the finite agent's life at all. God's activity is not the sole cause of any particular element (e.g. the recognition of a novel possibility for action) among the orienting conditions of the finite agent's action. Rather, God acts conjointly with the agent's past experience and present circumstances to generate this development. Hence, God's activity toward us introduces within the orienting conditions of our action an element that constitutes (a) a coherent development of what has gone before, but also (b) a creative, or generative, advance that can affect the array of possibilities that open out before us as we come to terms with this new element in action. By contributing to the network of influences that condition our actions, God can continuously shape the possibilities toward which we live and so can aim our self-creative activity toward the fulfilment God intends for us. In this way, God affects us not as an alien power that disrupts or compels but rather as an intimate contributor to our own creative activity.

Second, God cannot simply make whatever he will of the

material presented by the agent's past history and present circumstances. If God's action is to be an intelligible development of tendencies at work in the agent's life, then the range of possibilities open to God will be limited in certain ways. In this respect, God's action in us is like our own free acts, i.e. it is a novel development of given resources. Unlike our acts, however, each of God's contributions to our lives perfectly comprehends both what we have been and what we might become, and so engages us at just those points where God's purposes for us can best be advanced. The limits upon the range of possibilities open to God in his dealings with us, then, are fundamentally different from the limits we face in our finite self-creativity. The 'givenness' God confronts in the creature's life simply reflects God's free decision that there should be beings distinct from himself, a decision that involves a concomitant free restraint upon the uses of God's power. In contributing to the creature's history, God works within limits that God has established as the given possibilities for the creature's life.

Third, if God intends that there be finite free agents, then there will be a further constraint upon the uses of God's power: God's enactment of his purposes for the agent's life will respect the creature's purposes for himself. God's acts will introduce elements into the orienting conditions of human action that (a) we must take into account as we formulate our projects, and that thereby (b) affect the direction of action by shaping the range of possibilities we confront. But insofar as we are free, this contribution to the processes by which we recognise and choose among projects will not causally necessitate a particular outcome in action. We cannot do otherwise than receive and include these elements within the integrative process by which we generate our actions. But how God's influence upon us enters into our actions is something that we will have at least some power to determine in those of our actions that are free.[19]

---

[19] It seems to me that this affirmation of human freedom, and therefore of our genuine though limited co-creativity with God in determining the content of our lives, does not bar us from making some strong claims about 'salvation by grace alone', The issues here are notoriously difficult, and no simple solution is to be

This account makes it possible to say that God acts through our actions, though such language must be handled carefully. Austin Farrer speaks of the 'paradox of double agency' – i.e. the paradox of asserting that a single action is performed by two agents – and he tells us that this puzzle lies at the heart of reflection upon God's action in the world. Farrer acknowledges that 'two agents for the same act would be indeed impossible, were they both agents in the same sense and on the same level'.[20] The question, then, is how we distinguish and relate the 'senses' in which or the 'levels' on which God and creatures act, i.e. how do we differentiate *what* each agent does?

There are at least two instances in which we can say that an action is performed by two agents. First, we often speak of one agent acting on behalf of another (acting, we might say, as that agent's agent). This is relatively uncomplicated, it can be analysed in terms of two instrumental action hierarchies that (i) originate in distinct basic actions performed by different agents and (ii) overlap by including certain events in both action series (e.g. the event of one person reading a statement to the press on behalf of another). Second, we also speak of two agents performing a single action when they jointly contribute to the production of some effect. Once again, we can distinguish the basic actions they each undertake and note that these actions initiate chains of consequences that converge in a common result (e.g. as when two people together lift a heavy object).

expected. Nonetheless, it may be useful to note two interconnected points. First, to say that our lives as finite free agents are fulfilled is *not* to say that this fulfilment is brought about through the exercise of our freedom. Rather, our free actions (indeed, our entire personal history) may be brought to a completion that we do not produce through our actions but which is produced by God out of our actions. Second, this suggests a distinction between respects in which we do and do not contribute to the fulfilment, or completion, of our lives in relation to God: viz. it may be that (1) over the course of our lives as free agents we generate (in interaction with God) the history that is fulfilled, but (2) we do not, through our actions, bring about the fulfilment of that history. Hence it would be possible to say that while we cannot salvage our lives from their fragmentariness and involvement in evil, they are nonetheless redeemed as a free gift, i.e. they are given a final meaningfulness as the beneficiaries of a divine love that excludes nothing of what we have been.

[20] *Faith and Speculation*, p. 104.

These ordinary examples of 'double agency' do not exhaust the range of possible instances. In particular, the interaction of divine and human agency will not precisely fit either of these patterns, given the radical asymmetry of this relationship. But these ordinary cases of double agency do suggest a *prima facia* conceptual limit upon our talk of multiple agents performing a single action. In these two instances we have no difficulty maintaining the distinct identities of the agents because we ascribe different *basic actions* to them. But the situation becomes much more problematic if we claim that a single basic action is performed by more than one agent. In this case, we seem to have an inconsistent triad in which we cannot simultaneously affirm (1) that Agent $X$ and Agent $Y$ both perform action $A$, (2) that $A$ is a basic action, and (3) that Agent $X$ is distinct from Agent $Y$. Here our paradox of double agency is in danger of reducing to a conceptual incoherence.

On the account I have given, God can be understood to act in our actions in two respects (though my discussion in this essay has been directed only to the second). First, God is the ontologically creative source of our existence and operation as agents. We exist and act as finite free agents only because God holds us in existence at every moment, and so is the sustaining ground of all our actions. This does not entail, however, that God does what we do or that our acts can be ascribed to God. Rather, it is to say that God empowers us to be and to do at all. Second, God shapes the content and direction of our lives by contributing to the orienting conditions from which we act. God's actions within us become ingredient in our actions. In this way, what we do is in part God's achievement; indeed, if God's activity is knitted into the pattern of our personal histories as deeply as I have suggested, then our lives are in a significant way 'authored' by God.[21] Thus it is possible to say, as theists often have, that God may act toward one person through the actions of

---

[21] The analogy here, while obviously limited, is useful. For even a fictional character may come to have an integrity that its author respects and that generates developments in the plot to which the author must adjust in working out his overall intention for the story.

another; God acts *in* us by contributing to the background from which we act, and in so doing God acts *through* us toward the rest of his creation. But what God does and what we do can be differentiated. God does not enact our actions, but God does shape the processes by which we shape ourselves.

Chapter 10

# FAITH AND THE RECOGNITION OF GOD'S ACTIVITY

Diogenes Allen

Philosophers of religion are prone to ignore or to dismiss faith in their assessment of the truth or falsity of Christian theism. They usually consider the existence of the universe, the operations of nature, religious experience, and perhaps the events of history to see what support these provide for theism in general and for Christian theism in particular. The typical philosopher of religion does not find much support for either.

Austin Farrer's theory of 'double agency' and his view of the relation of faith to evidence accounts for the apparent weakness of the support for Christian theism from nature, history, and religious experience. In *Faith and Speculation* Farrer holds that to be or to exist is to act.[1] If God is a creator, then what he makes and preserves are creatures which are active through and through. Their *activities*, which are their very being, are *effects* of divine creative power. But it follows from the hypotheses that God is creator *and* that to be is to act, that we can never specify the line of demarcation between divine creative power and creaturely activity by an empirical examination of creatures because, though we have two agents (divine and creaturely), we have one activity, the empirically observable activity of creatures. Thus when creatures are examined empirically, all that is found is their own activities, and never the divine creative power which

[1] Farrer held this principle in his much earlier work *Finite and Infinite* (Westminster: Dacre Press, 1943) as well, but in that work he still held to an Aristotelian view of substance, albeit a modified one. Only with *Faith and Speculation* (London: A. & C. Black, 1967) did he shed it fully, and wrestle with the implications of 'double agency' and his version of the legitimate demand for empirical confirmation.

allegedly produces those creaturely activities as effects of its creative power. Farrer claims that even though it is theoretically impossible to observe the 'causal joint' at which the divine activity produces thoroughly active creatures it is possible to specify some things in nature, history, and individual lives, which *manifest* divine agency, such as the contingency of the universe, the general direction of biological evolution, and the history of Israel and the Church. But, again according to Farrer, a believer's faith is a necessary condition for identifying these and other phenomena in nature, history, and individual lives as manifestations of divine activity and thus providing evidential support for Christian theism. Unlike the typical philosopher of religion, from the time of *Saving Belief* (1964) Farrer takes the believer's faith to be essential for a proper assessment of the grounds for Christian theism. If Farrer is correct in his views of double agency and of the role of faith, it is not surprising that philosophers of religion usually find the evidence supplied by nature, history, and religious experience for both theism and Christian theism to be insufficient.

I shall show how, according to Farrer, the believer's faith is a necessary condition for the recognition of divine activity, and how on this view the usual relation between faith and evidence is reversed. Rather than examining nature, history and religious experience *first* to see whether they support theism, as is usually the case in the philosophy of religion, one is *first* to have faith in order to be in a position to recognise the manifestation of divine activity in nature, history, and individual lives. If faith is indeed a necessary condition for the proper assessment of the grounds for Christian theism, then philosophers of religion will have to take far more seriously the familiar theological procedure employed by Augustine, Anselm, and Aquinas who examine Christian theism *with faith* as they seek to understand it and to display its grounds.[2]

[2] For some recent examples in which faith is an indispensible ingredient in uncovering the intellectual warrant for Christian theism, see Robert Sokolowski, *The God of Faith and Reason* (Notre Dame: University of Notre Dame Press, 1882), and David Burrell, *Exercises in Religious Understanding* (Notre Dame: University of Notre Dame Press, 1974).

# I

According to Christian teaching, God is a reality with whom human beings can interact consciously. They may hear his Word, respond to his call, seek and find his will. Even a person, who has no knowledge of philosophy and little understanding of Christian doctrine and its philosophical implications, can consciously interact with God. A knowledge of the problems of critical history, much less the capacity to engage in critical historical study, are also not requisites for a person to respond to God.

This means that we are not restricted to a study of nature and history for manifestations of divine agency, but we can become aware of divine agency in our individual lives. In fact, we have better access to divine agency in our own lives than elsewhere because there is a harmony between the divine will and the physical world, and history (apart from that of Israel and the Church) is so complex that the divine intentions for it are largely opaque to us. Human wills, in contrast to physical nature, are wayward. We can become aware of divine agency in the tension between God's will and the waywardness of our own. Since we have been created for fellowship with God our needs and our aspirations give us still another arena for an awareness of God's agency as we find our needs and aspirations met. The place where divine agency is most accessible is thus in human lives and in our own individual lives in particular.

Brian Hebblethwaite is therefore on very solid ground when he claims that the believer's experience of divine agency forms the lynchpin of Farrer's defence of Christian theism.[3] He claims that even though it is 'private', it is part of the evidence for

---

[3] Brian Hebblethwaite, 'The Experimental Verification of Religious Belief in the Theology of Austin Farrer' in *For God and Clarity: New Essays in Honor of Austin Farrer*, (eds. Jeffrey C. Eaton and Ann Loades) (Allison Park, Pennsylvania.: Pickwick Publications, 1983), pp. 163–76.

Christian theism.[4] Hebblethwaite argues that Farrer achieves a balance between the believer's experience, which is private, and 'rational considerations' drawn from nature and history, which are public, to give a sound defence of Christian theism. He quotes with approval one of Farrer's sermons.

> I will tell you how to disbelieve in God. Split the evidence up and keep it apart. Keep the mystery of the world's origin carefully separate from your experience of God and then you can say that the cosmic facts are dumb . . . Keep the believer's experience of God by itself, and away from the general mystery of nature; then you can say that it is so peculiar, so odd a little fact in this vast indifferent universe, that to attach universal importance to it is too absurd . . .
>
> Now I will tell you how to believe . . . Poor [though our own lives may be] and too thin to bear the weight of evidence . . . they do not stand alone. We see clearly enough that what we have an inkling of, the saints apprehend and Christ simply achieves. Ah, but is not this whole phenomenon of life invaded by the divine a mere freak in the vast material solid of the universe? Nonsense, the universe isn't solid at all . . . it is, as a totality, unexplained, and subject to the appointment of creative will in all its infinite detail.[5]

But why are spirituality and 'rational considerations' for theism kept apart? Is it an oversight? No, says Hebblethwaite, it is because 'the believer's reasons' are private and philosophers of religion consider only public evidence. It is for this reason that Hebblethwaite discusses how non-believers might gain access to religious experience. Were some procedure of access specifiable, it would transform what has hitherto been said to be private evidence into public evidence. Hebblethwaite describes H. H. Price's speculations on how a non-believer might gain access to religious experience and why Farrer would disagree

[4] Hebblethwaite does not mean private in the solipsistic sense, in which private means that what is 'in me' is not directly accessible to others. Private means that a believer has experiences *qua* believer which a non-believer *qua* non-believer does not have. For something to be evidence it must be accessible in principle to everyone. Were a procedure specified which could make the believer's kind of experiences available to others, they would not be private even though not everyone has those experiences.

[5] ibid., pp. 175–6.

with Price. Hebblethwaite himself says that there is something to be said for both men's views, but probably more for Farrer's refusal to countenance what amounts to experimenting with deity.

Hebblethwaite specifies no procedure which might make what is private accessible to non-believers and hence make religious experience public in principle. But, he claims, it is not necessary for it to be public after all because Farrer has balanced private and public evidence in such a way as to make a strong case for Christian theism even though experience of divine agency in the believer's life is inaccessible to non-believers. He concludes,

> Farrer's reliance on genuine spirituality is very great in his overall apologetic, but it is not detached from rational considerations . . . At the point where our own experience seems implausibly to have to carry too much weight, attention is shifted to the public evidence of the saints and of Christ himself. Thus the rational arguments, the appeal to Christ and the saints and the appeal to our own experience are held in creative tension . . . I called the moment of experiential verification the lynchpin of Farrer's defence of Christian theism. Clearly, without that lynchpin the whole structure cannot stand, but equally clearly the lynchpin is no use by itself.[6]


## II

There is indeed a lynchpin to be found in Farrer's defence of Christian theism, and it is 'the believer's reasons', but it is improper to describe it as 'private'. Divine agency in an individual's life shares with divine agency in nature and history the scandal of double agency. The causal joint of divine and creaturely agency cannot be specified in an individual's life any more than it can be specified in nature and the events of history. But, as with nature and history, some divine activity is said to be manifest in nature, history, and individual lives. What, according to Farrer, are those manifestations? Farrer does not think that paranormal, weird, or parapsychological phenomena are the

[6] ibid., p. 176.

places to look for divine manifestations.[7] Nor does Farrer seem to have any interest in spectacular religious experiences. He severely criticises the theologians who interpret revelation as a personal encounter, and rather naughtily makes fun of those who face you eye-ball to eye-ball and say, 'He speaks to thee!' Farrer is sure that they are saying something, but still more sure that they are not speaking to his condition. In addition, he confesses to an experiment.

> I thought of myself as set over against deity as one man faces another across a table, except that God was invisible and indefinitely great. And I hoped that he would signify his presence to me by way of colloquy . . . I believe that at the time anything would have satisfied me, but nothing came: no 'other' stood beside me, no shadow of presence fell upon me.[8]

When Farrer describes 'the believer's reasons' in the first chapter of *Faith and Speculation* all that he mentions is that the believer embraces the gospel, and in embracing it finds himself or herself blessed. The blessings the believer experiences are the reasons the believer continues to embrace the gospel. There is no mention of ecstasies, whether one's own or those of the mystics and saints. Farrer is thus not speaking of something uncommon, inaccessible, or accessible only to an elite. The blessings to which he alludes, such as finding oneself judged and accepted, nourished and strengthened, and given guidance are terribly prosaic. Having a broken and ensnarled life healed is more dramatic but still rather common.

The saints and Christ are indeed looked to, but not because of their ecstasies or raptures. Nor are they appealed to because the religious experience of each of us is private and thus does not provide public evidence. Rather, it is because the lives of most believers conform so badly to the will of God that they provide little evidence for Christian theism for anyone, *including* the believer. We can all see that the saints love their neighbours to an impressive extent and that Christ does so paradigmatically. If no

[7] See David Brown's contribution to this volume for a criticism of Farrer on this point.

[8] Austin Farrer. *The Glass of Vision* (Westminster: Dacre Press, 1948), p. 7.

one loved his or her neighbour, it would be utterly implausible to claim that there is grace or a divine agency at work in people and in Christ. But God's sanctifying work in me as an individual is insignificant as evidence, not because it is private, but because it is so paltry. Were it greater in me, then my life would be joined to that of the saints and Christ and play with them the evidential role Farrer assigns to them in that part of a sermon we just quoted.

In Chapter One of *Faith and Speculation*, entitled 'The Believer's Reasons' Farrer does not mention the lives of saints nor the sanctity of Christ's life as evidence of divine agency. The believer's reasons are only the prosaic blessings promised by the gospel. And yet those blessings are said to give sufficient reason to be a believer, even though they are not evidence for the truth of the gospel. This suggests that the manifestations of divine agency in an individual's life are not limited to sanctification. To experience blessing is also a manifestation of divine action.

### III

The problem with the experience of divine blessings as part of the basis for belief is not that individual experiences are private nor that the blessings are too paltry to be evidence for Christian theism, but that blessings are the result of opening one's heart. If one's heart were open, one might experience the blessings of the gospel. Then one might be able to recognise and respond to the evidence provided by the natural world's existence and evolving order for divine agency and by history for his providential benevolence. To speak of the heart may seem to be remote to a philosophical defence of theism and Christian theism, so let us consider what Farrer says about the heart.

In the first chapter of *Saving Belief* we have one of Farrer's most sustained discussions of the relation of faith to evidence. He tells us that the notion of 'God', just like that of 'mother', is a loaded term: it contains built-in attitudes. He compares the situation of an orphan considering the possibility that his or her mother is alive to that of one considering the possibility of God.

> For the child, to think of a possible mother is to experiment in having a mother; to try filial existence. The experiment takes place in the realms of the imagination, but it is real enough to the heart. And similarly to think of a possible God is to experiment in having God. The attitude of creature to Creator, of doomed mortal to immortal saviour, is built into the very idea. The heart goes out to God, even a possible God . . .[9]

Farrer tells us that he does not know whether we should call this attitude 'faith' because it does not represent a commitment, since we realise that the thought of an existing God is a contested notion. Thus he suggests that it should be called 'initial faith', and he also refers to it as the 'faith-attitude'. Although the thought of God is a contested notion, nonetheless it is not like the figure in a dead mythology. Our minds are engaged. But our minds are divided.

> I say, 'There is a God', and a piece of my heart goes with it; I add 'perhaps', my state of being changes; I go on 'But then . . .' and my attitude swings into the opposite. Which of my thoughts, which of my attitudes, is I, or speaks for me? It is notorious that I may be deceived in thinking myself committed in one direction, when I am really committed in another. But so long as I know very well that I am not committed, I do not think of claiming to have faith. Yet the faith-attitude is there, if it is no more than one posture among several which I try by turns. To have faith in the full sense, I do not need to bring it from somewhere else, and apply it to the idea; all I need to do is to let it have its way, and subdue its rivals.[10]

The way to subdue rivals is by considering nature, history, and the gospel story. But one has to 'appreciate' the notion of deity if the evidence for deity in nature, history, and the gospel story is to be appreciated and be convincing. 'Without the readiness of [initial] faith, the evidence of God will not be accepted, or will not convince . . . [Initial] faith is the subjective condition favourable to the reception of the evidence.'[11]

But how does full faith, that is a commitment come about? What is the relation of evidence to it? In the short essay 'On

[9] *Saving Belief*, p. 18.
[10] ibid.
[11] ibid.

Credulity' Farrer describes four kinds of facts or truths.[12] They differ as facts or truths only because our access to them differs. The first domain is that of specialised studies. We limit our inquiry, for example, to the measurable dimensions of physical processes or to the economic aspects of human behaviour. When we do this, we recognise that we are dealing with abstractions; but the abstractions give us access to some facts. In the second domain we deal with actual people and things. There is a difference between interacting with an actual individual person or animal and dealing with the abstractions of our specialisations, which study only aspects of them. All specialisations taken together do not have the same impact on us or yield the same knowledge as interacting with actual individuals. The third and fourth domains, unlike the first two, include values and valuation. We can engage in abstract study and even interact with actual people and things without raising the question of whether the facts revealed are to be approved or deplored, or whether a person is, let us say, sincere or perverse. The domain of value is treated in part by a specialisation: ethics. Just as in the first domain, here too we think abstractly. But by observing the limitations of abstract thinking we have access to various truths about such things as the nature of obligation and moral rules, or at least we hope to. The fourth area is religion. As in ethics, we are concerned with values and valuation, but not abstractly. We deal with the entire person interacting with real beings. If we are willing to consider Christianity we may find that

> part of our minds [yields to] the inexorable truth that we are rebellious creatures under the eye of our Creator, and that our Creator has come upon us in Christ. Credulity, here, is the crime of pretending to believe that there is any way out of this situation but one – to reconcile ourselves to the truth of our nature, which demands our submission to the God who made us.[13]

---

[12] 'Prologue: On Credulity', *Interpretation and Belief* (ed. Charles Conti) (London: S.P.C.K., 1976), p. 2. This essay was first published in 1947.
[13] ibid., p. 5.

Of this domain Farrer writes,

> Now when the New Testament writers said that in Christ they
> met the truth, they meant that in him they recognised what was
> demanding admittance through this door [the fourth domain]. It
> is of no use, of course, for Christians to pretend that on this
> ground everybody is bound to agree with them straight away, but
> anyhow on this ground their position is immensely strong and
> need fear no antagonist. There is no constraint, no embarrassment
> here; here we can take on all comers.[14]

Farrer is here describing the effects on the individual of
encountering Christ or, if you prefer, of encountering the gospel.
It does not seem to me that there is any philosophical problem of
privacy here. We are not here troubled with what it takes to
produce a religious experience of the sort that is an esctasy, nor
any other sort of extraordinary experience, nor are we concerned
with the manifestations of sanctity which might help warrant talk
of divine agency in individual lives. There is nothing either
private or esoteric here. The problem is whether an individual
person is willing to expose himself or herself to a self-
examination in the light of what is said about Christ.

It is very easy to avoid such self-examination. All that a person
needs to say is 'Why should I examine myself in this light?' He or
she thereby refuses to grant admittance to the general category of
valuation because an answer is demanded in terms of only those
truths accessible through the first, the second, or at most, the
third domain. It is thus very easy to avoid the impact of Christ
on oneself.[15] On the other hand, it is not difficult to specify a
procedure that puts one in a position to be exposed to the effects
of divine agency on one's life. Anyone can open his or her heart,
just as anyone can close it.

What is meant by 'heart'? We sometimes use the word to refer

[14] Christ is here not considered in terms of the holiness of his life, as was done
earlier in talking about his sanctity and that of the saints as a necessary condition
for the plausibility of the claim that there is divine grace at work in some people.

[15] This is just what J. L. Mackie has done in his consideration of every alleged
rational ground for the truth of theism. See especially chapter 1 of his *The Miracle
of Theism* (Oxford: Clarendon Press, 1982), in which 'rationality' is so narrowly
construed as to exclude all the considerations Farrer had brought to bear on the
recognition of the grounds for Christian theism.

to being sensitive to another person's plight. 'Have a heart!' we say when we mean, 'Be merciful!' Another use of the word is found in Jesus' remark, 'Where your heart is, there is your treasure.' This use refers to what we value and seek to possess because of the good it will do and be for us. It is related to the human hunger or quest for life. The intellect is involved in this quest, but what is at stake is our own person: what we are, what we ought to be, what we may become, what we may hope for. It is this use of the term 'heart' that I am employing. To open the heart is to allow what is in the domain of value, and in particular self-evaluation, to affect one. One with an open heart may find in Christ and in the promises of God the good that we need and seek. But one without an open heart shall not.

Frequently we use the intellect to solve problems or to seek knowledge without the questions of the heart arising. We quite properly exclude considerations of the heart when we deal with questions of the properties of a physical process, or the economic factors in currency exchange rates (truths of type 1). It is even quite proper to restrain, though not utterly to exclude, questions of the heart when we consider the nature of obligation or the role of moral rules (truths of type 3). When we interact with people or things (truths of type 2), we can and do close our hearts. Sometimes this is improper. Finally, we can also quite easily avoid Christ's impact on us as judge and redeemer by keeping in check the human search for what is valuable and what gives life significance.

Disbelief then, according to Farrer, is not caused merely when we keep what we can find from investigation of nature and history apart from what we experience in religion. Prior to that is the question of whether our hearts are open or closed to religious matters. The mystery of the world's origin is kept separate from all else because some people have no relevant experience to connect it to. And without a heart that is open 'the cosmic facts are dumb,' as Farrer puts it. What is crucial is *what we seek with*. This has priority over *where we look*, whether to nature, history, or to Christ. Without an open heart nature and history are dumb, and Christ is not given admittance.

## IV

Assuming that we have opened our hearts, why should we look at nature, history, and our own lives for manifestations of divine agency? In the essay 'On Credulity', Farrer points out that we do not want to be credulous. He tells us that in the special sciences we are not to believe what evidence does not warrant; otherwise we are credulous. But when one exposes oneself to evaluation by Christ, credulity is the pretence of believing that one's life has validity.

> Unless our minds in fact function in these two ways: unless we sometimes see God as truth, and evasion of him as credulity, at other times the proved facts of the special sciences as truth, and the outrunning of them as credulity – unless this is so, we are not confronted with the specifically religious problem of truth.[16]

It is because our minds function in *two* ways that a believer investigates philosophical questions that are relevant to Christian claims and also considers historical questions, since 'we must have no bogus history'.[17] But the investigation is done in a particular way. Farrer points out that many historians limit their search to truths of the first and second type (specialised and without the dimension of value). Such people, he says, are not going to see truths of the fourth type breaking out at them through the facade of history because they have discounted them from the start.

> But the historian whose mind is open to the fourth type of truth, and who has some awareness of the abyss of divine being which underlies his own existence, may meet a voice and visitant out of that abyss, when he weighs the strange history of the year 30 as it is mirrored in the witness of those who most intimately responded to it.[18]

In less dramatic language, a person who has exposed him or herself to valuation by Christ, and who engages in intellectual

[16] ibid., p. 2.
[17] ibid., p. 6.
[18] ibid.

work in philosophy or history with a concern for Christian truth is a person *with* faith seeking understanding.

In the opening pages of *Faith and Speculation* Farrer says that he has dropped all pretence to a neutral approach, because neutrality is a fiction. In this work, as one who has faith, he is seeking to relate religious truths to which he is committed to truths in other domains. That is indeed a form of gaining confirmation because it shows how God is related to our understanding of nature, history, and human personality. But it is not to be understood as the search for evidence which will move one from unbelief to belief. Nor is it to be understood as seeking for something in nature and history which will tip the balance in favour of Christian theism, because what is precious to an individual is merely private. There is indeed a difference between the effects of divine agency in the lives of individuals and divine agency in nature and history, as I mentioned very early in this paper. But the difference is not to be characterised as that between what is private and what is public.

Full faith or commitment, then, does not imply that there is no intellectual work to be done. Quite the contrary. Initial faith becomes full faith only 'by subduing its rivals'. And we continue to look for manifestations of divine agency because of our desire to be honest, and *because* of our response to Christ. Because we have confidence in the truth of the gospel, we *expect* to find manifestations of divine agency in nature, history, and in people in all times and places.

It is not at all clear how much of divine agency must be manifest in nature and history for us to continue to have faith. Farrer clearly says in *Faith and Speculation* that nature must bear at least some marks of divine agency.[19] This contrasts with a position such as Bultmann's, in which the natural world is exactly the same whether there is a God or not. But Farrer does not tell us how much of the divine agency we must be able to detect for Christian theism to be true or plausible. Farrer himself did not speculate what the precise results of the enquiries of

---

[19] ibid., p. 13.

reason or philosophy must be for faith to be sustained. That perhaps would have been to engage in idle speculation for one whose openness of heart and strength of mind uncovered so much of the manifestations of divine activity.

Chapter 11

# DIVINE ACTION AND HUMAN LIBERATION

*Jeffrey Eaton*

One of the principal sources, if not the principal source, of theological vitality today is to be found in the several movements generally designated as 'liberation theology'. Although this term is most commonly associated with the work of Latin American theologians such as Gutierrez, Bonino, Segundo and Boff, it has other expressions as well. Liberation themes are a prominent feature of Asian and African theology, and in North America, Black theology and Feminist theology have developed the liberationist perspective in their own distinctive ways. These theologies are differentiated by the historical conditions of oppression out of which they emerge, but what is common to them all is the identification of the Christian gospel as essentially a word of freedom and a challenge to every idolatry by which human creatures oppress other human creatures. Each, in its own way, is a theology from below, a theological response from the point of view of persons who have been marginalised, left by the wayside by those who comprise the dominant class in society, whether 'class' be interpreted in terms of economics, race or gender.

One of the most troubling things about liberation theology for many who have been technically trained in academic theology is its adherence to Marx's eleventh thesis on Feuerbach, according to which the first priority is not to understand the world, but to change it. Good theology, on this telling, is a critical response to what is going on in the world in which we live, reflection on praxis. Such theology is theoretical only to the extent that theory

informs action. Its goal is not to probe the universal structure of
being, nor is it an apologetics to make God credible. Rather it is
an attempt to engender, 'active participation to liberate human
beings from all that dehumanises them and prevents them from
living according to the will of God'.[1]

The liberation theologies have been subjected to a variety of
critiques, many of which are little more than reactionary
dismissals on narrow ideological grounds, but some of which
raise substantive issues that are worthy of consideration by those
who hold the liberationist point of view.[2] One of the most crucial
questions has to do with the conception of God which these
theologies invoke. Is it the conception of God enshrined in
classical theism? Is it the neo-classical conception advanced by
process theology? Or is it actually the abandonment of God in
favour of political ideology? Or to put this question in the
starkest possible terms, does the God of the liberation theologies
enjoy personal agency?

Although liberation theologians are generally and understand-
ably suspicious of metaphysical speculation as a luxurious
diversion of energy from the immediately pressing theological
concern for liberation, or worse, as a means of sanctioning and
extending the historic alliance between Christianity and the
ruling classes in society, the questions which provoke such
speculation are nevertheless real questions and must be addressed.
It is understandable that liberation theologies, constructed from
below, from the perspective of non-persons, would show a
reluctance to spend time inquiring into the perfect personhood of
God, or to give much attention to the question of divine agency,
when that notion has been so effectively used to inhibit the
exercise of human agency for the realisation of liberation from
the social structures which crush the personhood of the
oppressed. It is entirely understandable that this be the case, and
yet, if the liberation theologies are actually theology and not

---

[1] G. Gutierrez, *A Theology of Liberation* (Maryknoll, New York: Orbis
Books, 1973; London: S.C.M. Press, 1974), p. 308.

[2] A categorisation and discussion of these several critiques may be found in
R. M. Brown's *Theology in a New Key* (Philadelphia: Westminster Press, 1978).

merely ideology, the issue of God's agency cannot be avoided. If God is not an agent engaged in the making of a world, then God is simply a metaphor for the way the one who uses that metaphor would like the world to go. Agency is the only image in which the otherness of God can be intelligibly maintained. If this image is given up, and with it the possibility of interaction with God's will, theology has become little more than 'sentimental atheism'.[3]

Take the case, for instance, of the biblical story of the Exodus, a story of crucial significance for all the liberation theologies. Is the passage from bondage to freedom in some way the result of God's activity on behalf of the oppressed, as surely the redactors of that story believed it to be, or is the story essentially a programmatic device in which God's name is invoked as a way of saying that justice will ultimately prevail? If it is the former, then some sense must be made of the way in which God's activity takes effect in the liberation of the oppressed. If it is the latter, it is difficult to know how the 'God of the oppressed' is anything other than the rationalisation of self-interest, which is to say, an ideological construction. But then what is the authority of this construction over rival ideologies. The fact that the story appears in the Bible is of small significance if the Bible is not in some measure the expression of God's will, but this brings us back again to the problem of conceiving of divine agency. The liberationist, like every critical theologian, is wary of mythic images and is concerned to avoid the confusion of the mask with the face in the use of those images, to avoid 'direct parabolic inference'[4] according to which divine agency is *nothing but* a simplistic and very likely alienating anthropomorphism. At the same time, however, substance must be given to the image of divine agency or else theology will dissolve completely into philosophical anthropology, at which point all motive for speaking of God will have been lost.

It is my intention to argue that this dissolution need not occur and that there is a way of conceiving God's activity which detracts neither from the divine initiative nor from the responsi-

---

[3] Austin Farrer, *Faith and Speculation* (London: A. & C. Black, 1967), p. 45.
[4] ibid., p. 51.

bility of human beings for their own destiny, or, to put this another way, which allows for the reconciliation of finite and infinite agency. Sharing as I do with liberation theologians the belief that liberation is the vocation of one who wishes to become a *co-operator Dei*, I shall attempt to show that far from requiring a retreat from belief in the God of theism, the liberation theologies actually depend upon the intelligibility of God's agency for their theological integrity. Indeed, it is only if God is agent that theology has a God worth having.

I

The liberation theologies fall into the category of what is today called constructive theology. Theological construction is required as a consequence of the breakdown of the doctrinal edifice of classical theology, which enshrined a sacred dimension distinct from the world of secular concerns. In the words of one liberation theologian: 'We have entered the era of the "demise of heaven" and the death of the "spiritual", and of the God who was defined in terms of one side of these dualisms. We are entering an era wherein man can affirm his sense of having deeper roots and higher horizons than those of the immediate *status quo* only by pouring back the traditional polarities into dynamic unities; dynamic unities between the historical and the transcendent; the spiritual and the somatic; the holy and the worldly.'[5] Such dualisms are viewed as sources of human alienation, as impediments to the realisation of full humanity for those caught in them.

That these dualisms represent a great deal of misunderstanding and misery cannot in good faith be gainsaid. Surely Marx was correct in his criticism of the religion which stupified its adherents to conditions in this world in the interest of securing their standing in the next, which abandoned historical exigencies for the sake of eternal hopes. Feminist criticism has shown beyond reasonable doubt the way in which the psycho-somatic

---

[5] Rosemary Ruether, *Liberation Theology* (New York: Paulist Press, 1972), p. 7.

dualism has been used to subordinate women, construed as the bodily principle in human existence, to men, as the spiritual-intellectual principle. And Latin American liberation theology has made a powerful case for an 'orthopraxis', according to which Christian spirituality is expressed, not in separating oneself from the world of human struggle, but in liberating activity in solidarity with the oppressed. The Church is not, accordingly, the bastion of orthodoxy, but the servant of the poor. One of the principle undertakings of the liberation theologies has been the attempt to move Christian faith beyond these dualisms, to a point where the reconciliation of finite and infinite can be envisioned.

When Austin Farrer undertook to discover a means of reconciling finite and infinite in the 1940s, he entertained no such programme as has been advanced by the liberationists. His point of departure was an analysis of the metaphysics of theism and in particular the question of what it is that constitutes a substance. The argument in Farrer's *Finite and Infinite* was in many respects the sort of arcane metaphysical discussion which many liberationists view as self-indulgent abstraction, a contribution to the believer's dialogue with non-believers perhaps, but of no significance to the non-person to whom the liberationist's work is addressed.

Farrer himself was not pleased with the outcome of *Finite and Infinite*, characterising it in later years as a perverse compromise between formalism and voluntarism. The weight of the argument in that book was mostly against a formalist conclusion in which the motive for theistic belief lies in the idea of sheer and absolute Being to which all beings are approximations to one degree or another. And yet, the formalist conclusion was drawn in the face of analysis that pointed in a very different direction. This was the 'perversity' of Farrer's early book, a perversity which liberationists would claim is characteristic of theology which is done 'from above'.

In *Finite and Infinite* Farrer drew together two kinds of argument in order to exhibit the relation of finite and infinite and thus to make a case for theistic belief. One set of arguments was derived from a distinction in finite nature in general and was called usiological; the other set was taken from a distinction in human being specifically, and called anthropological. The former moved along an external hierarchy of being in which God is the supreme existence; the latter worked from an interior hierarchy which finds expression in human aspiring. Both forms of argument were essential, according to Farrer. One could begin either with the usiological forms or the anthropological forms in order to arrive at a conception of God's creative activity. The usiological arguments follow the order of being, starting from a consideration of divine existence to which content is given from some mode of finite existence. The anthropological arguments begin from the modality of human existence and proceed along the order of knowing to the God who is the archetype of human existence. Both sets of arguments begin from a material division, and from this generate analogies along which the mind can move from the finite to the infinite plane, to the 'cosmological intuition' in which one apprehends the form of existent perfection which is God.

The odd thing about this conclusion was that the analysis of substance on which it was based was an analysis of agency, of which one's own voluntary activity is the most obvious instance. One might reasonably have expected a less abstract conclusion from an analysis of something so full-blooded as personal activity. But the argument went awry, departed from this initial insight and made of divine agency a formal operation which was not so much activity as accomplishment, leading Farrer to reformulate the traditional metaphysics of being-becoming in which the act of God is the radiation of an absolute essence. In this way, activity was abandoned for a causality of essence which was ahistorical and static, and which finally bore no relation whatsoever to the activity of finite agency which had prompted Farrer's prodigious exercise in rational theology. This had been the pattern of philosophical theology since it had adapted Aristotle to its purposes, and in *Finite and Infinite* Farrer showed himself to be well within this venerable tradition of theologising. The promise of that book for liberating rational theology from the metaphysical prison in which it had languished for so long was not kept. And until this liberation took place, theology itself would not be liberating.

Farrer recognised the difficulty in *Finite and Infinite* and, in one way or another, spent the rest of his life attempting to purge the 'Aristotelian leaven', as he called it, from his thought, which is to say, to extricate theology from metaphysical formalism and fulfil the promise of the analysis of activity that was carried out in his early book. In the last book he published, *Faith and Speculation*, he gave concerted effort to the problem, and there achieved an exposition of the metaphysics of theism that was more consistent with his earlier analysis of activity. The breakthrough in his thinking is, in many respects, expressed in the title of that book.

In *Faith and Speculation* he educed the 'voluntarist' account of Deity which he could not bring himself to state in his earlier book. 'Voluntarist' here does not mean fideism, a sheer willingness to believe regardless of evidence or coherence. Rather, the work identifies the sense in which theistic reflection is at every stage a reflection on will-activity, which begins in the splintered image of agency, which finds expression in our own activity, and proceeds analogically to the perfection of that image in the One who is all that One wills to be and who wills to be all that that One is.[6] One arrives at this conception through a dialectic of faith and speculation in which the life of faith is in every way prior to theological reflection. Farrer summed up his position in this way:

> ' "Unconditioned Will" is the historical core of practical theism and though irreducibly analogical, expresses the ideal terminus of human aspiration. *What gives it actuality is a life lived in relation to it; the very form of such a life being belief in God, in the same sense as that in which belief in one's neighbours is the form of intercourse with them.*'[7]

---

[6] *Faith and Speculation*, p. 118.
[7] ibid., p. 174, emphasis added.

The speculation which rises out of the life of faith is not metaphysical abstraction, but rather is an attempt to think through the life of faith in the conviction that, to paraphrase Kant, theological reflection without commitment is empty, as commitment without theological reflection is blind. The voluntarist response evinces the dialectical form which liberationists call praxis, the continuous interchange between action and reflection in which voluntary acceptance of the Creative Will of God comes in the course of one's engagement with that Will. In other words, knowledge of the God who is Sovereign Will is itself the exercise of will-activity, an interaction of agents, finite and infinite, by which God makes the world make itself, a state of affairs which Farrer called 'the paradox of double-agency'. The voluntarist account rests upon this paradox, according to which God wills into being creatures which are active in themselves. Farrer's analysis of finite substance had led him to the conclusion that activity is existence and that each kind of existent as well as each particular existent is what it is because of its distinctive pattern of activity. This conclusion, which is entirely respectable in light of the discoveries of modern physics, put Farrer in position to free his theology from the last vestiges of the Aristotelian formalism which assigned to creaturely existence the goal of becoming a true instance of its species, which set the ends of creaturely becoming in the forms of what the creature truly is, would the creature but realise it. The Christianisation of Aristotelian causal theory had afforded a means of accommodating creaturely freedom to the purposes of divine providence.

The paradox of double-agency was conceived by Farrer in order to preserve, on the one hand, the full integrity of creaturely activity, and, on the other hand, to do justice to the particular providence of God; to reconcile the act of finite and infinite agents without resorting to the ploy of Aristotelian causal theory. In advancing that paradox Farrer argued that the immediate will of God is for each created energy to be itself, to act in the manner which is the substance of that energy's existence. In so doing, the purpose of God is the realisation of a world of self-acting parts.[8] The special dignity of human creatures is that they can freely co-operate with the divine will for the purpose of this realisation or choose to oppose that will and serve other ends. In other words, the agency of God is such as to work through created agents, and to do so without in any way coercing or undermining creaturely activity. God's action is encountered in one's own action, in the embrace of the Divine Will as one's own will. One need not, of course, acknowledge the action of God in one's own activity. One can quickly dissolve the paradox of double-agency with a flat denial of divine effect, but to do so is to accept without demur the metaphysical insufficiency of finite agency. 'The brute-fact character of things can be swallowed; it can scarcely be disputed. To swallow it is much the same thing as to denounce for fantastic or vacuous that ultimate explanation, or First Causality, to which the life of belief gives substance and application.'[9] There is no contradiction in such a position, but there is nothing like completeness in it either. Nevertheless, unless a person is concerned with the Will of God as it affects him or her, it must be admitted that the contingency of finite agents will not be sufficient reason to accept the paradox of two agents for one act. The causal nexus between the activity of finite agents and the activity of God cannot be specified. This is only as one would expect if finite agents are genuinely free, but this will be a stumbling block to those who demand naturalistic definition of supernatural act. Be that as it may, the voluntary relation of the human and the divine is analogically intelligible and practically verifiable in the association of wills, finite and infinite.

### III

Farrer sought in his theology of will to be rid of every form of *apriorism*, philosophical and theological. His approach to the question of the relation of finite and infinite act was an attempt to be faithful to the empirical principle that we can have, 'no

---

[8] ibid., p. 110. See also: *A Science of God?*, *Saving Belief*, and *Love Almighty and Ills Unlimited*.

[9] ibid., p. 130.

thought about any reality about which we can do nothing but think'.[10] Farrer did not question that the initiative in this interaction lay with God, but he was just as positive that the human response to this initiative must be an active response, that human passivity can know nothing of divine activity, nor of anything else for that matter, inasmuch as real knowledge is itself interaction. But then what is it that one can do to encounter the action of God? Or to put this somewhat differently, what is it that God is doing that we may align our wills with the divine will? The great virtue of Farrer's work is in its statement and clarification of these questions. Less satisfying, however, is his proposal of what it is one ought to do to enter into the purposes of God.

For the most part, Farrer gave the conventional answers of a conventional Christian piety when he made his suggestions about where the Christian was to engage the action of God. The metaphysics he developed to conceive the possibility of inter-action with the divine was innovative and evocative, a challenge to Christian consciousness and conscience; the application he made of that metaphysics was generally individualistic and traditionally pastoral. There are occasional hints in his work that the Christian has a responsibility to act to transform unjust social structures, as well as repent of individual acts of injustice or attitudes of complacency. But these are rare. The vocation he practiced was that of a Christian apologist, and he mostly refrained from making topical application of his conclusions. He was, after all, functioning in a particular historical situation out of a particular historical experience, a situation and experience that was far removed from the struggles of theologians living and working in the midst of revolutionary situations. And yet Farrer's theology of will is applicable to the liberationists' struggles; it makes possible a conception of the relation of finite and infinite activity in those struggles that is more than rhetorical, and at the same time resists the tendency toward alienating theological abstraction of the sort that has made

[10] ibid., p. 22.

theistic metaphysics suspect among many liberationists. Moreover, the liberationist hermeneutic of engagement gives a practical expression to Farrer's theology of will that is not merely privatistic or parochial.

One of the most familiar charges against the liberation theologies is that they are hardly theological at all, that they are rather a tangle of ideological commitments which depend upon a specious reading of the scriptures and tradition(s) of Christianity for whatever authority they have. Or to put this somewhat differently, it is charged that the liberation theologies concentrate on political liberation to the virtual exclusion of the spiritual salvation wrought by God in Christ, which liberates humankind from the grip of sin and so reconciles the creation to its Creator. If such charges are to be countered it will have to be shown not only that the Christian faith allows of being read in terms of the theme of liberation, but that it needs to be read from this vantage point to do full justice to the God whose will it is claimed is for the liberation of the whole creation, whose Word is freedom. In short, the liberation theologies must be concerned with the nature of God, or more properly, the nature of God's activity. Farrer devoted much of his energy to this topic, and his labours are not without significance for the theological constructions of the liberationists. The following three points are of particular interest in this regard.

First, as has already been suggested, Farrer demolished the notion of passive substance. His ontological analysis led him to an activist conclusion which he compromised in his early work, but which he later embraced. This conclusion, which he characterised in the slogan, *esse est operari*, was confirmed wherever one looked, whether in the sub-atomic world of interacting energies, or in the world of persons whose identities are constituted by the interactions which they undergo and effect with the other activity-systems which comprise their world of experience. It is impossible, Farrer argued, to conceive of any entity whatsoever apart from a consideration of its interactions with other entities, and further, that no conception of God is possible other than as Agent, that to think about God is to think about an action with which our own activity, 'must be presumed to engage'.[11] The nature of God is Unconditioned Will, the perfect freedom of One who is all that One wills to be and who wills to be all that that One is. The model of liberation is to be found in the creative activity of God, according to which the creature is made to make itself: the paradox of double-agency. The divine will is that the creatures of that will act freely, and in the case of God's personal creatures, that they act in voluntary co-operation with the creative purposes of God. The force of Farrer's analysis was to show that such a conception was justifiable in terms of the facts of modern physics and our experience as essentially social selves.

Second, Farrer offered two palliatives of the paradox of double-agency, both of which are crucial for conceiving the divine nature. The first is logical. One had no choice in attempting to think about the relation of finite and infinite but to resort to analogy. Nothing that can be said about the action of God can possibly be adequate description. The only thing that can properly be said of God is that God is unique, and from this it follows that all other assertions about God must be analogical, expressed in images drawn from our own experience and stretched to infinity. Not all analogies, however, are equally good, and the shift Farrer makes from a formalist conception of Deity to a voluntarist conception is precisely a shift in analogies, based on the conclusion that the latter does greater justice to our experience of God's otherness. The analogy of divine agency allows one to conceive of God; the realisation that this conception is analogical prevents the idolatrous fixation on the image.

For example, the image of God as father was intended to give a certain character to divine activity, say, the character of providential care for the creatures God has made and is making.

[11] ibid., p. 36.

The image is a convention developed under the values of patriarchal culture, values which are today being challenged by feminist theologians for their role in the subordination of women to men, challenged as limiting God's action in the world to that which is allowed under the conditions of patriarchy. The agency of God is analogically conceivable, but this analogical conception is always and only analogical, and hence must not be used in such a way as to dissolve the paradox of double-agency. To do so results in idolatry, the sin which most liberation theologians contend is at the root of human oppression.

The second palliative is practical. God is known by interacting with God, and interaction which is inseparable from the exercise of one's moral responsibility for and with one's neighbours. Faith is the condition of this interaction inasmuch as God's existence is assumed in relating one's life to the good which is (believed to be) God's purpose. The substance of this assumption is the transforming action of faith in which one finds oneself engaged with the creative purposes of God. 'We can, in the only possible way, experience the active relation of a created energy to the Creator's action by embracing the divine will.'[12] Reflective faith, then, is a kind of praxis to which the faithful commits himself or herself. Its object is not the demonstration of first principles for subsequent adoption, but commitment to life in God, the interaction of agencies, creaturely and divine.

The contribution of the liberation theologies to the theological enterprise is their identification of Christian faith as *liberating* praxis and specifically as liberating praxis to transform the conditions of poverty and oppression which crush the image of God in the oppressed and the oppressor alike. The liberation theologies articulate a hermeneutical position from which to understand and respond to the creative activity of God in the world. They indicate points of engagement where the divine will for the creatures of that will seems to be most clear, insofar as they indicate where in the world the exercise of free creature-

[12] ibid., p. 66.

hood is being frustrated by human perversity.[13]

But of course the actual causal nexus between finite and infinite activity can never be definitively specified, and this fact brings us to our third point regarding the significance of Farrer's work for the theologies of liberation. The elusiveness of the causal nexus is the very heart of the paradox of double-agency. If the joint between finite and infinite activity could be pin-pointed, the paradox of double-agency would be dissolved. Such specificity would either reduce supernatural creativity to natural creativity, or obliterate free creaturehood in the omnipotent activity of God. In either case something would be eliminated which is necessary for a full account of the observed and experienced activity of finite agents. The paradox of double-agency is essential if there is to be real co-operation of finite and infinite agents in the making of the world.

An earlier age avoided this paradox by emphasising the absolute omnipotence of God in all things to the exclusion of human responsibility for anything at all. In the more secular climate of the contemporary world, the tendency has been to relegate the divine activity to the status of contextual influence in order to make room for full human freedom. Much of what is called 'liberation theology' has been subject to this tendency and accordingly, has seemed to be no theology at all. It is under-standable that compensation be sought for the theological sins of the past, but the exclusion of the independent activity of God from consideration would seem to be an over-compensation which theology can scarcely afford.

The paradox of double-agency makes possible a third position between the theological absolutism that leaves nothing for the creature to do and the promethean secularism which makes the action of God superfluous to human undertakings. How God's

[13] The essence of the liberating praxis of Christian faith is powerfully expressed by Gutierrez in a paraphrase of Pascal: 'All the political theologies, the theologies of hope, of revolution, and of liberation, are not worth one act of genuine solidarity with exploited social classes. They are not worth one act of faith, love, and hope, committed – in one way or another – in active participation to liberate (persons) from everything that dehumanises (them) and prevents (them) from living according to the will of (God). A Theology of Liberation, p. 308.

action takes effect is, to be sure, a mystery which cannot be approached without the admission of paradox. But this admission does nothing to detract from the reality of God's action for those who in faith have made the divine will a matter of practical concern. What one takes the divine will to be is conditioned by the situation in which one finds oneself and what in that situation one finds revealing of the divine intention. The theologies of liberation have emerged out of situations of human oppression and have interpreted the Christian message in terms of the struggle for human dignity against forces in the world which would deny that dignity to some. In this way, the liberation theologies claim to make explicit the implicit will of God. Whether or not this interpretation of the Christian message is correct, it depends for its intelligibility upon the action of the divine will in the lives of free creatures; i.e., it depends upon the reconciliation of finite and infinite activity. It was for the purpose of this reconciliation that Farrer proposed the paradox of double-agency.

## IV

One of the sophistications of modern theology is that theological inquiry can be carried on independent of a commitment to the God of theism. This view owes as much to Barth as it does to Hegel. The former was an apriorist who dogmatically assumed the God of theism and eschewed all philosophical inquiry into the matter. The theologian's business was to interpret divine revelation, leaving aside the question of how one knows that a moment of (supposed) enlightenment is of God, or even that God is such a One as to make revelations. The result of Barth's influence was that the concern for the object of faith increasingly gave way to concern for the function of faith in illuminating the boundaries of human existence. Theology could discuss these transcending boundaries at great length without ever having to take up the issue of whether or not it was the God of theism who was met at the border. The focus of theology became, as a result, more and more anthropocentric, a quest for human meaning in response to the anomie of modern existence.

Hegel, the other inspiration for modern theologising, interpreted transcendence in historical terms. The fulfilment of the
human spirit lay in the future realisation of the Absolute Spirit,
after the dialectics of history had worked themselves out. The
Absolute was non-personal, since it was the surpassing of every
category, including the personal. Theistic religion was a myth-
ologised rendering of Absolute Spirit, a stage in the progress
toward the realisation which the Hegelian system had at last
brought to light. Theology, under the influence of Hegel, tends
to construe transcendence horizontally, which is to say, theology
becomes eschatology; the reality of God is not above us but
rather before us, in the future which even now is weighing on the
present as an unborn child weighs upon its mother's womb. The
matter of divine agency is by-passed by a metaphysical formalism which is very different from the formalism of Greek
metaphysics, but which is no less formalistic for this difference.

These two strands of reflection come together in process
theology, which, as Farrer has charged, is a compromise between
positivism and metaphysics.[14] This compromise has a certain
attractiveness for liberation theologians in search of a metaphysical base for their theologies, offering as it does a theological
immanentism which, it is claimed, is not simply immanentist. It
might be supposed that the panentheist Fellow-Sufferer of
process theology would make possible the reconciliation of finite
and infinite in such a way as to avoid the hierarchical image of
God above and outside the world, an image which has done so
much to alienate humankind from the natural order in which it
subsists, and from itself as responsible for the making of a world
where love is more possible. It has attraction for feminist
theologians in the possibilities it presents for a theological
perspective that is both somatic and ecological and which resists

[14] *Reflective Faith*, ed. C. Conti (London S.P.C.K., 1972), p. 187. Farrer's
characteristion of process theology referred to a secularist positivism, according
to which whatever is of God is, 'exhaustively displayed in finite occurrences'. But
the characterisation is also applicable to the positivism of the fideist who, for
example, is concerned only with the coherence and applicability of a (supposed)
revelation, and who resists speculation about the intelligibility of such a
revealing; i.e. about the possibility of a relation of finite and infinite.

the tendency of classical theism to portray God in male-dominant images. It has attraction for Black and Latin American liberation theologies in its identification of the divine with the passion of the oppressed. God is the unsurpassable relativity whose fulfilment awaits the fulfilment of historical process, when humankind is at last emancipated and redeemed, when finally the duality of oppression/oppressed is overcome in a universal humanity. Indeed, the duality of finite and infinite will be overcome, because it is already overcome in the God who is the divine relativity.

The temptation of process metaphysics for the liberation theologies is plain enough. And it is a temptation to be resisted. Process theology is, in its own way, as formalistic as the classical theological absolutism it proposes to replace. The abstraction of the Scholastics in the cause of transcendence is mirrored in the abstraction of process theology in the cause of immanence. The God of remotion is exchanged for a principle of concretion, an *elan vital* bubbling up to animate the world, and there is as good reason for liberation theologians to reject the latter as the former. Neither will provide an image of God as One with whom finite agents have something to do. Both abandon the essential theistic idea of God as analogous to the living act which we ourselves are. This abandonment is disastrous from the liberationist point of view in which primacy is given to action in solidarity with the oppressed. If God is not an agent whose will for the liberation of God's human creatures can be engaged, then there is finally nothing to distinguish the theological from the ideological except that the former resorts to telling tales of the gods in order to motivate human commitment.

It is absolutely crucial that the liberation theologies be able to make a case for the agency of God. They should be able to give an account of the divine act with which and in which they propose to be engaged, an account which is at least as intelligible as the social analysis they bring to bear on the structures of oppression in the world. If theology is, as Gutierrez says, the 'second act', the effort to understand what it is that faith believes, then one of the things it must endeavour to understand is what it

means to say that God empowers people to work for a justice
that is God's justice. For this, there will have to be a theological
re-commitment to the God of theism on the part of liberation
theologians. Theology cannot restrict itself to performing critical
reflection on praxis and remain theology, even if that praxis is
identified in the language of the Christian faith. It cannot be
assumed, to paraphrase the scholasticism, that because God acts
on behalf of the oppressed that it is possible for God so to act;
i.e., that God is an agent at all. It may be entirely appropriate for
the liberation theologian, as a matter of procedure, to consider
first the matter of human oppression, but the procedural order
must not be allowed to foreclose upon the consideration of the
metaphysics of his or her theology, and specifically, on the
questions surrounding the theistic assertion of creative omnipotence.

The power of the witness of the liberation theologies cannot be
gainsaid. It is a witness that provokes a reassessment of Christian
commitment at every level and not least of all in the way
Christians conceive God. It is difficult to imagine that so activist
a witness could construe God in terms that are not activist, could
be satisfied with the conception of God that is less than that of
perfect agency, an agent who, for freedom, creates significantly
free creatures. But how express this conception without undermining the creaturely activity which is the point of departure for
the liberationists' theological reflection? How, in other words,
understand the relation of the human struggle for the liberation
of the oppressed to the action of God?

Years before the call for human liberation became theologically articulate Austin Farrer pondered the question of how one
might properly think about God in light of the cognitive
challenges to theism that emerged out of the Enlightenment. The
result was a theology of will in which creative and created act
were related in the paradox of double-agency. Speaking of this
paradox, Farrer said,

> 'But if we are told that our most free acts are those most purely
> and pelucidly expressive of a will sovereign over all, the paradox
> cannot dismay us; it cannot deny the effect of freedom which it

supposes and upon which it offers a theological comment. Still less shall we be dismayed to be reminded that the grace active in the human will so operates as to make us dependent upon one another, as well for the supernatural gifts of God, as for natural charities and blessings.'[15]

The liberation theologies teach us the meaning and implications of our dependence on one another in the struggle against human oppression; Farrer's work enables us to see that it is God's creative activity with which we have to do when we are engaged in the cause of liberating love.

[15] ibid., 'Grace and Human Will', p. 199.

# INDEXES
# TO THE MAIN WORKS
# OF AUSTIN FARRER

*Finite and Infinite*, 1st edition, 1943, 2nd edition, 1959, with a revised preface, A. & C. Black Ltd., Dacre Press, Westminster. Reissued 1979, Seabury Press, New York. (Capitalised roman numerals refer to the preface of the 1st edition; lower case roman numerals refer to the preface of the 2nd edition.)

## The Freedom of the Will (London: Adam & Charles Black), 1957.

*Love Almighty and Ills Unlimited*, Doubleday & Co., Garden City, NY, 1961. (The English editions by Collins and Fontana, 1962 and 1963 respectively, do not match the pagination.)

accident, 12, 34–5, 51, 54, 56, 70, 75, 101, 104, 109, 136, 144–5, 166–7
act, 42, 43, 52–3, 55, 58, 60, 62, 78, 82, 88, 92, 105, 108, 109, 113, 116, 125, 129, 144, 150, 162
action, 16, 37–8, 49, 52–4, 64, 69, 74, 80, 82, 84, 87–9, 92, 98, 100, 107, 109, 114–15, 117, 120, 127–9, 131, 150–2, 155–6, 165
actions, 64, 90, 125, 135, 140
active, 15, 47
activity, 13, 16, 30, 47, 89, 91, 158
agency, 120, 127
analogy, 28, 29, 40, 59–60, 62, 93, 109, 122, 129, 163
angel, 13, 37–39, 50, 56–7, 61, 63–4, 66–8, 71, 120–1, 129–31, 134, 140, 144–5
animal, 15, 21, 25, 31–2, 36, 48–9, 54, 63, 66, 71, 73–82, 84, 88, 90, 92–102, 104, 106, 108, 115, 129, 133–4, 136, 138, 146–8, 161, 166
apostle, 134
appetite, 72, 81, 138
apprehension, 164
Aristotle, 35, 87, 158
aspiration, 155
atheist, 155
Augustine, 23, 29–31, 119, 142–4
authority, 67

being (self, scale of, unitary, etc.), 12–14, 16–17, 24–7, 29–10, 33–4, 37, 40, 42, 44–6, 50–1, 53, 55, 57, 59, 63–5, 67–9, 74, 85, 87, 89, 91–3, 95, 97, 99–100, 105, 109–10, 114–16, 129, 187, 143, 151, 155, 163, 166

belief in God, 15
Bible, 162
blessing, 72–4, 96, 112, 133–4, 146, 150, 155, 162–4
body, 79, 82, 95, 97, 100–2, 107, 113–14, 134, 136, 148–9, 154
body of Christ, 114
brain, 33, 154, 166

Catholic, 119
causality, 42
cause (external, final, immanent, external, physical, real, etc.), 12, 15, 46, 48, 81, 83, 85, 90, 93–4, 105, 125–7, 129–30, 132, 138, 145, 160
character, 13–14, 18–19, 37, 43, 51, 53, 57, 67, 70, 75, 87, 98, 100, 133, 144, 146–7, 150, 162–3
choice, 36, 51, 58–61, 69, 103, 121–2, 124–6, 134, 136, 139
Christ, 92, 103, 111–15, 134–5, 141, 151, 153–5, 163
Church, 23, 39, 111, 113, 115, 153
clue, 122, 145
concentration, 50
conscious, 24–5, 97, 129
consciousness, 73, 96, 146, 148–51
consolation, 73, 96, 146, 148–51
contingency, 12
co-operation, 78, 105, 152
creation, 13–14, 16, 26, 33, 35, 37, 39, 49, 52, 57–9, 61–4, 67–8, 75–7, 83, 86, 90
Creator, 13–16, 20, 23, 35–6, 38, 40, 45, 48, 54–5, 60–1, 63–7, 78, 84, 86–7, 99, 103, 105, 109, 116, 119, 126, 132, 143, 163, 168
credible, 38

transfiguration, 106, 114
truth, 19, 60, 89, 95–6, 104, 119, 131–2, 139, 146, 155–6, 158, 162, 164

unbelief, 158–9
understanding, 20, 35, 67, 89, 122–3, 138, 145, 150
unit, 32–3
unity, 33–4

valuation, 51
virtues, 18, 43, 96, 104, 130, 134, 143, 147, 152

will
divine will, 15, 31, 36, 64–5, 62, 87, 90, 103, 105, 109, 132, 135, 144–5, 151–5, 163–4
freedom of will, 37, 92, 127
human will, 97, 102, 106, 110–11, 121, 124, 125, 135–6, 139, 141, 150, 153
wisdom, 21, 32, 58, 62, 65, 78, 81, 84, 89, 130, 143, 145, 147, 162
wishes, 73
wit, 92
word of God, 109
work of God, 16, 19, 34–5, 38–40, 42–5, 103, 150

## Saving Belief (London: Hodder & Stoughton), 1964.

accident(s), 38, 52, 69, 126
act(s), 20–2, 26, 38, 44, 49, 57–8, 63, 71, 75–7, 83, 88, 91, 97, 99, 104–5, 115–16, 124–5, 129, 132, 151
action(s), 14, 20, 23, 26, 34, 43, 49, 51–3, 57, 65, 73–5, 78–9, 82, 95, 97, 100, 104–5, 116, 118–19, 121–2, 124–5, 129–30, 132, 144, 155
active, 43, 94, 114
activity, 93, 96, 99, 121, 144
affirmation(s), 15, 18, 102
agnostic, 39, 41
almighty, 37, 43, 46, 50, 62, 96, 104, 114
analogy, 21, 28, 38, 50, 66, 92, 95, 104, 122
angel(s), 38, 53, 128, 130–1, 142
animal(s), 12, 23–5, 51, 56, 126, 129, 136–7
apostle(s), 73, 80, 150
archetype, 31, 66–8

arguments for God's existence, 16, 28–9, 31
aspiration, 74, 98, 129
atheism, 26, 43
atheist(s), 16, 19, 41, 94–5, 148
atonement, 53, 100–5, 113–16, 154
Augustine, 141–2, 145
authority, 100, 116, 149

baptism, 131
being (self, scale of, unitary), 14, 18, 20–2, 24, 26, 29–30, 33, 40–5, 47, 50–1, 54–5, 58, 63–6, 70–1, 76, 83, 90, 92, 102, 115, 124, 127, 129–31, 140–1, 143–9
belief in God, 5–6, 15, 31, 37, 39, 58, 150
Bible, 5, 49, 71–2, 96–100, 125, 140, 147, 155
blessing(s), 49, 83, 97, 126
body, 20, 30, 55, 128, 131, 140–2, 148
body of Christ, 113–14, 130–2, 155, 157

will (divine, human, uncondited, etc.),
12, 14, 16, 22, 25–7, 31–2, 34, 38,
43–5, 48, 54, 57, 74, 78, 88, 90,
92–7, 99–100, 103–4, 111–14,
116, 118–21, 124–5, 127, 132,
143–4, 150

wisdom, 20, 68, 78, 113–14
work of God, 54, 129
worship, 6, 66, 142

*A Science of God?*, London: Bles, 1966, and in the U.S.A. as *God Is not Dead*, Wilton, Ct.: Morehouse-Barlow, 1966.

*Faith and Speculation*, A. & C. Black, London, 1967, and New York University Press, New York, 1967. Reprinted by T. & T. Clark, Edinburgh, 1988.

*Reflective Faith: Essays in Philosophical Theology*, by Austin Farrer, edited by Charles C. Conti (London: S.P.C.K.), 1972 and (Grand Rapids, MI: Eerdmans), 1974.

accident(s), 71–2, 96–8
act(s), 7–8, 12, 19, 35–7, 46, 48, 51–3,
    55–8, 60–1, 63, 65–7, 69, 71–2,
    77, 80, 89, 94–5, 94–5, 102, 105,
    109, 111–12, 121, 123, 127,
    137–9, 150–1, 166, 176, 178,
    181–2, 186, 192, 196–7, 204,
    206–7, 220, 223–4
action(s), 7, 12, 23, 40, 52, 61, 79–80,
    95–7, 102–3, 105, 107–9, 111,
    116–17, 118, 121–4, 126–9,
    131–3, 138, 142, 149–50, 153–4,
    156, 159, 172, 176–84, 187–8,
    190–4, 197–9, 202, 205–8, 211,
    213, 219–22
active, 35, 40–1, 51, 58, 69, 93, 98,
    102–3, 133, 137–8, 150, 152,
    156, 158–60, 166, 170, 179–80,
    197–9, 205, 207, 210, 214
activity, 12, 17–20, 22, 39–40, 42–3,
    45, 52, 62, 89, 94, 98, 102, 111,
    116–18, 122, 141, 149, 172, 180,
    188, 191, 196, 220–4
agency, 51, 64, 122, 202
agnostic, 2, 7–8, 68
almighty, 31, 44, 189
Allen, Diogenes, 223–4
analogy, 2, 20, 22, 32–3, 35–7, 55–8,
    60, 64–90, 97, 109, 128, 138,
    147, 149, 153, 211, 219, 221–4
angel(s), 14, 21, 31, 35, 42–3, 79, 88,
    120, 141, 160–1, 167
animal(s), 12, 21, 37, 40, 58, 62–4, 71,
    98–9, 104, 149, 159, 187, 221–3
apex of the mind, 63
apostle(s), 4, 36, 49
appetite(s), 70, 118
apprehension, 9–12, 14, 18, 21, 27, 34,
    37, 48, 50–8, 60–3, 70, 72, 77,
    116, 219, 223–4

Aquinas, Thomas, 65–7, 69, 77, 146,
    221, 223
archetype, 54, 217
arguments for God's existence, 21, 39,
    44, 58, 108, 114–33, 141, 143,
    170, 200–1, 210, 215–17, 225
Aristotelianism, 66, 92, 107, 220, 222
Aristotle, 23, 33, 42, 93, 98, 107, 149,
    178, 181, 188, 190, 195, 207–9,
    225
aspiration, 2, 15–17, 23, 34, 49, 60,
    62–3, 195–6, 225
atheism, 8, 175, 177
atheist(s), 2, 160, 176–7, 217
Augustine, 192–6
authority, 93, 110, 119–20, 139, 177

baptism, 197
Barth, Karl, 68, 221
being (self, scale of, unitary, etc.), 7,
    18, 20–2, 31, 33–6, 39–42, 44–6,
    48–56, 59, 62–3, 65–80, 94, 96,
    103, 105, 109–10, 120–1, 123,
    131, 133, 137–8, 140–1, 153,
    158–61, 166–8, 170, 172–3,
    176–8, 180–4, 189–90, 198,
    200–1, 206–7, 221, 225
belief in God, 7–8, 12, 15, 18–19, 21,
    23, 39, 47, 50, 56, 65, 116–19,
    125, 127, 129–30, 138, 142, 144,
    161, 174, 182, 184, 201, 210, 217,
    223
Bergson, Henri, 164–5
Berkeley, George, 68–9, 84, 91,
    155–62, 219, 221
Bible, 3, 192
body, 40–2, 55–6, 64, 69–71, 94, 96,
    98–104, 109–10, 210, 221–2, 224
body of Christ, 3, 144, 148
brain, 99–100, 131

*Interpretation and Belief* (ed.) Charles Conti (London: S.P.C.K.), 1976.